BUILDING ON THE ROCK

Living the Sermon on the Mount

ROBERT GRIFFITH

GRACE AND TRUTH PUBLISHING
PO Box 338, Gunnedah NSW 2380 Australia
www.graceandtruthpublishing.com.au

All Bible quotes are from the New International Version (NIV) expect where
otherwise stated.

Other version quotes are from:

Quotes in square brackets are the author's comment.

ISBN 978-1-7635504-9-0

TABLE OF CONTENTS

PREFACE

There are very few passages of Scripture which are as widely recognized or as deeply transformative as what we know as the *Sermon on the Mount*. Contained in Matthew chapters 5-7, these are the most famous words ever spoken by Jesus, and perhaps the most influential moral and spiritual teaching in history. From the Beatitudes to the Golden Rule, from loving our enemies to building our lives on the rock, these three chapters have shaped individuals, societies, and even whole nations.

Yet for all their familiarity, the words contained in this Sermon are also incredibly challenging. They confront our assumptions, overturn our values, and reveal the radical nature of life in the kingdom of God. They are not comfortable platitudes or lofty ideals meant for admiration alone; they are a vital call to action, demanding nothing less than the surrender of our lives to Jesus Christ, the King Who preached them.

Why this Sermon matters

The Sermon on the Mount is not merely an inspiring message. It is the greatest sermon ever preached and a full manifesto of the kingdom of God. It tells us what it looks like when we live under the rule of Christ here and now, not just in eternity. It will answer pressing questions like:

➢ What does true righteousness look like?
➢ How should we relate to God in prayer and worship
➢ How do we love not only our friends but even our enemies?
➢ How do we trust God in a world filled with anxiety and uncertainty?
➢ What distinguishes true faith from empty religion?

Far from abstract theology, these are practical, everyday realities. Jesus addresses issues such as anger, lust, revenge, generosity, worry, relationships, and more. In fact, His words leave no part of human life untouched.

More than moral teaching

It is tempting to view this Sermon as a set of ethical principles to try harder to follow. But to do so is to miss its heart. The Sermon on the Mount is not primarily about what we must do but about who we are becoming as citizens of Jesus' kingdom. It describes the character of those transformed by His grace, filled with His Spirit, and walking in obedience to His Word.

This is why the Sermon begins with the Beatitudes: blessings not for the strong, the successful, or the self-sufficient, but for the poor in spirit, the meek, and the merciful. Jesus is not inviting us to earn His kingdom by good behaviour; Jesus is inviting us to receive it through humble faith and then live in its reality.

A journey through the greatest Sermon

This book is designed to guide you through the Sermon on the Mount in depth, chapter by chapter, phrase by phrase. Each chapter will explore a specific section of the Sermon, drawing out its meaning, its relevance today, and its implications for our lives as followers of Jesus.

Here's what you can expect:

➤ *Biblical depth:* Each chapter will unpack Jesus' teaching in context, explaining its meaning with clarity and care.
➤ *Practical application:* You will see how these ancient words speak directly into modern challenges - our relationships, priorities, anxieties, and decisions.
➤ *Christ-centred focus:* At every step, we will keep our eyes on Jesus, remembering that He not only spoke these words but lived them perfectly and empowers us to live them through His Spirit.

Why this message still transforms lives

The Sermon on the Mount remains as countercultural today as it was two thousand years ago. In a world driven by pride, power, and self-interest, Jesus calls us to humility, mercy, purity, and love even for our enemies.

In an age of anxiety and materialism, He invites us to trust our heavenly Father and seek first His kingdom. To take this Sermon seriously is to embark on a journey that will disrupt our comfort, challenge our assumptions, and ultimately lead us to the joy and freedom which is found in Christ alone. As you journey through these chapters, you will see that this is not just a Sermon to be studied - it is a life to be lived.

An invitation to build on the rock

At the close of His Sermon, Jesus issues a stark choice: Will we hear His words and obey them, building on the rock, or will we hear them and ignore them, building on sand? This question is not academic. It is very personal and urgent, and it frames the purpose of this book: to help you not only understand the words of Jesus but live them each and every day.

If we really take Jesus seriously here, our lives will change. Our relationships will deepen. Our priorities will shift. Our fears will loosen their grip. And most importantly, our foundation will be secure - not in shifting sand, but in Christ Himself, the Rock who cannot be moved.

A word to the reader

As you read this book, I encourage you to do more than analyse the words. Pray them. Wrestle with them. Let them search your heart. Approach them not as distant advice but as the living words of the King who calls you to follow Him.

This is more than just a study of a passage of Scripture - it is an invitation to be transformed; to live as salt and light in a dark world; to walk the narrow path that leads to life; and to reflect the character of our Father in heaven.

The Sermon on the Mount is not easy, but it is good. It is not comfortable, but it is freeing. It calls us away from a focus on self and toward Jesus Christ, the One Who alone fulfils its demands and makes us new.

1

INTRODUCTON

When Jesus ascended the hillside overlooking the Sea of Galilee and sat down to teach, He did more than deliver a collection of moral sayings. He was unveiling the manifesto of His kingdom, a radical call to live under God's reign in a way that defied all human convention. To understand the Sermon on the Mount in its fullness, we must first step into the world in which Jesus spoke those words, grasping the historical, cultural, and spiritual context that makes His teaching so revolutionary even today.

The Gospel of Matthew situates the Sermon early in Jesus' public ministry. After His baptism in the Jordan River by John the Baptist (Matthew 3:13-17) and His confrontation with the devil in the wilderness (Matthew 4:1-11), Jesus emerges proclaiming the central theme of His mission: *"Repent, for the kingdom of heaven has come near."* (Matthew 4:17). His words echo through Galilee, a region bustling with trade and diversity but marked by Roman occupation and a deep spiritual longing. People were weary of political oppression and hungry for hope. Into this climate of expectation, Jesus brought a message unlike any other: the reign of God was breaking into the present world.

Matthew says that Jesus began to teach, heal, and draw crowds from *"Galilee, the Decapolis, Jerusalem, Judea and the region across the Jordan."* (Matthew 4:25). His many miracles of healing and deliverance stirred much amazement, but His words demanded transformation. This dual emphasis - proclaiming the good news of the kingdom and demonstrating its power - prepared the way for His most profound teaching: the Sermon on the Mount.

As Jesus ascended the mountainside that day, His actions carried a profound symbolism. Mountains in Scripture often serve as places of divine encounter. In Exodus 19:20 Moses ascended Mount Sinai to receive the law from God amidst thunder and fire. In 1 Kings 19:11-12 Elijah heard the gentle whisper of God on Mount Horeb.

In choosing a mountain setting, Jesus was deliberately evoking these moments of revelation, signalling that what He was about to declare was no less significant. Here was the new and greater Moses, not simply delivering God's law but actually embodying its fulfilment (Hebrews 3:3–6). Where Moses mediated between God and the people, Jesus spoke with His own authority: *"You have heard that it was said… but I tell you."* (Matthew 5:21–22). The mountain backdrop set the stage for a divine declaration that would redefine righteousness itself.

The fact that Jesus *"sat down"* (Matthew 5:1) is easily overlooked, but it carried much weight in first-century Jewish culture. Rabbis customarily taught from a seated position, a posture signifying authority. To sit was to claim the role of an authoritative teacher, one whose words demanded attention. The disciples drew near, taking the position of eager learners. Around them gathered the crowds - curious, hopeful, and perhaps sceptical - listening in on what would become the most famous Sermon in history.

Here we see a vital truth: while this Sermon is directed first to disciples, its scope encompasses everyone who would hear and respond. It is both instruction for those already following Jesus and invitation for those standing at the threshold of faith.

Understanding this Sermon as kingdom teaching is crucial. Jesus is not merely giving ethical guidelines or abstract ideals; He is painting a picture of life under God's reign. This is why Jesus begins with the Beatitudes, pronouncing blessing on those who exhibit the values of His kingdom: humility, mercy, purity, and a hunger for righteousness. These qualities are not natural to the human condition; they are the fruit of grace.

This Sermon is not a ladder we climb to earn God's favour but a window into the kind of transformed life that flows from faith in Him. As Paul later wrote, *"For it is by grace you have been saved, through faith… not by works… For we are God's handiwork, created in Christ Jesus to do good works."* (Ephesians 2:8–10). The Sermon on the Mount clearly reveals to us that those *"good works"* are the natural expression of a redeemed heart.

The audience who heard these words of Jesus first lived under a religious system dominated by the scribes and Pharisees. These leaders were meticulous in their observance of the law, but their focus all too often lay on external compliance rather than inner transformation.

Jesus would later confront them directly: *"Woe to you... You clean the outside of the cup and dish, but inside they are full of greed and self-indulgence."* (Matthew 23:25). Against this backdrop, the Sermon exposes a deeper righteousness - one that penetrates to motives, desires, and the very core of who we are. It is a call to live not merely by rule-keeping but by wholehearted devotion to God.

This internal focus marks a significant shift from old covenant patterns. Under Moses, Israel's identity was defined largely by its separation from the surrounding nations and adherence to ceremonial laws.

But Jesus inaugurates a new kingdom that transcends ethnic and ritual boundaries. His words on the mountainside are not limited to Israel; they are addressed to all who would follow Him, Jew and Gentile alike. By sitting and teaching in this informal yet authoritative setting, Jesus signalled that the kingdom of heaven was not restricted to the temple or priestly class - it was breaking into ordinary life.

This phrase *"kingdom of heaven,"* is unique to Matthew's Gospel, and it underscores this reality. Rather than focusing solely on future glory, Jesus proclaimed that God's reign was present and active. This 'now and not yet' tension permeates the Sermon.

On the one hand, its promises - comfort for those who mourn, satisfaction for those who hunger for righteousness - are fulfilled even now as we experience the Spirit's transforming work. On the other hand, they point forward to the day when God's kingdom will be fully realized, and His will done perfectly *"on earth as it is in heaven."* (Matthew 6:10). So, the Sermon calls us to live as citizens of that future kingdom in the present world. This dual dimension is vital for modern readers.

Too often, this Sermon is reduced to either unattainable ideals or mere social ethics. But Jesus intended neither. He was neither describing some impossible utopia nor simply offering moral reform. Instead, Jesus was declaring what happens when God reigns in human hearts - when grace reshapes character and love fulfils the law (see Romans 13:10). This Sermon is aspirational because it lifts our eyes to what God's Spirit can accomplish in us. It is practical because it instructs us how to live now in light of that reality.

The authority of Jesus' teaching astonished His hearers. Matthew concludes the Sermon by noting, *"The crowds were amazed at his teaching, because he taught as one who had authority, and not as their teachers of the law."* (Matthew 7:28–29). The authority of Jesus was inherent, rooted in His identity as the Son of God. This is why His words still carry weight today. They confront us, expose us, comfort us, and compel us. They challenge superficial religion and offer the deep, transforming life that only Jesus can give.

For modern day disciples, this opening scene invites reflection. Are we approaching this Sermon as mere listeners in the crowd, intrigued but uncommitted? Or are we coming as disciples of Jesus, ready to be reshaped by the words of our King? The same Jesus Who sat on that Galilean hillside now speaks to us through these pages, summoning us into His kingdom and calling us to embody its values in a world which is do desperately in need of light and truth.

The Sermon on the Mount does more than describe life in God's kingdom - it confronts every false foundation upon which we are tempted to build our lives. In its sweeping scope, it addresses both our relationship with God and our relationships with one another. It presses beyond surface-level behaviour to the motives and desires of the heart.

Jesus' teaching pierces like a surgeon's scalpel, exposing sin not merely as wrongdoing but as a condition rooted deep within us. His words unsettle our comfort, dismantle our self-reliance, and draw us into complete dependence upon Him.

This is why the Sermon doesn't begin with commands but with blessings. The Beatitudes set the tone, describing the inward qualities of those who belong to the kingdom of heaven, such as humility, mourning over sin, meekness, hunger and thirst for righteousness, mercy, purity, peace-making, and perseverance in persecution. These are not human achievements but Spirit-wrought dispositions. In pronouncing such people *"blessed,"* Jesus reframes the world's definition of success.

While society will celebrate power, wealth, and self-sufficiency, Jesus calls blessed those who are weak, dependent, and despised in worldly eyes. This radical reversal signals that His kingdom is not an extension of human systems but a complete reordering of values under God's reign.

Understanding this inversion is essential. This Sermon is not a list of virtues we must try and produce through willpower. Rather, it describes what happens when God's grace grips a person's life. The poor in spirit are blessed because they know their need and receive His mercy. The meek inherit the earth because they trust in His strength rather than their own. Those who hunger for righteousness are filled because they are drawn to Christ, Who is Himself our righteousness (1 Corinthians 1:30). The Sermon on the Mount is not a call to self-improvement, it is a transformation invitation, rooted in faith and empowered by the Spirit.

Yet this Sermon also carries a sharp edge. Jesus' words expose the inadequacy and evil of religion. He says our righteousness must exceed that of the Pharisees (Matthew 5:20), the ones who meticulously obeyed external laws but neglected the weightier matters of justice, mercy, and faithfulness (Matthew 23:23). In declaring this, Jesus was not dismissing God's law but fulfilling it. His fulfilment involves perfect obedience *and* the unveiling of its deepest intent: not merely to restrain outward acts of sin but to transform inward desires. When Jesus equates anger with murder and lust with adultery, He shows that true righteousness involves a heart aligned with God's holiness. He does not relax the standard but drives it deeper, beyond what human effort can achieve apart from divine grace.

This penetrating diagnosis is unsettling, yet it is precisely what prepares us for the gospel. This Sermon is designed to strip us of our self-confidence and awaken us to our need for a Saviour. It shows us what kingdom life actually looks like, then reveals that we cannot hope to attain it apart from Christ. As Paul later wrote, *"Through the law we become conscious of our sin."* (Romans 3:20). Far from crushing us into despair, this realization drives us to the only One Who perfectly embodies the Sermon: Jesus Himself. He lived the life described in these chapters, displaying mercy, purity, humility, and perfect obedience to His Father. He not only preached the Sermon - He personified it.

This Christ-centred lens is vital. Without it, this Sermon becomes either crushing legalism or empty moralism. If we see it merely as a new law, we will despair of ever achieving it. If we treat it as inspirational ideals, we will reduce it to sentimental platitudes devoid of power. But when we view it through the gospel, we see both its impossibility apart from Christ and its fulfilment in Christ. He not only calls us to this life but also empowers it by His Spirit. This Sermon functions as both a mirror, showing us our need, and also a map, guiding our Spirit-enabled growth as kingdom citizens.

Its enduring relevance flows from this dual purpose. The world in which Jesus preached was severely fractured by oppression, corruption, and division - conditions all too familiar today. We, too, live in an age of great disillusionment, where many distrust institutions, question moral absolutes, and pursue autonomy at all costs. Into this context, the Sermon speaks with fresh clarity. It offers an alternative vision of human flourishing rooted not in self-assertion but in surrender to God's reign. It summons us away from the noise of competing ideologies and toward the simplicity of obedience to Jesus' words.

Consider how the themes of this Sermon confront modern life. In an age obsessed with image, Jesus calls for purity of heart, reminding us that God sees beyond appearances. In a culture which is quick to retaliate, He commands us to love our enemies and pray for those who persecute us.

Amid our consumerism and anxiety over material security, He teaches us to seek first God's kingdom, trusting Him to provide. Each line of the Sermon cuts across the grain of human instinct, challenging us to embrace values that can only be sustained by the grace of God.

Moreover, the Sermon's call to authenticity speaks powerfully to the ones disillusioned by hypocrisy. Jesus condemns outward religion performed just for show, whether in giving, praying, or fasting. He insists on secret devotion to the Father Who sees in secret. This resonates deeply in a time when public faith is often marred by scandal or self-promotion. True discipleship, Jesus teaches, is not about outward displays, it's all about the hidden faithfulness springing from a heart transformed by grace.

The closing image of the Sermon underscores its urgency. Jesus likens those who hear His words and put them into practice to a wise builder who lays a foundation on rock (Matthew 7:24–25). The storms come - the trials of life, the testing of faith - but the house stands firm. By contrast, those who hear His words yet ignore them are like a foolish builder on sand. When trouble comes, their lives collapse. This final picture makes clear that the Sermon is not for casual admiration but for decisive action. It is not enough to nod approvingly at Jesus' teaching; we must build our lives upon it.

This challenge confronts us still today as it forces us to ask: What foundation are we building upon? Are we rooting our lives in shifting sands like success, approval and possessions, or in the unshakable bedrock of the teaching of Christ? The Sermon on the Mount compels a response. It is not an optional appendix to the gospel but the very heart of Jesus' call to discipleship.

For this reason, the Sermon remains both deeply comforting and profoundly unsettling. It comforts because it assures us that the broken, the humble, and the overlooked are blessed in God's kingdom. It unsettles because it leaves no room for half-hearted allegiance. Jesus' words demand our whole selves: our hearts, our motives, our obedience.

Yet this demand is inseparable from His promise. He who calls us to this life also promises to be with us, to forgive our failures, and to empower our obedience through His Spirit.

As we prepare to walk through this Sermon line by line, we must hold fast to this very real tension. The Sermon is neither a distant mountain we cannot climb nor a gentle hill we can ascend in our own strength. It is a portrait of life under the rule of King Jesus - a life that begins with repentance and faith, continues in Spirit-led transformation, and then culminates in eternal joy when His kingdom comes in fullness. Each word He spoke on that Galilean hillside carries this dual weight: exposing our sin, then pointing us to the grace that meets us in our need and lifts us to new life.

This is why the Sermon on the Mount continues to captivate and confront every generation. Its vision of human flourishing stands apart from every political platform, philosophical system, and cultural trend. It is not bound to time or place, because it flows from the timeless authority of the King Who reigns forever. When we hear Jesus say, *"Blessed are the poor in spirit,"* we hear not a slogan but the voice of the One Who calls us into His eternal kingdom. His words are life, and His summons is clear: *come, follow Me.*

The Sermon on the Mount begins not only with teaching but with invitation. It beckons us to draw near to Jesus and listen, just as those first disciples did. Matthew writes that *"his disciples came to him, and he began to teach them."* (Matthew 5:1–2). This simple description carries profound implications: discipleship starts with proximity to Christ. Before we can live out His words, we must come close enough to hear His voice. This is the essence of Christian life - not merely adopting a moral code but walking in daily fellowship with the living Lord Who speaks with authority and grace.

This posture of coming to Jesus is not just a one-time act but an ongoing reality. The Sermon on the Mount is not addressed to the casual observer or occasional listener; it is aimed at those who are willing to sit at His feet.

Luke's Gospel underscores this when he writes, *"Why do you call me, 'Lord, Lord,' and do not do what I say?"* (Luke 6:46). Hearing without obeying is hollow, but obedience begins with hearing. The crowds heard His words too, but only the disciples drew near. This distinction reminds us that this Sermon is not abstract philosophy - it is relational teaching, flowing from the intimacy between the Master and His apprentices.

To really hear Jesus properly, we need to come with humility and openness. The crowds who gathered around Him were diverse: fishermen and farmers, tax collectors and zealots, the sick and the poor, even curious Pharisees. They brought their questions, hopes, and assumptions, and Jesus addressed them all with a piercing clarity. His teaching cut across social lines, addressing both personal sin and systemic injustice. He spoke to the proud and to the broken, to the religious elite and to the spiritually lost, levelling all distinctions in light of God's kingdom.

This inclusivity highlights the breadth of His message: no one is beyond its reach, and yet no one can approach it without being challenged and changed. This Sermon confronts every person with a decision: will we align our lives with this kingdom vision or remain tethered to the values of the world? Jesus warns that there are two gates, two roads, two kinds of builders, and then ultimately two outcomes. This dualism leaves no room for us to sit on the fence.

As we progress through these chapters, we will see again and again that Jesus presses us to choose light or darkness, God or mammon, the narrow way or the broad road. He makes it clear that there is no middle path in His kingdom. This sharp division unsettles our modern sensibilities that favour ambiguity and compromise, but it is precisely this clarity that makes the Sermon so powerful. It calls us to a decisiveness, and to a wholehearted allegiance to the King Who speaks.

Yet even as it challenges us, this Sermon comforts us with its promises. The blessings that open the Sermon are declarations of grace, not demands for achievement.

Jesus does not say, *"Become poor in spirit so that you may earn the kingdom,"* but *"Blessed are the poor in spirit, for theirs is the kingdom of heaven."* (Matthew 5:3). These blessings describe what God gives to those who depend upon Him. They remind us that we enter the kingdom not by climbing upward but by bowing low. This is the paradox of the gospel: the way down is the way up. Those who humble themselves will be exalted (Luke 14:11), while those who cling to self-sufficiency will be excluded.

This emphasis on grace is critical as we approach the Beatitudes. These opening statements are not merely poetic introductions - they are the very heart of the Sermon, painting a portrait of those transformed by God's reign. Each blessing is both descriptive and invitational. They describe the realities of kingdom life while inviting us to embody them all through faith. The poor in spirit, those who mourn, the meek, those who hunger and thirst for righteousness - these are not eight different categories of people, but eight interwoven traits of every true disciple. Together, they provide a picture of what it really means to belong to Jesus and to reflect His character in the world.

Consider the striking contrast between these blessings and the values we see in our contemporary culture. Where society prizes self-confidence, Jesus blesses those who recognize their need. Where the world avoids pain, He blesses those who mourn over sin and suffering. Where our age rewards assertiveness and dominance, He calls the meek heirs of the earth. Where material abundance is celebrated, He blesses those who hunger and thirst not for wealth but for righteousness.

These reversals are not simply counterintuitive; they reveal a kingdom that is utterly different from human systems of power and prestige. To embrace them is to live as citizens of another realm, embodying in the present the all values of God's future kingdom. This means that reading the Sermon on the Mount requires us to view it not simply as personal advice but as a call to an entirely new identity. Jesus is not merely offering us better techniques for living; He is inviting us to become a new kind of people - a kingdom people.

Paul captures this transformation when he writes, *"If anyone is in Christ, the new creation has come: The old has gone, the new is here!"* (2 Corinthians 5:17). This Sermon will describe what this new creation looks like in practice: reconciled relationships, pure motives, trust in God's provision, and resilient hope amid trials.

This transformation cannot be achieved through human effort alone. Left to ourselves, we will always fall short of the standard Jesus sets. That is why this Sermon must always be read in the light of the cross. The One Who preached it would soon fulfil it perfectly, then bear the penalty for our failure to do so. His death and resurrection secure both our forgiveness and the Spirit's indwelling power to live out His words. The Sermon on the Mount is thus inseparable from the gospel - it both reveals our need for Christ and shows us what life in Him looks like.

This connection to the cross also grounds the Sermon's call to costly discipleship. When Jesus calls us to love our enemies, to turn the other cheek, to forgive without limit, He is describing the very pattern of His own life and death. He loved His enemies even as they crucified Him; He prayed for His persecutors; and he bore our sins to reconcile us to God.

To follow Him, then, is to walk the same road, empowered by His Spirit and sustained by His grace. This is why the Sermon on the Mount cannot be reduced to a set of rules - it is a summons to relationship, a call to union with Christ in His life, death, and resurrection.

In this light, the Sermon is deeply practical. It speaks to everyday realities: anger and reconciliation, lust and purity, prayer and worry, generosity and secrecy, judgment and discernment. It touches on the very things that shape our lives and relationships, offering wisdom that is as relevant in a modern city as it was on a Galilean hillside. Its simplicity belies its depth: these are words that a young child can memorize, yet theologians can study for a whole lifetime. They invite us into a lifelong journey of learning, unlearning, and relearning under the gentle and yet demanding tutelage of Jesus.

As we embark on this detailed study, we must approach it with both reverence and expectancy. Reverence, because these are the words of the King Who speaks with divine authority, and also expectancy, because His words are living and active, continuing to transform hearts and lives today. Each passage we encounter will challenge us to examine our assumptions, repent of our sins, and yield more fully to His reign. But in doing so, we will discover the joy and freedom of kingdom living - a life shaped not by fear or striving but by the love and lordship of Christ.

This opening chapter invites us, therefore, to now take our place among those early disciples on the hillside that day. Picture yourself seated there, the wind off the Sea of Galilee rustling the grass, the murmur of the crowd fading as Jesus begins to speak. His voice carries both tenderness and authority, His eyes search the very depths of your soul, and His words cut through every pretence. He calls you - not merely to listen, but to follow. And as He opens His mouth and pronounces those first unexpected blessings, you sense that nothing will ever be the same again.

In the next eight chapters, we will work our way through these blessings one by one, exploring their meaning, their biblical roots, and their implications for our lives today. We will see how they form the foundation of the entire Sermon, shaping not only our understanding of righteousness but our identity as citizens of God's kingdom.

The path ahead will challenge you and convict you, but it will also comfort and inspire you, for it is nothing less than the path Jesus Himself has walked and now calls you to follow. With ears open and hearts ready, let's begin where Jesus began: with the words, *"Blessed are the poor in spirit, for theirs is the kingdom of heaven."*

2

'BLESSED ARE THE POOR IN SPIRIT'

Matthew 5:3

"Blessed are the poor in spirit, for theirs is the kingdom of heaven."

With these startling words, Jesus commences His Sermon on the Mount. It is no accident that this is the first Beatitude. In a single sentence, He overturns human expectations and then lays the foundation for everything that follows. Entry into His kingdom begins not with strength, or achievement, or merit, but with the recognition of our own spiritual poverty. This is the gateway to grace, the posture without which no one can approach God.

The phrase *"poor in spirit"* is easily misunderstood. It does not refer to material poverty, though Scripture often reminds us of God's special concern for the poor and oppressed (Proverbs 14:31; Luke 4:18). Nor does it describe timidity or weakness of personality. Instead, it speaks of a conscious awareness of our spiritual bankruptcy before God. To be *"poor in spirit"* is to know that we really have nothing to offer Him, that we are entirely dependent on His mercy and grace. This is the exact opposite of self-sufficiency and pride.

This idea runs throughout Scripture. Isaiah declares, *"These are the ones I look on with favour: those who are humble and contrite in spirit, and who tremble at my word."* (Isaiah 66:2). King David echoes the same truth in his prayer of repentance: *"My sacrifice, O God, is a broken spirit; a broken and contrite heart you, God, will not despise."* (Psalm 51:17). Both passages remind us that God draws near to those who know their need of Him. Spiritual poverty is not a flaw to be overcome - it is the very soil in which God's grace takes root and grows.

Jesus Himself illustrated this truth vividly in the parable of the Pharisee and the tax collector (see Luke 18:9–14). The Pharisee, confident in his religious observance, stood and prayed about himself: *"God, I thank you that I am not like other people."*

By contrast, the tax collector, standing at a distance, would not even look up to heaven but beat his breast and said, *"God, have mercy on me, a sinner."* Jesus concluded, *"I tell you that this man, rather than the other, went home justified before God."* Here is the essence of being poor in spirit: acknowledging our unworthiness and casting ourselves entirely on God's mercy.

This humility stands in stark contrast to the spirit of the age - both in Jesus' day and also in ours. The world prizes self-reliance, independence, and personal achievement. From childhood, we are taught to believe in ourselves, assert ourselves, and trust in our own abilities. But the kingdom of heaven belongs to those who abandon self-reliance and cling instead to God. The gospel begins where human pride ends. As James writes, *"God opposes the proud but give grace to the humble."* (James 4:6).

To be poor in spirit, then, is not merely an attitude we adopt once at conversion; it is a continual posture of the heart. We never outgrow our dependence on God. Even Paul, near the end of his ministry, confessed: *"I know that good itself does not dwell in me, that is, in my sinful nature."* (Romans 7:18). Spiritual maturity does not lead to self-sufficiency but to deeper awareness of our need for grace. The closer we draw to God, the more clearly we see His holiness and our own inadequacy apart from Him.

Importantly, Jesus ties this poverty of spirit directly to the kingdom of heaven. *"Blessed are the poor in spirit,"* He says, *"for theirs is the kingdom of heaven."* Notice the present tense: *"is,"* not *"will be."* This blessing is not merely a future hope but a present reality. Those who come to God empty-handed will find that the doors of His kingdom are already wide open. The reign of God belongs to them because they have renounced every rival claim. They no longer seek to build their own kingdoms or trust in their own righteousness. They are free to receive everything God has prepared for them.

This is why this Beatitude comes first. Without spiritual poverty, none of the other blessings make sense. We cannot mourn over sin if we think we are sufficient in ourselves.

We cannot be meek if we are still clinging to pride. We will not hunger for righteousness if we believe we already possess it. Spiritual poverty is the foundation upon which the rest of this Sermon is built. It is the doorway into the life Jesus describes.

We see this beautifully illustrated in the lives of those who encountered Jesus during His ministry. Consider Peter's reaction after the miraculous catch of fish in Luke 5. Confronted with Jesus' power, Peter fell at His knees and said, *"Go away from me, Lord; I am a sinful man!"* His instinct was to shrink back, yet Jesus responded by calling him to follow. Similarly, Isaiah, when he saw the Lord high and exalted in the temple, cried out, *"Woe to me! … I am ruined! For I am a man of unclean lips."* (Isaiah 6:5). Yet God touched his lips with a coal and sent him forth as a prophet. In both cases, awareness of unworthiness was a prelude to divine commissioning. Poverty of spirit is never an end in itself; it is always met by God's mercy and empowerment.

This truth is particularly striking when we contrast it with the self-assuredness of the Pharisees in Jesus' day. They had prided themselves on their meticulous observance of the law and their outward piety. But in Matthew 23:25, Jesus exposed their hearts: *"You clean the outside of the cup and dish, but inside they are full of greed and self-indulgence."* Their arrogant confidence in their own righteousness blinded them to their need for grace. This is why Jesus declared in Matthew 9:12–13, *"It is not the healthy who need a doctor, but the sick… I have not come to call the righteous, but sinners."* Only those who accept that they are sick will ever seek the physician.

Spiritual poverty also shapes how we relate to others. When we see ourselves as recipients of undeserved mercy, we become less judgmental and a lot more compassionate. We recognize that we stand before God not because of anything we have done, but because of what Jesus Christ has done for us. This frees us from comparison and pride. Paul captures this beautifully: *"What do you have that you did not receive? And if you did receive it, why do you boast as though you did not?"* (1 Corinthians 4:7). The poor in spirit live with gratitude rather than entitlement, generosity rather than avarice.

This posture of humility is also essential when we want to pray. Jesus illustrates this in His parable of the tax collector, whose simple cry - *"God, have mercy on me, a sinner"* - is the model of genuine prayer (Luke 18:13). Such prayer flows from poverty of spirit, from the recognition that we cannot barter or negotiate with God. We come with empty hands, dependent entirely on His grace. And He delights to answer. As Psalm 34:18 assures us, *"The Lord is close to the broken-hearted and saves those who are crushed in spirit."*

The blessing attached to spiritual poverty is profound: *"for theirs is the kingdom of heaven."* This bold phrase is not merely a poetic expression ; it is the central promise of Jesus' opening words. The kingdom of heaven is not granted to the powerful, the wealthy, or the accomplished, but to those who acknowledge their need.

In God's economy, the doorway into His reign is humility, not achievement. This is the paradox of grace: those who admit they are empty are the ones who are filled; those who confess their weakness are the ones who receive strength.

The present tense of Jesus' statement - *"theirs is the kingdom"* - underscores that this is not simply a future hope but a present reality. To be poor in spirit is to live *now* under the rule of God, enjoying the privileges of His reign even in a fallen world.

The blessings of this kingdom are both 'now' and 'not yet.' We taste them in this life through forgiveness, reconciliation, and the transforming work of the Holy Spirit, and we anticipate their fullness in the age to come. This tension invites us to live in joyful dependence, knowing that while the kingdom of God is not yet consummated, it has already broken into the present through Jesus Christ.

This present reality has practical implications. When we are poor in spirit, we approach every aspect of life - from relationships to work to worship - with a posture of dependence. We then see ourselves not as self-made or self-sufficient, but as recipients of mercy and grace. This then transforms how we relate to God.

Instead of coming to Him with bargaining or entitlement, we come empty-handed, echoing the hymn writer's words: *"Nothing in my hand I bring, simply to Thy cross I cling."* This dependence is never weakness; rather it is the deepest kind of strength, because it anchors us in the One who is unfailing.

In Matthew 18:3-4 Jesus illustrated this when He was teaching about children. He said, *"Truly I tell you, unless you change and become like little children, you will never enter the kingdom of heaven. Therefore, whoever takes the lowly position of this child is the greatest in the kingdom of heaven."* Children are not strong or independent; they are marked by trust and dependence. To be poor in spirit is to approach God this way, with the humility and receptivity of a child who knows his need for his father's care.

This perspective will also reshape how we view righteousness. Many in Jesus' day believed they could achieve righteousness through meticulous obedience to the law. The Pharisees were the prime example, convinced that their scrupulous rule-keeping would earn them favour with God. Yet Jesus declared that our righteousness must surpass that of the Pharisees (Matthew 5:20), not because we outperform them, but because the righteousness of the kingdom is of an entirely different kind. It is not earned from below but given by God from above. Paul explains this in Philippians 3:8-9: *"I consider everything a loss because of the surpassing worth of knowing Christ Jesus my Lord... not having a righteousness of my own that comes from the law, but that which is through faith in Christ - the righteousness that comes from God on the basis of faith."*

Poverty of spirit, therefore, is inseparable from the gospel. It is the recognition that we cannot ever save ourselves, that our best efforts fall short of God's holiness, and that we must receive His righteousness as a gift. This is why Jesus could declare that tax collectors and sinners were entering the kingdom ahead of the religious leaders (Matthew 21:31). They knew their need. They came broken and desperate. They came ready to receive grace. The Pharisees, by contrast, clung to their imagined goodness and missed the invitation entirely.

This same dynamic is at work around us today. The gospel is still offensive to human pride because it insists that we bring nothing to the table. It levels the ground at the foot of the cross, stripping away every illusion we might have of self-sufficiency. Whether outwardly respectable or openly rebellious, we stand before God equally bankrupt apart from Christ. As Paul wrote, *"There is no difference… for all have sinned and fall short of the glory of God, and all are justified freely by his grace."* (Romans 3:22–24). Poverty of spirit is simply the honest acknowledgment of this reality.

Yet this acknowledgment is liberating. When we stop pretending that we are strong enough or good enough, we are finally free to rest in God's provision. Spiritual poverty is not a dead end but a doorway. It leads us away from the exhausting treadmill of self-reliance and into the peace of trusting in Christ's finished work. It allows us to say with Paul, *"When I am weak, then I am strong."* (2 Corinthians 12:10), because our weakness drives us to the One who is strong.

This daily dependence is not passive resignation; it is active trust. It looks like beginning each day with prayer, acknowledging our need for God's wisdom and strength. It looks like confessing our sins quickly and receiving His forgiveness rather than hiding in shame. It looks like seeking His guidance in all decisions, His provision in needs, and His presence in trials. Poverty of spirit cultivates a rhythm of life centred on reliance, where every success is attributed to His grace and every burden is laid at the feet of our Lord and King.

It also shapes how we view others. When we are poor in spirit, we are less likely to look down on those who struggle. We see ourselves as fellow beggars who have found bread, not as self-made successes who can boast. This humility fosters empathy, patience, and kindness. We also become less critical and more forgiving because we know how much we have been forgiven.

As Jesus taught in Luke 7:47, *"Whoever has been forgiven little loves little,"* but those who know the depth of their own need are quick to extend mercy.

Furthermore, poverty of spirit will free us from the tyranny of comparison. In a world obsessed with status, achievement, and appearances, we can rest in our identity as beloved children of God. We no longer strive to prove our worth or outshine others. Our value is anchored not in what we accomplish but in what Christ has already accomplished for us. This security liberates us to celebrate the successes of others and serve without seeking recognition.

In practical terms, this means cultivating habits that remind us of our dependence on God. Regular confession of sin keeps us grounded in grace. Immersing ourselves in Scripture renews our perspective, reminding us of God's holiness and our continual need for Him.

Worship lifts our eyes from ourselves to His majesty, fostering humility and gratitude. Even fasting, as Jesus commended later in the Sermon (Matthew 6:16–18), is a tangible reminder of our weakness and our need to be sustained by God rather than by our appetites.

The blessing promised to the poor in spirit is not merely spiritual satisfaction but participation in God's reign. When Jesus says, *"theirs is the kingdom of heaven,"* He is declaring that those who come empty-handed receive everything. They are welcomed into the Father's household, adopted as His children (John 1:12–13), and made co-heirs with Christ (Romans 8:17).

This inheritance is not earned but bestowed, not deserved but freely given. To be poor in spirit is to exchange the fleeting riches of this world for the immeasurable riches of God's grace.

To live in poverty of spirit is to walk daily in the shadow of the cross. It is to be constantly reminded of who we are apart from Christ and who we have become in Him. This awareness is not meant to crush us but to keep us firmly anchored in the truth that everything we are and everything we have is a gift of grace. Such a posture then fundamentally reshapes the way we follow Jesus, because it keeps us dependent, teachable, and grateful.

Poverty of spirit combats one of the greatest dangers in the Christian life: pride. Pride is subtle and insidious, creeping in even after we have been humbled by the gospel. It whispers that our spiritual progress is our own doing, that our victories are signs of personal strength rather than God's sustaining grace. It thrives on comparison, measuring ourselves against others and concluding that we are doing well because we are not as bad as them. In Luke 18:11, we see this mindset in the Pharisee in Jesus' parable, who prayed, *"God, I thank you that I am not like other people."* But Jesus declared that it was the tax collector, not the Pharisee, who went home justified, because he understood his need and cast himself on God's mercy.

Poverty of spirit dismantles pride because it keeps us ever aware of our dependence on God. Paul himself modelled this attitude. Despite his extraordinary ministry, he described himself as *"the least of the apostles"* (1 Corinthians 15:9) and *"the worst of sinners"* (1 Timothy 1:15). This was not false humility it was an honest assessment of his own sinfulness in in the face of God's holiness. His awareness of grace deepened his love for Christ and his willingness to serve others. This is the fruit of poverty of spirit: we see ourselves rightly before God, so we can then serve God and others without seeking any recognition and love without demanding repayment.

This humility also makes us teachable. Those who are poor in spirit know they do not have all the answers. They approach Scripture and prayer not as masters seeking to confirm their own opinions but as learners eager to be shaped by God's truth. This was the attitude praised in Isaiah 66:2: *"These are the ones I look on with favour: those who are humble and contrite in spirit, and who tremble at my word."* Such trembling is not fear of judgment but reverent openness to correction and guidance. In a world that prizes self-assurance, poverty of spirit keeps us soft-hearted and responsive to the Lord's leading.

In daily discipleship, this means continually returning to the basics of the gospel. We never move beyond our need for God's mercy or our reliance on His Spirit.

Each day becomes an opportunity to rehearse the truth that apart from Christ we can do nothing (John 15:5). This is why prayer is indispensable for those who are poor in spirit. It is the language of dependence, the daily acknowledgment that we need God's wisdom, strength, and provision. Prayerlessness is often a clear sign of pride because it assumes that we can manage life on our own. But the poor in spirit pray continually because they know they cannot.

This dependence will also shape our response to trials. When hardships come, pride resists them, demanding answers and insisting on control. Poverty of spirit, by contrast, sees trials as reminders of our need for God's sustaining grace. It allows us to echo Paul's words in 2 Corinthians 12:9–10: *"My grace is sufficient for you, for my power is made perfect in weakness... For when I am weak, then I am strong."* Weakness becomes an occasion for God's power to be displayed, and suffering becomes a teacher that deepens our reliance on Him. Rather than resenting our need, we learn to rejoice that it drives us closer to Christ.

This posture also frees us from the crushing burden of personal performance. So much of modern life revolves around proving ourselves - whether in careers, relationships, or even ministry. We measure worth by productivity, and our identity is often formed by our accomplishment. But poverty of spirit liberates us from this relentless striving. It reminds us that our value is not in what we achieve but in whose we are. We are beloved children of God, accepted not because of our merit but because of Christ's finished work. This frees us to work diligently without anxiety, serve faithfully without fear of failure, and rest securely in the love of our Father.

Living this way also prepares us for the rest of the Beatitudes. Spiritual poverty is not only the first step but the root from which the other blessings grow. Those who know their need will mourn over sin, not only in themselves but in the world. They will be meek, trusting God rather than asserting themselves. They will hunger and thirst for righteousness, recognizing their lack and longing for His fullness.

They will extend mercy freely because they have received mercy freely. They will be pure in heart, not pretending to be more than they are but seeking integrity before God. They will make peace, having themselves been reconciled. When persecution comes, they endure with hope because their security is in the kingdom, not in this world. In short, all the Beatitudes flow from the first: a heart that knows its poverty and clings to God's grace.

This also explains why Jesus begins the Sermon here. Before He speaks of anger, lust, forgiveness, prayer, or any other aspect of righteousness, He first addresses the heart's posture before God. If we do not begin with spiritual poverty, we will hear the rest of the Sermon as burdensome demands rather than invitations to life. Only when we recognize that we are poor in spirit can we receive the Sermon not as a list of impossible standards but as a description of what God produces in those who trust Him.

This is why it is essential for us to see that this Beatitude is not a command but a declaration. Jesus does not say, *"Be poor in spirit,"* as if we could manufacture such humility ourselves. He says, *"Blessed are the poor in spirit."* He is describing what is true of those who have encountered God's grace.

Poverty of spirit is the natural response of seeing ourselves clearly in light of His holiness and our sin. It is not something we perform to earn blessing; it is evidence that His blessing has already reached us.

This distinction matters deeply for how we live each day. All too often, Christians fall into the trap of trying to imitate kingdom qualities whilst lacking kingdom power. We see the beauty of meekness or mercy and attempt to cultivate them in our own strength. But without the foundation of poverty of spirit, such efforts quickly turn into prideful self-improvement projects.

We begin to think we are the ones producing righteousness, and our gaze shifts from Christ to ourselves. The result is either pride when we think we succeed or despair when we inevitably fail.

The remedy is to return again and again to this first Beatitude. It calls us to empty our hands daily so that we might be filled anew. It invites us to confess our need continually so that we might receive afresh the sufficiency of Christ. It keeps us rooted in grace, the soil from which every other virtue grows.

As Martin Luther famously wrote in the first of his ninety-five theses, *"When our Lord and Master Jesus Christ said, 'Repent,' he willed the entire life of believers to be one of repentance."* Repentance is the ongoing expression of poverty of spirit: acknowledging our need and turning to the One Who meets it.

In this way, poverty of spirit is not a place we visit but a home we live in. It is not the first rung on a ladder we leave behind but the foundation we build upon daily. Every time we open God's Word, approach Him in prayer, or serve in His name, we do so as those who have nothing apart from Him. It is in that posture, we discover the paradoxical joy of the kingdom: that those who come empty are filled, those who confess their weakness are made strong, and those who humble themselves are lifted up.

This is why Jesus' opening words here are so crucial. They do not simply introduce the Sermon on the Mount; they unlock it. To be poor in spirit is to stand in the doorway of the kingdom, ready to receive all that follows. It is to hear Jesus' words not as a distant ideal but as a living promise: *"Blessed are the poor in spirit, for theirs is the kingdom of heaven."*

With this foundation laid, we are now ready to explore the next Beatitude: *"Blessed are those who mourn, for they will be comforted."* If spiritual poverty confronts our pride, mourning confronts our complacency. It calls us to grieve over sin and suffering with hearts tuned to God's mercy, taking us deeper into the process of kingdom transformation.

3

'BLESSED ARE THOSE WHO MOURN'

Matthew 5:4

"Blessed are those who mourn, for they will be comforted."

At first glance, these words seem to be contradictory. How can mourning be a blessing? In our culture, mourning is associated with grief, loss, and pain - things we instinctively want to avoid. Yet Jesus declares that those who mourn are not cursed, they are blessed, and that their mourning will lead to divine comfort. As with the first Beatitude, He is overturning our assumptions and pointing us toward a deeper spiritual reality.

To understand this Beatitude, we must first ask: what kind of mourning is Jesus talking about? This is not mere sadness over unfortunate circumstances or natural grief over personal loss, though those are experiences addressed elsewhere in the Bible. Rather, this is mourning rooted in spiritual awareness. It flows from the recognition of sin - our own and the world's - and from the longing for God's righteousness to prevail. It is the sorrow of those who see the brokenness of creation and yearn for God to make it right.

This is why the Beatitudes build upon each another. Poverty of spirit leads naturally to mourning. When we finally see ourselves clearly before God - acknowledging our spiritual bankruptcy - we cannot help but grieve over our sin and its consequences.

The closer we draw to the holiness of God, the more we become aware of the gap between His perfection and our failings. This awareness is not meant to drive us to despair but to repentance.

As the Apostle Paul writes in 2 Corinthians 7:10, *"Godly sorrow brings repentance that leads to salvation and leaves no regret, but worldly sorrow brings death."* The mourning Jesus talks about is not destructive guilt but godly sorrow that turns us back to Him.

We see this kind of mourning vividly in the life of King David. After his sin with Bathsheba and the subsequent confrontation by the prophet Nathan, David penned Psalm 51 - a psalm of repentance that captures the heart of this Beatitude. He prays, *"Against you, you only, have I sinned and done what is evil in your sight."* (Psalm 51:4). His grief is not merely over the consequences of his actions but over the offense against God's holiness. This is mourning that looks upward, grieving not only for what has been lost but for how our sin wounds the heart of God.

The prophet Isaiah also reflects this posture in his vision of the Lord's glory. Confronted with God's holiness, he cries out, *"Woe to me! ... I am ruined! For I am a man of unclean lips, and I live among a people of unclean lips."* (Isaiah 6:5). His mourning is personal *and* communal: he laments his own sin and that of his people. Yet it is precisely in this moment of confession that God acts in mercy, touching Isaiah's lips with a coal and declaring, *"Your guilt is taken away and your sin atoned for."* (Isaiah 6:7). Mourning over sin becomes the gateway to forgiveness.

Jesus Himself modelled this kind of mourning. He wept over Jerusalem, lamenting its hardness of heart and blindness to the things that would bring peace (Luke 19:41–42). He was *"deeply moved in spirit and troubled"* at the tomb of Lazarus, entering into human grief and sorrow (John 11:33–35). In these moments, we see that mourning is not weakness, but compassion aligned with God's heart. To mourn as Jesus did is to feel the weight of a fallen world, to be grieved by what grieves Him, and to long for His redeeming work.

This Beatitude also has a corporate dimension. True disciples not only mourn their own sin but also the sin and suffering around them. Like Nehemiah, who wept over the ruins of Jerusalem (Nehemiah 1:4), or Daniel, who confessed the sins of his people as his own (Daniel 9:4–5), the poor in spirit do not distance themselves from the brokenness of the world. They intercede for it, grieving over injustice, violence, and rebellion against God. This is not despairing cynicism but prayerful lament, born from love for God and neighbour.

This mourning is deeply countercultural. Our society is adept at distraction, numbing discomfort with entertainment, pleasure, or busyness. We prefer denial to lament, positivity to penitence. But Jesus calls us to face reality: to see sin for what it is, to recognize its destructive power, and to feel its weight. Only then can we truly appreciate the grace that meets us in our grief. As Jesus later said (Luke 7:47) of the sinful woman who anointed His feet, *"Her many sins have been forgiven - as her great love has shown."* Those who mourn deeply over sin always love deeply the Saviour Who forgives that sin.

Yet this Beatitude is not merely about sorrow; it is about comfort. *"Blessed are those who mourn,"* Jesus says, *"for they will be comforted."* This promise echoes Isaiah 61:1–3, a passage Jesus Himself read in the synagogue at Nazareth: *"The Spirit of the Sovereign Lord is on me... He has sent me to bind up the broken-hearted... to comfort all who mourn... to bestow on them a crown of beauty instead of ashes."* This is the comfort of redemption, the exchange of grief for joy, sin for forgiveness, ashes for beauty. It is not shallow consolation, but deep restoration rooted in God's saving work.

This comfort comes first through the gospel. When we mourn our sin and turn to Jesus Christ in repentance, He meets us with pardon. As John assures us in his first letter, *"If we confess our sins, he is faithful and just and will forgive us our sins and purify us from all unrighteousness."* (1 John 1:9). The Spirit of God applies the forgiveness which is ours in Christ to our hearts, lifting the burden of guilt and replacing it with peace. This is the comfort of knowing that our sins are remembered no more, that we are clothed in Christ's righteousness, and are reconciled to God.

This deep comfort also looks ahead to the future. Jesus' promise is both present and eschatological. Even now, we experience the Spirit's comfort as the *"Counsellor"* or *"Comforter"* who dwells within us (John 14:16). Yet we also look forward to the day when mourning will be no more, when God *"will wipe every tear from their eyes."* (Revelation 21:4). Our present mourning over sin and suffering anticipates that final renewal, when Christ will make all things new.

In this sense, to mourn is to align ourselves with the groaning of creation itself, which *"waits in eager expectation"* for redemption (Romans 8:19–23).

Mourning, then, is not hopeless grief but hope-infused lament. It is the cry of those who know that things are not as they should be but who trust that God will set them right. This kind of mourning is essential for spiritual health. Without it, we risk becoming numb to sin, indifferent to injustice, or complacent in our walk with God. Mourning keeps us sensitive to His holiness and compassionate toward a hurting world. It keeps us longing for His kingdom to come in fullness.

Practically, cultivating this kind of mourning involves a number of key elements. First, it requires honest self-examination. Like David praying in Psalm 139:23, *"Search me, God, and know my heart,"* we must invite the Spirit to reveal areas where we fall short and grieve over them appropriately. This is not morbid introspection but Spirit-led conviction that leads to confession and renewal. Second, it involves empathy and intercession.

When we see suffering or wrongdoing around us, we do not simply shake our heads; we bring it before our God in prayer, standing in the gap as those who mourn and plead for His mercy. Finally, it demands that we resist the temptation to anesthetize our souls with distraction. We must create space to feel - to weep, to lament, to bring our brokenness and the world's brokenness before the Lord.

Jesus' promise of comfort for those who mourn is not theoretical; it is deeply personal and experiential. When we grieve over sin - our own or the brokenness of the world - God Himself draws near. This is why Scripture repeatedly links His presence to those who are lowly and contrite.

Psalm 34:18 declares, *"The Lord is close to the broken-hearted and saves those who are crushed in spirit."* Mourning does not drive God away; it draws Him close. Our tears are not wasted - they are met by His tender compassion and redeeming power.

This comfort is multi-layered. First of all, it is the comfort of forgiveness. When we mourn our sin and confess it to God, we experience the relief of knowing that our guilt has already been removed. This is not merely a change in legal status but a felt reality. David captures this in Psalm 32:1-2: *"Blessed is the one whose transgressions are forgiven, whose sins are covered. Blessed is the one whose sin the Lord does not count against them."* His mourning over sin in Psalm 51 leads to this declaration of joy in Psalm 32. There is a profound comfort in knowing that our past will no longer condemn us, that we are now clothed in Christ's righteousness and fully reconciled to God.

This forgiveness is not just a theoretical knowledge - it is deeply experiential. Those who have wept over their sin and then tasted God's grace often speak of their indescribable peace, a lightness of the soul, and a profound relief that surpasses any human understanding.

Jesus' parable of the prodigal son (Luke 15:11-32) captures this dynamic beautifully. The son's journey home should be marked by deep shame, but he is met not with condemnation but with embrace. Any mourning he may have over his sin flows directly from the Father's joyous welcome: *"Quick! Bring the best robe and put it on him... For this son of mine was dead and is alive again."* (Luke 15:22). Here we see God's heart of comfort: it is restorative, celebratory, and full of love.

Second, this is the comfort of transformation. Mourning over sin is not merely about forgiveness for past failures; it is also about longing for change in the present. God meets us in our grief not only to console us but to transform us. This is the dynamic of repentance described in 2 Corinthians 7:11, where Paul writes, *"See what this godly sorrow has produced in you: what earnestness, what eagerness to clear yourselves, what indignation, what alarm, what longing, what concern, what readiness to see justice done."* Godly mourning leads to renewed zeal for holiness and a much greater sensitivity to sin. It drives us to depend more fully on God's Spirit, who comforts us not only with pardon but with power to walk in newness of life.

This transformation deepens our intimacy with Christ. When we truly mourn our sin and draw near to the Lord in repentance, we encounter a sympathetic Saviour, not a distant judge. Hebrews reminds us, *"For we do not have a high priest who is unable to empathize with our weaknesses, but we have one who has been tempted in every way, just as we are—yet he did not sin."* (Hebrews 4:15). Jesus is not aloof from our struggles; He enters into them. He understands our frailty, bears our burdens, and ministers grace in our need. Mourning opens our hearts to receive this comfort, drawing us closer to His heart.

Indeed, mourning aligns us with the very heart of Jesus, who was *"a man of sorrows, and familiar with suffering."* (Isaiah 53:3). He wept over Lazarus's tomb, even though He knew He would raise him from the dead (John 11:35). He lamented over Jerusalem, crying out, *"How often I have longed to gather your children together, as a hen gathers her chicks under her wings."* (Matthew 23:37). His mourning was born out of compassion and love, and when we mourn as He did, we share in His character. This intimacy with Christ is itself a profound comfort, for in our grief we discover that He is not only our Saviour but our companion.

Third, this Beatitude points to the great comfort of eschatological hope. While we experience forgiveness and transformation now, the ultimate fulfilment of Jesus' promise is awaiting His return. Revelation 21:4 offers this breathtaking vision: *"He will wipe every tear from their eyes. There will be no more death or mourning or crying or pain, for the old order of things has passed away."*

The mourning we experience in this life, even when redeemed, is only temporary. One day, God Himself will banish all causes of sorrow and usher us into everlasting joy. The comfort we taste now is a foretaste of that future glory, anchoring our hope in the certainty that our mourning will give way to rejoicing.

This eschatological perspective is crucial for enduring in faith. We live in a world still marred by sin, suffering, and injustice. Even as we experience personal forgiveness and transformation, we continue to witness pain and brokenness around us.

Without hope in God's ultimate restoration, such mourning could easily overwhelm us. But with eyes fixed firmly on Christ's return, we can grieve honestly without despair. As Paul writes in Romans 8:18, *"I consider that our present sufferings are not worth comparing with the glory that will be revealed in us."* This hope infuses our mourning with purpose and motivates us in pressing forward in faith.

Mourning also has a communal dimension. The comfort Jesus promises is not merely individual but shared among His people. The church is called to be a community where mourning is met with compassion and comfort. In Romans 12:15, Paul exhorts all believers to, *"Rejoice with those who rejoice; mourn with those who mourn."* This shared life means that we do not grieve alone.

In times of repentance, suffering, or lament over the brokenness of the world, we are upheld by the prayers and encouragement of fellow believers. Likewise, when we see others mourning, we are called to embody Christ's comfort to them through empathy, presence, and words of hope.

This is why confession and mutual encouragement are so vital within the church. James 5:16 says, *"Therefore confess your sins to each other and pray for each other so that you may be healed."* When we are honest about our struggles and mourn together, we create space for God's healing grace to be experienced in community. Far from isolating us, mourning will bind us together in shared dependence on God's mercy. The comfort we receive from Him is meant to overflow to others, as Paul declares, *"Praise be to... the Father of compassion and the God of all comfort, who comforts us in all our troubles, so that we can comfort those in any trouble with the comfort we ourselves receive from God."* (2 Corinthians 1:3-4)

This dynamic also extends to how the church engages the world. Mourning over sin and suffering fuels compassionate action. When we lament injustice, poverty, or violence, we are moved not only to prayer but to service. Like Nehemiah, whose tears over Jerusalem led him to rebuild its walls (Nehemiah 1–2), our mourning propels us into mission.

True mourning like this is never passive resignation; it is active alignment with God's redemptive purposes. It compels us to become agents of His comfort, extending mercy, advocating for justice, and proclaiming the hope of Christ in a hurting world.

In this sense, those who mourn play a prophetic role. Their tears bear witness to the fact that the world is not as it should be. They refuse to accept brokenness as normal. Their lament is a form of protest against sin and its effects, a cry for God's kingdom to come. This is why Jesus pronounces them *blessed:* because their mourning is evidence that their hearts are tuned to His. They feel what He feels, long for what He longs for, and are therefore assured of His comfort.

Practically, embracing this Beatitude means cultivating space for lament in both our personal and corporate worship. Too often, modern Christianity emphasizes triumph and positivity to the neglect of sorrow. Yet Scripture is full of lament: nearly one-third of the Psalms are prayers of mourning. Incorporating these into our lives - whether through private prayer, fasting, or communal lament in the gathered church - keeps our hearts tender and our hope anchored in God's promises. Such practices remind us that mourning is not a sign of weak faith, it is a pathway to deeper dependence and comfort.

Mourning over sin and brokenness is not merely an emotional response; it is a means by which God matures us in Christ. The spiritual life is not one of unbroken happiness detached from reality, but one of honest engagement with the world as it really is, coupled with faith in what God is doing to make it new. By calling His followers to mourn, Jesus is shaping their character, training them to see life through His eyes and to long for His redemptive purposes.

This Beatitude reminds us that Christian growth often comes not through ease and comfort but through wrestling with sorrow in the presence of God. This kind of mourning teaches us to hate sin not simply because of its consequences but because of its offense against God.

Too often, our grief over sin is shallow, rooted in regret that we were caught or that our actions brought us pain or shame. But true mourning moves us beyond self-interest to a God-centred sorrow. We grieve because sin distorts God's good creation, separates us from Him, and wounds others. This is why David, after his grievous failure, prayed, *"Against you, you only, have I sinned and done what is evil in your sight."* (Psalm 51:4).

Even though his sin had harmed many people, David's primary anguish was that he had offended his holy God. This perspective is the essence of spiritual maturity: seeing sin as God sees it and feeling its weight accordingly.

Yet this mourning does not paralyze us; it leads to repentance and renewal. God uses our sorrow over sin to draw us back to Himself, restoring fellowship and reshaping our desires. This is the pattern Paul describes in 2 Corinthians 7:10–11, where godly sorrow produces earnestness, eagerness to make things right, and zeal for righteousness. Mourning softens our hearts, uproots our complacency, and turns us toward holiness. In this way, sorrow is not opposed to joy but is actually a pathway to it. Those who grieve their sin most deeply will rejoice most fully in God's grace because they know the depth of their own forgiveness.

Mourning also matures us by cultivating compassion. When we experience brokenness firsthand - whether through our own sin, the suffering of others, or the world's injustice - we become more empathetic toward those who hurt. Our tears teach us to weep with those who weep (Romans 12:15), to bear one another's burdens (Galatians 6:2), and to extend grace freely. Those who have been comforted by God are uniquely equipped to comfort others. They know what it means to be crushed and restored, wounded and healed. Their words carry weight because they speak from experience, not theory.

This is why seasons of mourning, though painful, often deepen our ministry to others. Those who have walked through grief or repentance with God emerge with a tenderness that cannot be manufactured.

They become living testimonies of His comfort, able to enter into others' pain without fear or judgment. The Apostle Paul tells us in 2 Corinthians 1:3-4 that God, *"comforts us in all our troubles, so that we can comfort those in any trouble with the comfort we ourselves receive from God."* Mourning therefore can become a means of multiplying grace, as the comfort we receive overflows into the lives of others.

Furthermore, mourning keeps our hope fixed on eternity. In a world prone to distraction and superficiality, sorrow will have a clarifying effect. It strips away illusions, reminding us that we are pilgrims passing through a broken world. When we grieve over sin or suffering, we are reminded that this is not our home and that something better is coming.

This longing for restoration echoes the deep groaning of creation described in Romans 8:22-23: *"We know that the whole creation has been groaning as in the pains of childbirth right up to the present time. Not only so, but we ourselves… groan inwardly as we wait eagerly for our adoption to sonship, the redemption of our bodies."*

This eschatological dimension gives mourning its redemptive shape. We do not grieve as those who are without hope, because our sorrow is tethered to God's promise that He will wipe away every tear. Every lament whispered in prayer is ultimately an expression of faith that the world will not remain as it is. Our mourning becomes a yearning cry: *"Your kingdom come, your will be done, on earth as it is in heaven."* (Matthew 6:10). This forward-looking hope sustains us in the present and prevents our grief from turning into despair.

In this way, mourning not only matures us but also aligns us with the heart of Jesus. He was not indifferent to the brokenness around Him; He entered into it fully. He bore our griefs and carried our sorrows (Isaiah 53:4), and in His humanity, He felt deeply the weight of sin's consequences. His tears over Jerusalem reveal His compassion for those blind to their need (Luke 19:41-42), while His anguish in Gethsemane shows His willingness to bear the cost of redemption (Matthew 26:36-39).

When we mourn, we follow in His steps, learning to see the world as He does and to respond as He did - with both grief and hope. This Beatitude, therefore, calls us to a spirituality that is both realistic and hopeful. It resists the shallow optimism that ignores sin and suffering, but it also rejects the cynicism that sees no way forward.

It invites us to live in the real tension of the 'now' and 'not yet'- already comforted by God's forgiveness and presence, but not yet free from the world's pain and imperfection. To live here is to be honest about our need and steadfast in our hope, mourning what is wrong while clinging to the One Who will make it right.

Practically, how do we cultivate this posture? One key is to make space in our lives for honest lament. Our prayers should include confession and sorrow over sin, both personal and communal. This is not some morbid fixation but healthy acknowledgment of reality before God. Psalms of lament such as Psalm 6, Psalm 32, and Psalm 51 provide the language for this, teaching us how to grieve in faith. In worship, we can recover the biblical rhythm of lament and praise, holding sorrow and joy together.

We also cultivate mourning through our engagement with the world's brokenness. When we encounter injustice, poverty, or suffering, our first response should not be to turn away or grow numb, but to bring those realities before God in prayer and to ask how the Lord might use us as instruments of His comfort. Mourning should move us towards action - feeding the hungry, comforting the grieving, advocating for the oppressed. Our tears then become seeds of service, compelling us to embody God's kingdom in tangible ways.

Finally, mourning prepares us for meekness, the next Beatitude. As we grieve over sin and yet depend on God's grace, we are humbled. Mourning strips us of arrogance and self-assertion, softening our hearts and teaching us to submit to God's will. This humility is the true essence of meekness: strength under control, yielded to God. In this sense, the Beatitudes form a very natural progression.

Spiritual poverty leads toward mourning; mourning leads to meekness; and meekness opens up the way for a life of deeper righteousness and mercy. Each step builds upon the one before, painting a coherent picture of kingdom character.

In the end, this Beatitude assures us that those who mourn are not forgotten. God Himself is attentive to every single tear. As the Psalmist declares, *"Record my misery; list my tears on your scroll — are they not in your record?"* (Psalm 56:8). Our mourning is precious to Him, and His promise is sure: those who mourn will be comforted. This comfort begins now in the assurance of His presence and forgiveness and will be completed in the day when sorrow and sighing shall flee away forever (Isaiah 35:10).

Thus, mourning is not the opposite of blessing but its pathway. It is how we learn to depend on God, to hate sin, to love mercy, and to long for His kingdom. Far from being a sign of weakness, it is evidence that our hearts are alive to God's Spirit and attuned to His holiness. It is a sign that we are truly His.

As we move forward to the next Beatitude - *"Blessed are the meek, for they will inherit the earth"* - we see how this process of humility deepens. The one who mourns over sin is the one who has been broken of pride and is ready to submit to God's authority. This is the path of genuine discipleship: downward in humility and dependence, upward in grace and blessing. It begins in poverty of spirit, passes through mourning, and blossoms in meekness - a journey that reflects the very character of Christ Himself.

- 4 -
'BLESSED ARE THE MEEK'

Matthew 5:5

"Blessed are the meek, for they will inherit the earth."

With this brief statement, Jesus is continuing to dismantle all the world's values and redefine what it means to live under God's reign. Meekness is not a trait commonly celebrated in our culture - or in any culture, for that matter. From the ancient world to today, strength is what is admired, dominance is respected, and assertiveness is rewarded. Yet Jesus declares that it is the meek - not the powerful - who will inherit the earth. With these words, Jesus confronts both our assumptions about strength and our understanding of what true blessing looks like.

To grasp this Beatitude, we must first understand what Jesus means here by meekness. In everyday speech, meekness is often confused with weakness, passivity, or timidity. But the biblical concept is far richer and far stronger. Meekness is not the absence of power, but it is restraint. The best way to describe meekness is: *'Strength under control, surrendered to God's will.'* A meek person is not spineless or ineffectual; rather, they possess a quiet strength that refuses to assert itself in pride or aggression. They are willing to wait on God, trust His timing, and yield their rights rather than grasping for their own advantage.

The Greek word translated *"meek" (praus)* carries this nuance of controlled strength. In classical usage, it described a wild animal tamed by its master - not broken or weakened but harnessed and disciplined. Similarly, biblical meekness is not about us being powerless, it's about submitting power to God. It is a deliberate choice to lay down self-assertion in favour of trustful obedience.

This is why meekness is closely tied to humility. It flows from the poverty of spirit we studied in the first Beatitude and the mourning over sin we encountered in the second. The meek are those who, humbled before God and grieved by their sin, no longer seek to elevate themselves but to serve and obey.

Scripture provides several powerful portraits of meekness. One of the clearest is Moses, described in Numbers 12:3 as *"a very humble man, more humble than anyone else on the face of the earth."* Yet Moses was no weakling. He confronted Pharaoh, led Israel out of Egypt, and stood between the people and God's wrath. His meekness was not timidity – it was submission. When he was criticized by Miriam and Aaron, Moses did not defend himself or retaliate; he entrusted the situation to God, Who vindicated him. His strength lay not in self-assertion but in quiet reliance on God's justice.

The supreme example of meekness, of course, is Jesus Himself. He described His own heart in Matthew 11:29: *"Take my yoke upon you and learn from me, for I am gentle and humble in heart."* Here, the word *"gentle"* is the same Greek word as *"meek"* in Matthew 5:5. Jesus embodied this quality perfectly. He wielded full divine authority, commanding storms and casting out demons, yet He also came *"gentle and riding on a donkey"* (Matthew 21:5). He did not force Himself upon others but invited them: *"Come to me"* (Matthew 11:28). Even in His passion, He demonstrated this meekness. When reviled, *"he did not retaliate; when he suffered, he made no threats. Instead, he entrusted himself to him who judges justly."* (1 Peter 2:23). Meekness in action is strength restrained; power submitted to God; trust triumphing over self-defence.

This definition now helps us see why meekness follows naturally from poverty of spirit and mourning. The poor in spirit know they have nothing apart from God; those who mourn their sin are broken of pride. Meekness is the outworking of these realities in how we relate to others and to God's providence. The meek do not need to dominate or control because they trust God to be their defender and provider. They are freed from the restless striving that characterizes so much of our human life. Instead of clawing for position or recognition, they can just serve quietly, endure mistreatment without bitterness, and wait for God's vindication. This is profoundly countercultural. In nearly every sphere of life, from politics to business to social relationships, those who push hardest often seem to get ahead. Assertiveness is celebrated as a virtue; meekness is dismissed as weakness.

Yet Jesus declares that the meek are blessed – they are not merely tolerated but favoured by God. His promise that they *"will inherit the earth"* is a stunning and bold reversal of worldly logic. While the powerful scramble to seize control and secure their place, Jesus says it is those who humbly submit to God who will receive it as a gift.

This language of *"inheritance"* draws from the Old Testament. Psalm 37, which most likely underlies this Beatitude, repeatedly contrasts the fate of the wicked and the meek. *"The meek will inherit the land and enjoy peace and prosperity."* (Psalm 37:11). In this psalm, the *"land"* refers to the promised land of Israel, symbolizing God's provision and blessing.

The psalm exhorts the reader not to fret over evildoers who seem to prosper but to *"trust in the Lord and do good... Commit your way to the Lord; trust in him and he will do this."* (Psalm 37:3–5). This is the essence of meekness: trusting God rather than striving in self-reliance.

Jesus expands this promise beyond Israel to encompass *"the earth."* Ultimately, this points to the new creation described in Revelation 21:1–7, when God will renew heaven and earth and dwell with His people. Those who live in meek submission now will reign with Christ in His restored world. This eschatological dimension gives meekness its hope. Those who are meek may be overlooked or trampled in this age, but their vindication is sure. Their inheritance is secure not because they seize it but because God has promised it.

In the meantime, meekness transforms how we live here and now. It shapes our relationships by freeing us from the need to assert our rights or win every argument. Paul exhorts believers in Ephesians 4:2 to *"be completely humble and gentle; be patient, bearing with one another in love."* This is meekness applied: humility that restrains pride, gentleness that diffuses conflict, patience that endures wrong without retaliation. Far from making us passive, meekness makes us peacemakers, for we no longer need to prove ourselves at others' expense.

Meekness also reorients our attitude toward God's providence. A meek person does not resent the twists and turns of life but submits to God's wise hand. They echo Job's words: *"The Lord gave and the Lord has taken away; may the name of the Lord be praised."* (Job 1:21). This is not fatalism but faith. It trusts that God is sovereign and good even when circumstances are hard. Such meekness enables us to rest rather than rage, to endure rather than grasp, because we believe that *"all things work together for the good of those who love him."* (Romans 8:28).

This is why meekness requires strength. It is far easier to retaliate than to refrain, to push forward than to wait, to seize control than to surrender. Meekness demands discipline of heart and mind, forged in the furnace of dependence on God. It is not natural; it is supernatural, produced by the Spirit's work in us. Paul, in Galatians 5:23, lists gentleness (or meekness) as a fruit of the Spirit, evidence that our lives are being shaped by His presence. Only those who know God as Father and Christ as Lord can truly lay down their pride and rest in His care.

The promise attached to meekness - *"they will inherit the earth"* - reminds us that our future is secure in Him. We do not need to grasp for what God has already pledged to give. The inheritance is not earned by force but granted by grace. Just as Israel did not conquer the promised land by their own power but by God's hand, so we will inherit the renewed earth not through ambition or striving but through meek trust in Christ. This frees us to live differently now, unburdened by the scramble for status and control that defines so much of human life.

Meekness profoundly changes the way we relate to others. Because it flows from humility and trust in God, meekness frees us from the relentless need to assert ourselves or compete for recognition. Instead of seeing others as rivals or obstacles, we begin to view them as fellow image-bearers of God, deserving of dignity and compassion. This transformation is so beautifully described in Philippians 2:3-4: *"Do nothing out of selfish ambition or vain conceit. Rather, in humility value others above yourselves, not looking to your own interests but each of you to the interests of the others."*

Meekness is the outworking of this mindset - it shifts our focus from self-promotion to service. This does not mean we become passive or indifferent, but rather that we learn to exercise strength for the good of others rather than ourselves. Meekness restrains the instinct to dominate or retaliate, replacing it with gentleness and patience.

Paul exhorts believers in Colossians 3:12: *"Clothe yourselves with compassion, kindness, humility, gentleness and patience."* Notice how these virtues cluster together. Meekness is not isolated; it is woven into a fabric of Christlike character that reshapes how we interact with the world.

One of the clearest expressions of meekness in relationships is our response to conflict and offense. Our human pride demands vindication; it resists insult and insists on being proven right. Meekness, however, is willing to absorb wrong without seeking revenge. Proverbs 15:1 reminds us, *"A gentle answer turns away wrath, but a harsh word stirs up anger."*

Meekness diffuses tension rather than escalating it. It chooses restraint over retaliation, even when mistreated. This is not weakness, but strength submitted to God's will, echoing Jesus' own response when He *"did not retaliate"* but *"entrusted himself to him who judges justly"* (1 Peter 2:23).

This does not mean meekness condones injustice or tolerates abuse. It's really important to distinguish biblical meekness from passivity or enabling wrongdoing. True meekness does not ignore sin or injustice; rather, it addresses them both without resorting to prideful aggression or self-serving anger.

Jesus Himself, though meek and gentle, confronted wrongdoing with courage. He drove the money changers from the temple (John 2:13-17) and denounced the hypocrisy of the Pharisees (Matthew 23). His meekness was not the absence of strength but the perfect alignment of strength with righteousness and love. In our own lives, meekness equips us to endure unfair treatment without bitterness.

Whether in workplaces, families, or communities, there will be times when we are overlooked, misunderstood, or wronged. The natural impulse is to fight back, assert our rights, and demand recognition. But the meek, trusting God's justice, can choose a different path.

They resist the urge to retaliate or manipulate outcomes, resting instead in the assurance that God sees and will vindicate in His time. This is why Psalm 37, the backdrop of this Beatitude, exhorts us: *"Be still before the Lord and wait patiently for him; do not fret when people succeed in their ways."* (Psalm 37:7).

This waiting on God is not passive resignation but active faith. It refuses to take matters into our own hands because it trusts that God's timing and ways are better than ours. Abraham is an example of this trust. When strife arose between his herdsmen and Lot's, Abraham, though older and entitled to choose first, meekly allowed Lot to select the land he wanted. Abraham's confidence in God's promise set him free from grasping for advantage. As a result, God reaffirmed His covenant with him and blessed him abundantly. Meekness rests in this same confidence: that what God has promised, He will surely provide.

Meekness also manifests in teachability. Those who are meek are open to instruction, correction, and growth. They do not resist wise counsel or bristle at rebuke because they are not enslaved to pride. Proverbs 9:9 says, *"Instruct the wise and they will be wiser still; teach the righteous and they will add to their learning."*

Meekness creates a posture of humility that welcomes learning and recognizes that we do not know everything. This is essential for discipleship, for only those willing to be taught can be shaped into Christ's likeness.

Furthermore, meekness reflects the very character of Jesus. As we saw earlier, He described Himself as *"gentle and humble in heart."* (Matthew 11:29). His invitation - *"Take my yoke upon you and learn from me"* - is not merely about receiving rest but about adopting His way of life.

To be meek is to walk in His footsteps, to embody His gentleness and restraint in how we engage with others. This is also not something we can achieve in our own strength; it is the fruit of His Spirit working in us. Galatians 5:23 includes gentleness as part of the Spirit's fruit, evidence that He is shaping us to resemble our Lord.

One of the most striking aspects of Jesus' meekness was His voluntary submission during His arrest and crucifixion. He told Peter in Matthew 26:53, *"Do you think I cannot call on my Father, and he will at once put at my disposal more than twelve legions of angels?"* Yet He restrained His power and chose the path of suffering for our sake.

His meekness was not weakness; it was strength willingly laid down out of love and obedience to the Father. When we respond to provocation with restraint, or to hostility with grace, we mirror this same Christlike meekness to a watching world.

This witness is powerful because it is so rare. In a society that prizes dominance, control, and self-assertion, meekness stands out as a radical alternative. It demonstrates that our confidence is not in ourselves but in God. It invites others to see a different way of living - a life unburdened by the frantic scramble for status and recognition. It points to the One who said, *"Learn from me,"* and whose strength was revealed through His humility.

Moreover, meekness has a ripple effect on our communities. When we forgo retaliation and respond with gentleness, we create space for reconciliation and peace. Meekness de-escalates conflicts that pride would inflame. It fosters unity in the church, where believers are called to *"make every effort to keep the unity of the Spirit through the bond of peace."* (Ephesians 4:3).

In marriages, families, and friendships, meekness nurtures environments of trust and safety, where disagreements can be resolved without hostility. Its quiet strength helps stabilize our relationships and builds bridges rather than walls.

The promise attached to meekness - *"they will inherit the earth"* - deeply anchors this way of life in hope. It assures us that even if meekness may seem costly now, its reward is guaranteed. The inheritance language signals both present and future blessings. Even now, those who are meek experience a foretaste of this inheritance as they rest in God's care and enjoy His provision. They are freed from the exhausting pursuit of self-exaltation and from the anxiety of defending their own interests. They live with the settled confidence that their lives are in God's hands. And one day, when Christ returns, they will fully inherit the renewed earth, reigning with Him in perfect peace and joy.

This future-oriented perspective empowers meekness in the present. Because we know our ultimate inheritance is secure, we can afford to relinquish our grip on temporary claims. We can resist the urge to fight for every advantage or prove ourselves in every conflict.

We can respond to provocation with grace because we know that God is our defender and our rewarder. Our confidence in His promises enables us to lay down our pride and embrace the way of meekness, even when it runs against the grain of our instincts and our culture.

In this way, meekness is both deeply practical and profoundly theological. It shapes how we treat other people in everyday interactions, but it also reveals what we truly believe about God. Do we trust His justice enough to forego retaliation? Do we trust His provision enough to release our grip on control? Do we trust God's promises enough to wait patiently for His vindication? Meekness answers *"yes"* to each of these questions. It is faith made visible in our posture toward God and people alike.

Meekness is essential for true discipleship. It is the quality that enables us to follow Jesus not only when His path is easy but also when it is costly. Discipleship involves surrendering our will to His. It means setting aside our own agendas and ambitions to embrace His call, even when it demands sacrifice. Meekness is what allows us to say, as Jesus did in Gethsemane, *"Not my will, but yours be done."* (Luke 22:42).

Without meekness, our pride resists this surrender, clinging to control and insisting on our own way. With meekness, however, we are freed to entrust ourselves fully to God's wisdom and care.

This is why Jesus repeatedly linked discipleship to self-denial. *"Whoever wants to be my disciple,"* He said, *"must deny themselves and take up their cross daily and follow me."* (Luke 9:23). Such denial is impossible without meekness. The proud heart recoils at the idea of yielding authority or enduring hardship for another's sake. But the meek heart, having already been humbled before God, is willing to lay down rights, privileges, and even life itself in obedience to Christ. This is not resignation but joyful submission, born of confidence that His path leads to life and His promises will not fail.

Meekness also protects us from the lure of worldly power. In every age, the world has equated strength with dominance, authority with coercion, and leadership with control. We see it in politics, business, and even within a number of our religious institutions: the drive to climb higher, to outmanoeuvre rivals, to secure influence at any cost.

Yet Jesus calls His followers to a radically different model of greatness. *"You know that the rulers of the Gentiles lord it over them,"* He said, *"but it shall not be so among you. Instead, whoever wants to become great among you must be your servant."* (Matthew 20:25–26).

Meekness embodies this upside-down greatness. It rejects the grasping ambition that so often corrupts power and instead embraces servanthood. It is willing to take the lowest place, confident that God will exalt in His time. This is precisely what Jesus modelled: *"He humbled himself by becoming obedient to death - even death on a cross! Therefore, God exalted him to the highest place."* (Philippians 2:8–9).

His exaltation followed His humiliation, and the same pattern holds true for His disciples. The meek may appear unimpressive to the world, but their reward is certain: *"they will inherit the earth."*

This inheritance, however, is not merely future-oriented. Even now, meekness liberates us from the relentless anxiety and striving that dominate so much of life. When we no longer feel compelled to defend our reputation or secure our own personal advancement, we can live with a peace that others envy but do not understand. Isaiah 26:3 captures this serenity: *"You will keep in perfect peace those whose minds are steadfast, because they trust in you."* Meekness flows from this trust, and it produces a calmness that cannot be shaken by circumstances or by the actions of others.

This calm, however, does not mean complacency. Meekness is not passivity or withdrawal from engagement with the world. It is precisely because the meek trust God that they can act boldly when He calls them to. Consider Jesus cleansing the temple: His zeal for His Father's house led Him to act decisively against corruption (John 2:13–17). His meekness did not prevent this; it defined it. He was not motivated by personal anger or pride but by holy zeal and submission to God's will. True meekness empowers us to act courageously for righteousness because our confidence is not in ourselves but in God.

This is why meekness leads naturally into the next Beatitude: *"Blessed are those who hunger and thirst for righteousness, for they will be filled."* (Matthew 5:6). The meek, having been humbled before God and freed from pride, now they long to see His righteousness prevail - in their own lives and also in the world. Meekness clears the ground for this hunger. It empties us of self-sufficiency, making room for God's purposes to take root. Those who are meek do not rely on their own power to accomplish righteousness but yearn for God to bring it about through His Spirit.

This hunger is more than a desire for moral improvement; it is a longing for God's justice and holiness to saturate every part of life. Meekness aligns our hearts with this longing by reorienting our ambitions. Instead of seeking dominance or recognition, the meek seek righteousness. They want to be conformed to Christ's image and to see His kingdom values manifested on earth.

Their focus shifts from building their own little empires to now participating in God's global redemptive mission. This is the natural progression of the Beatitudes: poverty of spirit empties us, mourning cleanses us, meekness humbles us and now hunger and thirst fill us.

But meekness not only prepares us to hunger for righteousness; it also equips us to pursue it rightly. Without meekness, even our pursuit of good things can be distorted by pride. We might seek righteousness merely to appear virtuous, to win arguments, or to assert moral superiority over others. But meekness purifies our motives. It teaches us to hunger for righteousness not for our own glory but for God's. It keeps us gentle and humble even as we seek justice or confront wrongdoing, ensuring that our zeal is tempered by grace.

This is particularly vital in our polarized world, where moral and political conflicts often devolve into anger, hostility, and prideful posturing. Meekness offers a different way, and it refuses to compromise truth but also refuses to wield it harshly. Paul captures this balance in 2 Timothy 2:24–25: *"The Lord's servant must not be quarrelsome but must be kind to everyone, able to teach, not resentful. Opponents must be gently instructed, in the hope that God will grant them repentance."* Here we see meekness at work: steadfast in truth, yet gentle in tone; firm in conviction, yet gracious in approach.

This Christlike meekness is desperately needed today. It is a witness in itself, pointing people to a kingdom not of this world. In a society where outrage often drowns out reason, where harshness masquerades as strength, the strength of meekness shines all the brighter. It demonstrates that our hope is not in winning earthly battles but in inheriting the earth when Christ returns. It shows that our confidence is not in our own ability to control outcomes but in the God who rules over all.

Cultivating this meekness requires intentional practice. It begins with daily surrender to God's will, echoing the prayer Jesus taught: *"Your kingdom come, your will be done"* (Matthew 6:10).

It involves learning to pause before reacting in anger, entrusting offenses to God rather than retaliating. It means choosing to listen before speaking, to serve before seeking recognition, to forgive rather than hold grudges. Over time, these small acts of humility train our hearts to rest in God's sovereignty and reflect His gentleness.

Prayer and Scripture meditation are vital in this process. As we soak in passages like Psalm 37 or Philippians 2, our vision of God's greatness and faithfulness expands, and our pride shrinks in comparison. The more we contemplate Christ's meekness - His restraint, His patience, His willingness to suffer for us - the more we are moved to imitate Him. Meekness is not self-generated; it is the fruit of our relationship with Jesus and being transformed by His Spirit (2 Corinthians 3:18).

In the end, meekness is both a gift and a calling. It is a gift because it springs from God's work in us, replacing pride with humility and anxiety with trust. It is a calling because it invites us to live in ways that seem foolish to the world but that align perfectly with the kingdom of heaven. The meek are blessed not because they grasp power but because they have relinquished it, confident that God will provide what they cannot secure for themselves.

As we move to the next Beatitude - *"Blessed are those who hunger and thirst for righteousness"* - we see how this humility fuels a deep longing for God's reign. Meekness empties us of self so that God can fill us with His righteousness. It positions us not as those striving to dominate but as those yearning for His will to be done. In this way, meekness is not an end in itself but a gateway into deeper dependence, deeper desire, and deeper joy in God's kingdom.

- 5 -

'BLESSED ARE THOSE WHO HUNGER AND THIRST FOR RIGHTEOUSNESS'

Matthew 5:6

"Blessed are those who hunger and thirst for righteousness, for they will be filled"

With this fourth Beatitude, Jesus shifts from the inward attitudes of humility, mourning, and meekness to the outward posture of desire. Having emptied ourselves of pride and self-reliance, we find our deepest craving redirected toward God's righteousness. This Beatitude speaks to longing - an intense yearning described not in mild terms of interest or preference but in the language of hunger and thirst, the most basic and urgent human needs.

Jesus is not addressing casual curiosity or occasional interest in righteousness. Hunger and thirst are primal drives that demand satisfaction. They are relentless and unavoidable. To be hungry or thirsty is to feel compelled toward what you lack, to recognize your need so sharply that it shapes your every thought and action. By using this imagery, Jesus is describing a deep spiritual appetite, an all-consuming desire for righteousness that is as vital to the soul as food and water are to the body.

This raises an important question: what does Jesus mean by righteousness? In the Scriptures, righteousness has a rich and multifaceted meaning. At its core, it refers to us being in right relationship with God - measured not by human standards but by His holiness. It is both positional and practical.

Positionally, righteousness is the gift we receive when we are justified by faith in Christ: *"This righteousness is given through faith in Jesus Christ to all who believe."* (Romans 3:22). So practically, righteousness refers to the ethical and moral conduct that flows from this restored relationship: living in alignment with God's will and reflecting His character in our actions.

This dual sense is key to understanding this Beatitude. Those who hunger and thirst for righteousness yearn both to be right with God and to live rightly before Him. They crave the righteousness that is imputed to us in Christ, knowing that apart from Him, *"there is no one righteous, not even one."* (Romans 3:10). But they also long for the righteousness that is imparted by the Spirit - holiness of heart and life that transforms how we think, speak, and act. This hunger is both forensic (our standing before God) and transformational (our daily growth in Christlikeness).

We must be clear: this hunger does not earn righteousness; it is evidence of God's grace already at work. Just as physical hunger signals life, spiritual hunger signals the presence of spiritual vitality. Dead people do not hunger. Likewise, those who are spiritually dead in sin feel no longing for God's righteousness. But those who have been made alive in Christ develop a new appetite - a deep dissatisfaction with sin and a restless desire for holiness. This hunger is a sign of new birth, the fruit of the Spirit drawing us toward God's will.

This longing also reflects the structure of the Beatitudes thus far. Spiritual poverty humbles us, showing us that we bring nothing to God. Mourning over sin breaks us, leading us to repentance. Meekness softens us, yielding our will to God's. Now, emptied of pride and self-sufficiency, we find ourselves hungry for what only God can give: His righteousness.

This progression is crucial. Only those who recognize their lack will hunger. Only those who have mourned over sin will crave holiness. Only those who are meek will submit to God's way of providing it.

Scripture is filled with imagery of this kind of hunger and thirst for God. The psalmist declares, *"As the deer pants for streams of water, so my soul pants for you, my God. My soul thirsts for God, for the living God."* (Psalm 42:1–2). In Psalm 63:1, David cries out from the wilderness, *"You, God, are my God, earnestly I seek you; I thirst for you, my whole being longs for you, in a dry and parched land where there is no water."* These are not casual words. They express desperation, intensity, and dependence.

To hunger and thirst for righteousness we need to be spiritually desperate for God's presence and His transforming work. This hunger is not self-generated. Just as our physical hunger is an involuntary response to the body's need for nourishment, our spiritual hunger is awakened by the Holy Spirit. It begins when God opens our eyes to His holiness and our inadequacy. Isaiah's vision in the temple is a powerful example: confronted by God's glory, he cries, *"Woe to me! ... I am ruined! For I am a man of unclean lips."* (Isaiah 6:5). That recognition of unworthiness leads to a longing for cleansing, which God graciously provides. Hunger for righteousness arises from the same place - an awareness of our sin combined with a vision of God's holiness and grace.

We see this hunger in the Apostle Paul's words, *"I want to know Christ - yes, to know the power of his resurrection and participation in his sufferings, becoming like him in his death."* (Philippians 3:10). Paul's desire is not simply to be forgiven but to be transformed, to know Christ deeply and be conformed to His image. This is the real essence of hungering and thirsting for righteousness: an insatiable longing to be like Jesus, to live in communion with Him, and to reflect His character in every aspect of life.

Importantly, this hunger is not limited to personal holiness; it extends outward into the world. Those who hunger and thirst for righteousness are grieved by injustice, oppression, and evil. They long for God's justice to be established on earth. This is why the prophets often connected righteousness with social concern: *"Learn to do right; seek justice. Defend the oppressed. Take up the cause of the fatherless; plead the case of the widow."* (Isaiah 1:17). Righteousness is not merely private morality; it is also public fidelity to God's standards of justice and mercy.

Jesus embodied this hunger. He was zealous for His Father's house (John 2:17), compassionate toward the marginalized, and unwavering in His commitment to truth and holiness. His mission was to bring righteousness to a world mired in sin. As His followers, we are called to share His hunger - to long not only for personal transformation but also for the renewal of society under His reign.

This is why His prayer, *"Your kingdom come, your will be done, on earth as it is in heaven."* (Matthew 6:10), is the natural outflow of this Beatitude.

The promise attached to this hunger is stunning: *"they will be filled."* The Greek verb here suggests complete satisfaction, like a banquet that leaves no craving unmet. This is the assurance that those who long for righteousness will not hunger in vain. God Himself will satisfy their desire. He does so in part now, through justification and sanctification, as He forgives our sins and transforms our lives. Yet this promise also looks forward to the consummation of His kingdom, when righteousness will dwell fully and permanently (2 Peter 3:13). The hunger of this age will give way to the fullness of the next, when we see Christ face to face and are made like Him (1 John 3:2).

Hunger and thirst for righteousness are the driving forces behind spiritual growth. Just as physical hunger compels us to seek nourishment, this spiritual hunger draws us deeper into the things of God. It is what fuels our pursuit of holiness, our desire for intimacy with Christ, and our longing to see His kingdom manifest in the world. Without this hunger, our spiritual lives become stagnant and complacent. But when our souls ache for righteousness, we are propelled forward, eagerly pressing on toward maturity in Christ.

This hunger transforms how we approach the disciplines of the Christian life. Prayer, for example, ceases to be a mere duty or ritual. It becomes the cry of a longing heart. When we hunger for righteousness, we pray not only for our needs but for God's will to be done, His kingdom to come, and His righteousness to prevail. Our prayers take on the urgency of David's urgent plea: *"I spread out my hands to you; I thirst for you like a parched land."* (Psalm 143:6). We pray because we are desperate, because we know that only God can satisfy the deep longing within us.

This hunger also reshapes our worship. True worship is born from desire - from hearts that yearn for God's presence and delight in His beauty.

When we hunger and thirst for righteousness, our worship becomes vibrant and authentic. We no longer simply sing words; we pour out our souls to the One who alone can satisfy us. We join the psalmist in saying, *"Because your love is better than life, my lips will glorify you."* (Psalm 63:3). Such worship is not confined to Sunday services but spills over into daily life as an expression of our continual dependence and delight in God.

Moreover, this hunger fuels our engagement with Scripture. The Bible is not merely a text to study but food for our souls. When we hunger for righteousness, we come to God's Word not as scholars dissecting information but as beggars seeking bread. We echo the words of Jeremiah: *"When your words came, I ate them; they were my joy and my heart's delight."* (Jeremiah 15:16). We read and meditate on Scripture not simply to accumulate knowledge but to be nourished, transformed, and aligned with God's will.

Hunger for righteousness also sharpens our sense of sin and drives us to continual repentance. Those who long to be filled with God's righteousness are strangers to compromise or half-hearted devotion. Like Paul, they cry out, *"What a wretched man I am! Who will rescue me from this body that is subject to death?"* and then rejoice, *"Thanks be to God, who delivers me through Jesus Christ our Lord!"* (Romans 7:24-25).

This dynamic - sorrow over our sin followed by overwhelming joy of forgiveness - is not a one-time experience but an ongoing rhythm of the entire Christian life. Hunger for righteousness keeps us returning to the cross, where we find fresh grace and renewal.

This Beatitude also speaks profoundly to our hope. While we experience isolated tastes of God's righteousness now - through justification, sanctification, and glimpses of His kingdom breaking into the world - we also live with a holy dissatisfaction. We know that our hunger is only partially satisfied in this age. We long for the day when Jesus Christ will return, when *"righteousness will be at home."* (2 Peter 3:13). This future hope sustains us in the present. It keeps us from despair when we see evil prosper or justice delayed.

We live in anticipation of the day when *"the earth will be filled with the knowledge of the glory of the Lord as the waters cover the sea."* (Habakkuk 2:14). This forward-looking perspective is of vital importance because the pursuit of righteousness is often met with opposition. Those who hunger for holiness in their own lives face internal battles against the flesh. Those who hunger for righteousness in the world encounter resistance, criticism, and sometimes persecution.

Jesus Himself warned of this later in the Beatitudes: *"Blessed are those who are persecuted because of righteousness, for theirs is the kingdom of heaven."* (Matthew 5:10). Our hunger for righteousness may make us out of step with the world's values, but this is precisely why Jesus calls it blessed. It marks us as citizens of His kingdom, distinct from the world around us and closely aligned with His purposes.

This hunger also compels us toward action. It is not enough to simply desire righteousness in theory; true hunger moves us to pursue it in practice. This means actively resisting sin and cultivating virtue through the power of the Holy Spirit. It means pursuing justice and mercy in our communities, advocating for the vulnerable, and living lives of integrity and compassion. The prophet Micah captures this integration of desire and action: *"He has shown you, O mortal, what is good. And what does the Lord require of you? To act justly and to love mercy and to walk humbly with your God."* (Micah 6:8). Our hunger for righteousness is not merely inward; it expresses itself outwardly in concrete ways.

One of the clearest signs of this hunger is dissatisfaction with superficial substitutes. Just as junk food can dull our appetite for what is truly nourishing, worldly pursuits can numb our longing for God. When we hunger and thirst for righteousness, however, we refuse to settle for lesser things. We recognize that wealth, success, or personal pleasure cannot satisfy our souls. We echo Augustine's famous confession: *"You have made us for yourself, O Lord, and our hearts are restless until they rest in you."* This hunger purifies our desires, reorienting them toward what is eternal rather than fleeting.

Practically, cultivating this hunger involves intentional practices. Asking God to deepen our longing for His righteousness is a starting point. Psalm 119 is filled with such prayers: *"My soul is consumed with longing for your laws at all times."* (v. 20); *"Turn my heart toward your statutes and not toward selfish gain."* (v. 36). Fasting is another discipline that trains our hearts to hunger for God above all else. By temporarily denying ourselves physical food, we remind ourselves of our deeper spiritual need and learn to direct our cravings toward Him.

Fellowship with other believers is also really important. Hunger is contagious; when we are around others who passionately pursue God, their desire fuels our own. This is why Hebrews 10:24-25 urges us to *"consider how we may spur one another on toward love and good deeds, not giving up meeting together... but encouraging one another."* The community of faith is a place where our hunger is stirred, sharpened, and satisfied as we seek God together.

Above all, our hunger is fed by beholding Christ. The more we see of Him - His beauty, holiness, mercy, and majesty - the more we long to be like Him. This is why Paul, after decades of knowing and serving Jesus Christ, could still say, *"I want to know Christ."* (Philippians 3:10). His desire had not diminished but grown. This is the paradox of spiritual hunger: the more it is satisfied, the more it intensifies. Unlike physical hunger, which ends in satiation, spiritual hunger deepens even as it is fulfilled, because God continually reveals more of Himself and draws us further in.

Hunger and thirst for righteousness are not only signs of life but safeguards against spiritual complacency. One of the greatest dangers in the Christian life is becoming content with a shallow experience of God. It is possible to settle for minimal faithfulness, doing just enough to maintain appearances while lacking deep passion for God's presence and purposes. This Beatitude exposes such complacency by holding before us a vision of longing that refuses to be satisfied with mediocrity.

Those who hunger and thirst for righteousness do not rest on past experiences or prior growth; they continually press forward, knowing that there is always more of Christ to know, more holiness to pursue, and more of His kingdom to see realized.

Paul exemplifies this restless pursuit in Philippians 3:12–14: *"Not that I have already obtained all this, or have already arrived at my goal, but I press on to take hold of that for which Christ Jesus took hold of me... Forgetting what is behind and straining toward what is ahead, I press on toward the goal to win the prize for which God has called me heavenward in Christ Jesus."* Even after all those years of ministry and profound encounters with Christ, Paul still longs for more.

This holy dissatisfaction is not discontentment with God but rather a recognition that His fullness is inexhaustible and our experience of Him is always incomplete on this side of eternity.

This hunger guards against the false security of religious routine. We can easily substitute external activity for internal vitality - attending services, performing duties, even reading Scripture mechanically - without truly seeking God's righteousness. But when we hunger and thirst, such routines become insufficient. We are not content to merely go through motions; we desire reality. We yearn for righteousness not just in form but in substance: real transformation, authentic intimacy with God, and genuine fruit in our lives.

This longing also keeps our focus sharp amid the distractions of the world. So many voices compete for our attention, promising satisfaction in wealth, pleasure, power, or approval. Yet none of these can quench the deep thirst of the soul. Hunger for righteousness clears our vision and helps us discern what truly matters.

As Jesus later warns in Matthew 6:33, *"Seek first his kingdom and his righteousness, and all these things will be given to you as well."* When righteousness is our priority, lesser things fall into their proper place. We no longer chase after what cannot satisfy because our desires are anchored in what is eternal.

This hunger not only shapes us personally but it will propels us outward in mission. Those who long for righteousness cannot remain indifferent to the brokenness of the world. They see the gap between God's will and earthly realities and are moved to act. This is why righteousness in Scripture is so closely tied to justice. The prophets continually cried out against oppression and corruption, calling God's people to live His righteousness in their communities. Isaiah 58:6–7 captures this vision: *"Is not this the kind of fasting I have chosen: to loose the chains of injustice… to set the oppressed free… Is it not to share your food with the hungry and to provide the poor wanderer with shelter?"*

Hungering for God's righteousness means longing not only for personal holiness but also for God's justice to prevail in society. It compels us to advocate for the vulnerable, confront injustice, and work for peace. This outward dimension of righteousness flows naturally from our inward transformation. As we become more like Christ, we share His compassion for the marginalized and His zeal for truth. His mission becomes our mission. We pray, *"Your kingdom come,"* and then we step into the world as agents of that kingdom, bearing witness in word and deed to its reality.

This hunger also sustains perseverance in mission. Working for righteousness in a fallen world is often slow, discouraging, and opposed. Without deep hunger rooted in God's promises, we might easily give up. But those who hunger and thirst are not deterred by delay because they know their longing will ultimately be fulfilled. They look beyond temporary setbacks to the certainty of Christ's return, when justice will roll on like a river and righteousness like a never-failing stream (Amos 5:24). This eschatological hope fuels endurance. We labour not in vain but in anticipation of the day when our hunger will be fully satisfied in the new heavens and the new earth.

Furthermore, hunger for righteousness fosters compassion and mercy, leading naturally into the next Beatitude: *"Blessed are the merciful."* (Matthew 5:7). When we deeply desire righteousness, we become acutely aware of how far we fall short of it.

This awareness humbles us and makes us patient with others. We realize that just as we are dependent on God's grace, so are they. Instead of self-righteous condemnation, we extend mercy. We yearn not only for our own growth but for those around us to experience God's forgiveness and transformation as well.

This connection between hunger and mercy is crucial. Without mercy, hunger for righteousness can devolve into harsh legalism or moral superiority. We might begin to equate righteousness with rigid rule-keeping and look down on those who fail to meet our standards. But true hunger for righteousness is tempered by the gospel. It remembers that righteousness is first a gift received, not an achievement earned. It leads us to pray not only *"Lord, make me holy"* but also *"Lord, be merciful to them,"* as we become instruments of His compassion.

This interplay between hunger and mercy reflects the character of Christ Himself. He embodied perfect righteousness yet was known for His mercy. He confronted sin without compromise, but He also welcomed sinners with open arms. He was *"full of grace and truth."* (John 1:14), holding both together in perfect balance. As we hunger for righteousness, we become more like Him - zealous for holiness but gentle toward the broken, longing for justice yet quick to forgive.

Practically, how can we cultivate and sustain this hunger? One key is continual exposure to God's holiness through Scripture and prayer. The clearer our vision of His character, the sharper our appetite for righteousness becomes. Isaiah's cry of *"Woe to me!"* arose when he saw the Lord high and exalted (Isaiah 6:1–5). Similarly, beholding God's glory stirs within us both awe and longing. Regularly meditating on passages that reveal His holiness - such as the Ten Commandments, the Sermon on the Mount, or the powerful visions of Revelation - keeps our desire for righteousness alive.

Another key is confession and repentance. Sin dulls our appetite for righteousness in the same way junk food ruins our appetite for nourishing meals.

When we tolerate compromise or neglect repentance, our hunger wanes. But when we bring our sins honestly to God and receive His cleansing, our desire is renewed. We begin again to long for the purity and the closeness that sin obscures. This rhythm of confession and grace keeps our hearts tender and hungry.

Serving others also stirs this hunger. When we engage in acts of mercy, justice, and love, we are participating in God's righteous purposes and taste the joy of His kingdom in action. This not only satisfies but deepens our longing, because we see both the beauty of righteousness and the brokenness that still remains. Our hunger grows sharper as we long for God to finish what He has begun.

Finally, we must pray for this hunger. Desire for righteousness is not something we manufacture; it is a gift of the Spirit. We can ask God, as David did in Psalm 51:10, *"Create in me a pure heart, O God, and renew a steadfast spirit within me."* We can pray for Him to enlarge our desires, to wean us from lesser things, and to make us restless until we are satisfied in Him. Such prayers are always answered, for they align perfectly with His will.

The promise remains: *"they will be filled."* This filling is both present and future. Even now, God satisfies us with His grace, His presence, and His transforming work. Yet our hunger is not fully quenched until the day when Christ returns and ushers in the new creation. On that day, the longing that has driven us will finally be met in full. We will see Him as He is, we will be like Him, and righteousness will reign unchallenged forever. Our hunger will be satisfied, not because it ceases, but because it is eternally fulfilled in beholding and enjoying God Himself.

As we turn next to the Beatitude on mercy, we see how this hunger naturally overflows into compassion. Those who deeply crave righteousness become agents of mercy, reflecting the grace they have received. Hunger for righteousness leads not to pride but to gentleness, not to judgment but to mercy. It transforms us into people who not only long for God's righteousness but extend His mercy to a world in desperate need of both.

- 6 -

'BLESSED ARE THE MERCIFUL'

Matthew 5:7

"Blessed are the merciful, for they will be shown mercy"

With this Beatitude, Jesus now turns our attention outward once again. Having spoken of hunger and thirst for righteousness - a longing that draws us closer to God - He now addresses how this transformed heart expresses itself in our relationships with others. True righteousness is never isolated or purely inward. It always bears fruit in how we treat people, particularly those in need or those who have wronged us. At the very centre of this outward expression is mercy.

To understand this Beatitude, we must first grasp what Jesus means by *"mercy."* In the Bible, mercy is always closely tied to compassion, forgiveness, and kindness - shown to those who are undeserving. It is not pity or sentiment but active goodness that relieves suffering or forgives offence. The Greek word used here, *eleos*, speaks of tender-heartedness in action. To be merciful is to extend grace where judgment is deserved, to offer help where there is need, and to embody love in tangible ways.

Mercy flows directly from the character of God. Throughout the Bible, He is revealed as *"compassionate and gracious, slow to anger, abounding in love."* (Exodus 34:6). His mercy is not a minor attribute but central to His dealings with humanity. The psalmist repeatedly celebrates this truth: *"The Lord is good to all; he has compassion on all he has made."* (Psalm 145:9). God's mercy is His willingness to withhold the judgment we deserve and instead offer forgiveness, restoration, and care.

It is the Lord's mercy that moved Him to redeem Israel from slavery, to forgive their repeated rebellion, and ultimately to send His Son for our salvation. This divine mercy reaches its climax in Jesus Christ. Paul writes in Titus 3:5, *"He saved us, not because of righteous things we had done, but because of his mercy."*

Mercy is the reason the gospel exists. Though we were sinners, alienated from God and deserving of condemnation, He acted in compassion: *"Because of his great love for us, God, who is rich in mercy, made us alive with Christ even when we were dead in transgressions."* (Ephesians 2:4–5). Every believer stands as a living testimony to God's mercy. We have received forgiveness we did not earn, grace we could never repay, and love we could not deserve.

This is why mercy is at the heart of discipleship. Jesus is calling His followers to reflect the mercy they have received. Those who truly grasp the magnitude of God's mercy cannot help but become merciful toward others. Just as hunger for righteousness grows from awareness of our poverty and need, mercy grows from awareness of the mercy shown to us. We forgive because we have been forgiven. We show compassion because God has been compassionate toward us. Mercy is the overflow of grace received.

The parable of the unmerciful servant in Matthew 18:21–35 illustrates this truth powerfully. A servant owes his master an unpayable debt but is forgiven completely. Yet that same servant then seizes a fellow servant who owes him a small sum and demands repayment. When the master hears of this, he is outraged: *"Shouldn't you have had mercy on your fellow servant just as I had on you?"* (v. 33). Jesus' point is unmistakable: those who have received mercy are expected to extend it. Mercy withheld reveals that mercy was never truly understood.

Mercy encompasses both forgiveness and compassionate action Forgiveness is central. To be merciful is to release others from the debts they owe us, whether those debts are emotional, relational, or material. It means letting go of resentment and vengeance. This is why Jesus later commands, *"Love your enemies and pray for those who persecute you."* (Matthew 5:44). Mercy does not wait until someone deserves forgiveness; it just forgives because we ourselves have been forgiven. It reflects the heart of God, who *"demonstrates his own love for us in this: While we were still sinners, Christ died for us."* (Romans 5:8).

But mercy is more than forgiveness; it is also compassion for those in distress. The merciful see suffering and are moved to act. Jesus' parable of the Good Samaritan (Luke 10:25–37) embodies this. A man is beaten and left for dead, ignored by those who should have helped.

But a Samaritan - despised by the Jews - stops, tends his wounds, and pays for his care. Jesus concludes, *"Go and do likewise."* Mercy notices pain and it responds with tangible help. It is not content with words alone but expresses itself in deeds.

This mercy extends to every sphere of life. It means kindness to the poor, generosity to those in need, and patience with those who fail us. It means empathizing with the hurting, welcoming the outcast, and standing with the oppressed. Mercy is not passive; it steps into messy situations and bears burdens. Paul exhorts us to *"clothe yourselves with compassion, kindness, humility, gentleness and patience."* (Colossians 3:12). Qualities like these, put together, paint a portrait of mercy in action.

It is important to understand that mercy is not weakness. It takes tremendous strength to forgive those who hurt us, to love those who wrong us, and to give to those who cannot repay us. Mercy resists the instincts of pride and revenge. It mirrors Jesus, who prayed from the cross, *"Father, forgive them, for they do not know what they are doing."* (Luke 23:34). Mercy does not deny justice; it transcends it. It acknowledges wrong but chooses grace over retaliation, trusting God as the ultimate judge.

Jesus' promise - *"for they will be shown mercy"* - is both present and future. In the present, those who practice such mercy often experience mercy in return, because kindness breeds kindness, and relationships marked by forgiveness and compassion tend to flourish. But this promise ultimately looks ahead to the final judgment. Those who show mercy now demonstrate that they have truly received God's mercy, and thus they will find mercy from Him on that day. James 2:13 underscores this: *"Judgment without mercy will be shown to anyone who has not been merciful. Mercy triumphs over judgment!"*

Our mercy does not earn salvation, but it evidences that we belong to the God who is merciful. This Beatitude challenges us profoundly because it confronts two deep tendencies of the human heart: our reluctance to forgive and our indifference to suffering. We often prefer to hold grudges rather than release them, to pass by need rather than engage with it.

Mercy disrupts these patterns. It calls us to a higher standard, one rooted not in our natural instincts but in God's supernatural grace. To be merciful is to imitate our Father in heaven, who *"causes his sun to rise on the evil and the good, and sends rain on the righteous and the unrighteous."* (Matthew 5:45).

Mercy is also countercultural in our world, which often prizes retribution over forgiveness and self-interest over compassion. In a society where a 'cancel culture' is thriving and vengeance is celebrated in media and politics; mercy stands out as radically different. It is disarming.

Mercy will silence hostility and open doors for reconciliation. It embodies the gospel in visible form, pointing people to the One who forgave His enemies and bore our sins in His body on the cross.

As we reflect on this Beatitude, we must ask: How does mercy manifest in my life? Do I forgive readily, or do I tend to cling onto grievances? Do I notice the needs around me, or do I pass by like the priest and Levite in the parable? Am I quick to judge or quick to show compassion? These questions expose whether we merely admire mercy or actually practice it.

Mercy is not merely an abstract virtue; it is intensely practical, transforming how we live and relate to others daily. When Jesus says, *"Blessed are the merciful,"* He is calling His followers to a way of life that mirrors God's own heart in every interaction.

Mercy is meant to shape our homes, our workplaces, our churches, and our communities. It is through small, consistent acts of mercy that we bear witness to the kingdom of God.

Mercy in relationships

Mercy has a deep, profound impact on personal relationships. It softens conflicts, heals wounds, and builds strong trust. In any relationship - marriage, family, friendship, or community - offenses and misunderstandings are just inevitable. Our natural inclination is to demand repayment or to withhold kindness until others meet our standards. But mercy interrupts this cycle. It chooses forgiveness over resentment and grace over grudges.

Paul's words in Ephesians 4:31–32 capture this beautifully: *"Get rid of all bitterness, rage and anger, brawling and slander, along with every form of malice. Be kind and compassionate to one another, forgiving each other, just as in Christ God forgave you."* Mercy is not simply overlooking faults; it is actively forgiving because we have been forgiven. It is remembering that God's mercy toward us far outweighs any debt owed to us by others.

Forgiveness is one of the clearest expressions of mercy, but it is also one of the hardest. We often resist forgiving because we fear it minimizes the wrong done to us. Yet forgiveness does not excuse sin; it entrusts justice to God. Romans 12:19 reminds us, *"Do not take revenge, my dear friends, but leave room for God's wrath, for it is written: 'It is mine to avenge; I will repay,' says the Lord."* When we forgive, we release ourselves from the bondage of bitterness and open the door for healing, ours and potentially that of the one who wronged us.

Mercy also expresses itself through patience. In a hurried and impatient world, mercy takes the time to understand, to listen, and to bear with others' weaknesses. It resists harshness in favour of gentleness. Proverbs 19:11 says, *"A person's wisdom yields patience; it is to one's glory to overlook an offence."* Often, what people need most is not judgment but kindness, especially when they are struggling or failing. Mercy meets them where they are.

Mercy in the Church

Mercy is essential within the life of the church. The church is not a gathering of perfect people but of forgiven sinners who are still being sanctified.

Without mercy, churches quickly become cold and judgmental, dominated by criticism rather than grace. But when mercy permeates a congregation, it will create an environment where people can be honest about their struggles, receive forgiveness, and grow.

Paul exhorts believers in Galatians 6:1-2: *"Brothers and sisters, if someone is caught in a sin, you who live by the Spirit should restore that person gently. But watch yourselves, or you also may be tempted. Carry each other's burdens, and in this way you will fulfil the law of Christ."* This is showing mercy at work within the body of Christ - restoring gently, bearing burdens, and fulfilling the law of love.

Mercy also fuels generosity within the church. Luke gave us this picture of the early believers, *"There were no needy persons among them... those who owned land or houses sold them... and it was distributed to anyone who had need."* (Acts 4:34-35). Their mercy was not abstract; it took the form of practical compassion, meeting material needs. James underscores this in his warning: *"Suppose a brother or sister is without clothes and daily food. If one of you says to them, 'Go in peace; keep warm and well fed,' but does nothing about their physical needs, what good is it?"* (James 2:15-16). True mercy is more than words - it is action.

When mercy saturates a church, it becomes a powerful witness to the world. Jesus said in John 13:35, "By this everyone will know that you are my disciples, if you love one another." Mercy is love in action. It shows that our community is shaped not by worldly values but by the gospel. A merciful church is a safe haven for the broken, a place where sinners find grace and where compassion overflows into the surrounding community.

Mercy in everyday life

Mercy is not confined to our relationships with fellow believers; it extends to everyone we encounter. Jesus' teaching about loving our enemies in Matthew 5:44 is perhaps the most radical application of mercy: *"But I tell you, love your enemies and pray for those who persecute you."* This command dismantles any notion of mercy being limited to those we like or who deserve it.

Mercy is most clearly seen when it is extended to those who least deserve it. This includes showing kindness to those who mistreat us, offering help to those who cannot repay us, and choosing not to retaliate when wronged. It also involves being alert to the needs around us: noticing the lonely coworker, the struggling neighbour, or the marginalized in our communities. Mercy sees people not as inconveniences or problems but as individuals made in God's image, worthy of compassion.

Practical expressions of this mercy can be simple yet powerful: offering a listening ear, sharing resources with those in need, volunteering your time to serve others, or speaking words of encouragement. In a world that often values self-interest, even small acts of mercy stand out as countercultural reflections of Christ's love.

Mercy and justice

Mercy doesn't ignore justice, it works in harmony with it. Biblical mercy is not sentimental tolerance of wrongdoing; it seeks restoration and reconciliation. Micah 6:8 holds these together: *"What does the Lord require of you? To act justly and to love mercy and to walk humbly with your God."* Justice addresses wrongs; mercy always extends grace. The two are not opposites, they are complementary. Where justice seeks to set things right, mercy heals wounds and offers hope.

Jesus exemplified this in His encounter with the woman caught in adultery (John 8:1–11). He upheld the seriousness of her sin, yet He did not condemn her: *"Neither do I condemn you... Go now and leave your life of sin."* Mercy did not dismiss the moral demand for righteousness; it offered grace and called her to transformation. This balance is crucial for us. Our mercy must be anchored in truth, and our truth must be tempered by mercy.

Mercy and evangelism

Mercy also plays a vital role in our witness to the world. Many people come to faith not simply through arguments or preaching but through experiencing God's mercy embodied in His people.

When we forgive those who wrong us, when we serve without seeking recognition, when we care for the hurting, we display the gospel in action. Our mercy becomes a living testimony of the mercy we have received.

Jesus tied mercy to our influence in the world. Immediately after the Beatitudes, He said, *"You are the light of the world... let your light shine before others, that they may see your good deeds and glorify your Father in heaven."* (Matthew 5:14,16). Our merciful deeds point people not to us but to Him, illuminating His grace and drawing others to His salvation.

➤ *Volunteer,* give generously, or simply be present for someone in need.

➤ *Resist judgmentalism:* When tempted to criticize or condemn, remember your own need for grace. As Jesus warns, *"Do not judge, or you too will be judged."* (Matthew 7:1).

➤ *Celebrate mercy in others:* When you see acts of compassion and forgiveness, affirm them. Encouraging mercy in others reinforces it in our own lives and builds a culture of grace.

The blessing of mercy

The blessing Jesus promises - *"they will be shown mercy"* - is both present and future. In this life, the merciful often experience God's nearness and peace in profound ways. As Proverbs 11:17 says, *"Those who are kind benefit themselves, but the cruel bring ruin on themselves."* Mercy releases us from bitterness, frees us from cycles of retaliation, and fills our lives with grace. But this blessing will be fully realized when we stand before God. On that day, His mercy will envelop us completely, and we will marvel at how every act of mercy in this life pointed to His greater mercy in eternity. Mercy will not be the basis of our salvation, but it will be the evidence that His mercy truly transformed us.

From mercy to purity of heart

As we turn to the next Beatitude - *"Blessed are the pure in heart"* - we see how mercy prepares the way. Having experienced and extended God's mercy, our hearts are cleansed and made tender.

Mercy removes the many stains of bitterness, envy, and self-righteousness, allowing us to see God more clearly. The merciful heart is a purified heart, one that has learned to mirror God's compassion and is thus ready to behold Him.

In this way, mercy serves as a bridge in the Beatitudes: it flows out of hunger for righteousness and leads into purity of heart. The one who hungers for righteousness is filled with God's grace, which overflows in mercy toward others, and this mercy then purifies the heart, preparing it to see God. This is the beauty of Jesus' teaching here: each Beatitude is not isolated but interconnected, painting a progressive portrait of kingdom life.

7

'BLESSED ARE THE PURE IN HEART'

Matthew 5:8

"Blessed are the pure in heart, for they will see God"

Of all the Beatitudes, this one carries an extraordinary promise: to see God. Throughout Scripture, the vision of God is presented as the ultimate hope and joy of His people. Moses longed for it when he prayed, *"Now show me your glory."* (Exodus 33:18).

David cherished it, declaring, *"One thing I ask from the Lord, this only do I seek: that I may dwell in the house of the Lord all the days of my life, to gaze on the beauty of the Lord."* (Psalm 27:4). And in Revelation, this hope is fulfilled: *"They will see his face, and his name will be on their foreheads."* (Revelation 22:4).

Yet Jesus ties this promise to a condition: purity of heart. To see God is not granted to everyone indiscriminately; it is for those whose hearts are pure. This raises two vital questions: what does it mean to be *"pure in heart,"* and how does such purity enable us to see God?

The meaning of purity of heart

Biblical purity is not merely ceremonial or external; it is inward and moral. The heart, in Scripture, refers to the core of who we are - our thoughts, desires, will, and affections. Thus, to be pure in heart is to have a heart that is undivided, sincere, and wholly devoted to God. It is the opposite of duplicity and hypocrisy. Purity of heart is about integrity: being the same in private as we are in public, aligning our inner life with God's truth.

David expresses this clearly in Psalm 24:3-4: *"Who may ascend the mountain of the Lord? Who may stand in his holy place? The one who has clean hands and a pure heart, who does not trust in an idol or swear by a false god."* Here, purity is contrasted with idolatry and deceit. A pure heart is free from divided loyalty; it is singularly focused on God.

James echoes this idea: *"Come near to God and he will come near to you. Wash your hands, you sinners, and purify your hearts, you double-minded."* (James 4:8). Purity involves ridding ourselves of doublemindedness and orienting our hearts fully toward God. Purity of heart is not mere moralism or outward rule-keeping. The Pharisees, whom Jesus often rebuked, were scrupulous about external rituals but neglected the heart. Jesus told them, *"You clean the outside of the cup and dish, but inside they are full of greed and self-indulgence."* (Matthew 23:25). True purity is not just cosmetic; it begins inwardly and works its way outward. It is not satisfied with appearances but seeks transformation from within.

The connection to mercy and righteousness

This Beatitude follows naturally from the one before it: *"Blessed are the merciful."* Mercy tenderizes the heart, uprooting bitterness and pride, which cloud our vision of God. A merciful heart is freed from resentment and self-absorption, making it receptive to God's presence. Similarly, purity flows from the hunger for righteousness described earlier in this Sermon. Those who truly long for righteousness are cleansed and refined, their hearts progressively aligned with God's holiness.

Purity of heart is not perfection in this life but sincerity and direction. It describes those who, though still flawed, earnestly desire to please God and seek His cleansing. David prayed, "Create in me a pure heart, O God, and renew a steadfast spirit within me" (Psalm 51:10). His plea came after his grievous sin with Bathsheba, reminding us that purity is not about a sinless past but about ongoing repentance and renewal. A pure heart is one continually washed in grace, quick to confess sin, and steadfast in seeking God.

Seeing God: The promise of purity

The promise attached to this Beatitude - *"they will see God"* - is breathtaking. To *"see God"* speaks of intimacy, fellowship, and ultimate satisfaction. Throughout Scripture, seeing God is both the longing of the faithful and the reward of the righteous. It carries both present and future dimensions.

➤ *A present experience:* Even now, those who are pure in heart experience God in a deeper, clearer way. Jesus said, *"Whoever has my commands and keeps them is the one who loves me. The one who loves me will be loved by my Father, and I too will love them and show myself to them."* (John 14:2). Purity will open our spiritual vision, enabling us to perceive God's presence, guidance, and His work in our lives. Sin clouds our vision, dulling our sensitivity to Him. Purity sharpens it, removing the fog and allowing us to behold Him more clearly.

➤ *A future fulfilment:* Ultimately, this promise will be fulfilled in the age to come. John describes the consummation of this Beatitude: *"They will see his face."* (Revelation 22:4). This is the radiant vision, the ultimate joy of heaven, to see our God unhindered, to behold His glory without veil or shadow. This is what John anticipates when he writes, *"We know that when Christ appears, we shall be like him, for we shall see him as he is."* (1 John 3:2). The pure in heart will not only see God's works or His reflections but His very face.

Purity is thus both the pathway and preparation for this vision. Hebrews 12:14 urges us: *"Make every effort to live in peace with everyone and to be holy; without holiness no one will see the Lord."* Holiness is not optional for those who hope to see God; it is essential. Not because our holiness earns God's presence but because His presence is incompatible with sin. A pure heart is one that has been cleansed by grace and made fit for His fellowship.

Purity and integrity

Purity of heart is also closely tied to integrity. In biblical terms, purity implies wholeness. That is, being undivided, consistent, and genuine. A pure heart is never split between devotion to God and devotion to idols, or between public piety and private compromise. Jesus condemned hypocrisy precisely because it violated this integrity: outwardly appearing righteous while inwardly being corrupt (Matthew 23:27–28). Purity demands congruence between our inner and outer lives.

This integrity has practical implications. It means being honest in our dealings, faithful in our commitments, and transparent in our relationships. It rejects duplicity and hidden agendas. The pure in heart do not manipulate or deceive; they live openly before God and others. This kind of integrity is rare in a world marked by pretence and image management, but it is precisely what marks those who will see God.

Cultivating purity of heart

Purity begins with the cleansing work of God through Christ. We cannot purify ourselves by sheer willpower. As David prayed after his sin, *"Wash away all my iniquity and cleanse me from my sin."* (Psalm 51:2).

Purity starts here: with confession, repentance, and the washing of our hearts by God's grace. John assures us, *"If we confess our sins, he is faithful and just and will forgive us our sins and purify us from all unrighteousness."* (1 John 1:9). The foundation of purity is forgiveness.

From this starting point, purity is nurtured through devotion and discipline. Daily prayer, time in Scripture, and fellowship with other believers keep our hearts oriented toward God. Jesus prayed in John 17:17, *"Sanctify them by the truth; your word is truth."*

Immersing ourselves in Scripture shapes our minds and affections, renewing our hearts and aligning them with His will. Purity is not only about avoiding sin but about filling our hearts with what is good, noble, and true (Philippians 4:8).

Purity also requires vigilance. Proverbs 4:23 warns, *"Above all else, guard your heart, for everything you do flows from it."* Our hearts are constantly being shaped by what we take in - what we watch, read, listen to, and dwell upon. If we feed on impurity, our hearts will be clouded, and our vision of God will be dimmed. To be pure in heart is to guard what influences us, choosing instead to focus on what draws us nearer to Him.

Purity versus hypocrisy

Jesus frequently confronted the hypocrisy of the Pharisees, who appeared outwardly righteous while their hearts were far from God. In Matthew 15:8 He quoted Isaiah's indictment: *"These people honour me with their lips, but their hearts are far from me."* Hypocrisy is always the enemy of purity. It prioritizes image over reality, external reputation over internal transformation. It masks sin rather than dealing with it honestly before God.

The danger of hypocrisy is that it deceives not only others but ourselves. We can become so skilled at projecting an image of holiness that we neglect the inward work of the Spirit. Jesus warned in Matthew 23:27: *"You are like whitewashed tombs, which look beautiful on the outside but on the inside are full of the bones of the dead."* Purity of heart, by contrast, seeks authenticity.

It invites God's searching gaze, praying with David: *"Search me, God, and know my heart; test me and know my anxious thoughts. See if there is any offensive way in me, and lead me in the way everlasting."* (Psalm 139:23–24).

True purity refuses to settle for external religiosity. It presses for inward renewal, knowing that God is not fooled by appearances. He desires truth in the innermost being (Psalm 51:6). Purity of heart is the opposite of duplicity - it is a single-minded devotion to God that refuses to be divided between Him and the world or between public image and private reality.

Purity and single-minded devotion

One of the greatest hindrances to purity is divided loyalty. Jesus later declared, *"No one can serve two masters... You cannot serve both God and money."* (Matthew 6:24). While He used wealth as an example here, the principle also applies broadly: we cannot simultaneously give our hearts fully to God and to competing loves.

Purity requires a singular focus. As James 4:8 commands, *"Purify your hearts, you double-minded."*

Double-mindedness manifests in subtle ways: trying to maintain faith while clinging to worldly ambitions; professing devotion to God while nurturing secret sins; attending worship outwardly while our hearts chase lesser affections. Purity of heart confronts these divided loyalties and calls us to wholehearted surrender. It echoes the Shema: *"Love the Lord your God with all your heart and with all your soul and with all your strength."* (Deuteronomy 6:5).

This single-minded devotion produces stability and clarity. When our hearts are undivided, our lives are integrated rather than fragmented. We are not pulled in conflicting directions, nor do we live compartmentalized lives — one version of ourselves in public, another in private. Purity aligns our inner and outer selves, anchoring us in integrity and freeing us from the exhausting effort of maintaining appearances.

The purifying work of trials

Interestingly, God often uses trials to purify our hearts. Peter writes, *"These have come so that the proven genuineness of your faith - of greater worth than gold, which perishes even though refined by fire - may result in praise, glory and honour when Jesus Christ is revealed."* (1 Peter 1:7). Just as gold is refined in fire to remove impurities, our faith is refined through difficulties. Trials strip away false supports and expose what truly resides in our hearts, leading us to deeper dependence on God and greater clarity of vision.

Suffering often purges us of superficiality. It reminds us of what matters most and loosens our grip on worldly attachments. Those who walk through deep valleys often emerge with a sharper sense of God's presence and a deeper longing for Him. Their hearts are purified by hardship, their vision clarified by need. As Job declared in the midst of his trials, *"When he has tested me, I will come forth as gold."* (Job 23:10).

Seeing God in the present

While the ultimate fulfilment of this Beatitude lies in eternity, purity of heart enables us to *"see"* God even now. This seeing is not physical but spiritual: perceiving His hand in creation, His guidance in providence, and His presence in our daily lives.

The pure in heart live with a heightened awareness of God's nearness. Their spiritual senses are attuned to His voice, their vision unclouded by sin or distraction.

This present vision of God is cultivated through intimacy. As we walk closely with Him in prayer and obedience, we begin to discern His fingerprints in ordinary moments. We see Him in answered prayers, in unexpected blessings, in the beauty of creation, and in the quiet assurance of His Spirit.

Jesus promised, *"Whoever loves me will obey my teaching. My Father will love them, and we will come to them and make our home with them."* (John 14:23). Purity creates space for this indwelling fellowship.

Moreover, purity enables us to see God at work in others. When our hearts are cleansed of cynicism and pride, we become more attuned to His image in those around us. We notice His grace transforming lives, His mercy breaking chains, His Spirit producing fruit in the lives of fellow believers. Instead of being blinded by criticism or jealousy, we rejoice in seeing God's activity in His people.

The cost and reward of purity

Pursuing purity is not without cost. It requires self-examination, repentance, and a willingness to let go of anything that competes with our devotion to God. It often means swimming against cultural tide that celebrates compromise and moral ambiguity. It calls us to higher standards than those around us, not to earn God's love, but because we belong to Him.

Yet the reward is incomparable: *"they will see God."* This promise is both breathtaking and deeply motivating. To see God - to experience His presence now and behold His glory forever - is the supreme blessing. Nothing else can compare.

This vision is what we were created for, and it is what sin obscures. Purity clears the lens, enabling us to see clearly the One who is our ultimate joy.

Pursuing purity of heart: practical Steps

Pursuing purity of heart is a work of God and a responsibility we actively embrace. It is not achieved in an instant but through daily surrender, steady discipline, and dependence upon the Holy Spirit.

While we cannot purify ourselves apart from God's grace, we are called to cooperate with His sanctifying work.

Here are several practical ways to cultivate purity of heart:

> *Regular confession and repentance:* Confession is vital for purity. We must be quick to bring our sins into the light, not hiding or excusing them but acknowledging them honestly before God. David's prayer in Psalm 51:10 - *"Create in me a pure heart, O God, and renew a steadfast spirit within me"* - reminds us that purity is God's work, but it manifests when we humble ourselves and seek His cleansing. Confession keeps our hearts tender, preventing sin from hardening or dulling our spiritual vision.

> *Immersion in God's Word:* Scripture is both a mirror and a purifier. As we read, meditate upon, and obey God's Word, it exposes impurities in our hearts and points us toward righteousness. Jesus prayed, *"Sanctify them by the truth; your word is truth."* (John 17:17). The Word confronts sin, renews our minds, and deepens our love for what is holy. Daily engagement with the Scriptures is essential for maintaining the reality of purity in our lives.

> *Guarding our hearts and minds:* Proverbs 4:23 says, "Above all else, guard your heart, for everything you do flows from it." Purity requires vigilance over what we allow into our hearts. This includes being discerning about conversations, the media, entertainment, and influences that shape our desires and thinking. What we feed our hearts daily will eventually define our affections and actions. Guarding our hearts means intentionally focusing on what is *"true, noble, right, pure, lovely, admirable."* (Philippians 4:8).

➢ *Cultivating single-minded devotion to God:* Purity of heart is closely tied to undivided devotion. Jesus said, *"Love the Lord your God with all your heart."* (Matthew 22:37). This involves continually examining whether there are competing loves or idols in our lives - anything that draws our allegiance away from Him. Practically, this means placing God first in our priorities, our time, and our decisions. It is about living a life fully oriented around His will.

➢ *Prayer for transformation:* Purity cannot be achieved by sheer human determination. We need the Spirit's renewing work. Prayer invites God's refining fire into our hearts. We can pray as the psalmist did: *"Search me, God, and know my heart; test me and know my anxious thoughts."* (Psalm 139:23). Through prayer, we surrender areas of compromise and ask God to align our desires with His.

➢ *Accountability and community:* Purity always flourishes in the context of godly relationships. Being part of a community of believers provides encouragement, accountability, support, and the blessing of family. Hebrews 10:24-25 urges us to *"spur one another on toward love and good deeds... encouraging one another."* Accountability helps us resist temptation, while fellowship with others who share our pursuit of holiness keeps our hunger for God strong.

➢ *Worship and awe of God:* Purity is sustained in our life when we maintain a vision of God's holiness and majesty. Isaiah's encounter with God's glory in Isaiah 6 led to both conviction and cleansing. Worship magnifies God and diminishes the allure of sin, filling our hearts with wonder that draws us closer to Him. When we behold His beauty, our desires are reordered, and impurity loses its grip.

Purity and holiness

Purity of heart is inseparable from holiness. Hebrews 12:14 exhorts: *"Make every effort to live in peace with everyone and to be holy; without holiness no one will see the Lord."* Purity is not a private virtue; it is the essence of living as those set apart for God.

Holiness means belonging wholly to Him, separated from sin and consecrated to His purposes. Holiness is not about mere rule-keeping but about intimacy with God. The holy person is not primarily someone who avoids certain behaviours but someone who walks closely with God in love and obedience. Purity is the fruit of this closeness. As we draw near to Him, His holiness transforms us, and our hearts become increasingly pure.

This pursuit of holiness also deepens our longing for God's presence. When our hearts are cleansed and focused on Him, worship becomes richer and prayer more intimate. We begin to live with a constant awareness of His nearness and support, as Jesus promised: *"Blessed are the pure in heart, for they will see God."* Purity enables a clarity of spiritual sight that allows us to perceive His hand even in the ordinary moments of life.

Purity and worship

Purity of heart is foundational for true worship. Jesus told the Samaritan woman, *"God is spirit, and his worshipers must worship in the Spirit and in truth."* (John 4:24). Worship flows from a heart aligned with God's Spirit and cleansed by His truth. When our hearts are pure, our worship is not mere ritual or performance - it becomes a genuine outpouring of love and adoration.

David understood this connection when he prayed, *"Who may ascend the mountain of the Lord? Who may stand in his holy place? The one who has clean hands and a pure heart."* (Psalm 24:3-4). Purity prepares us to draw near to God in worship with confidence, unburdened by hidden sin or divided affections. It allows us to approach Him boldly, not as those weighed down by guilt, but as those whose hearts have been washed by His grace.

Purity's preparation for peace-making

This Beatitude naturally leads us into the next: *"Blessed are the peacemakers, for they will be called children of God."* (Matthew 5:9). Purity of heart prepares us for peace-making because it clears away the pride, bitterness, and hidden agendas that often fuel conflict.

A pure heart will always seek reconciliation rather than division, forgiveness rather than retaliation, unity rather than strife. Because the pure in heart see God more clearly, they reflect His character more fully-becoming channels of His peace in a fractured world. Their vision of God's holiness and mercy drives them to pursue peace not merely as the absence of conflict but as the active presence of harmony rooted in righteousness. Peace-making requires sincerity, humility, and integrity - all hallmarks of purity. A pure heart is free from duplicity and self-interest, enabling it to mediate conflicts honestly and with genuine care. Thus, purity does not simply prepare us to see God in eternity, it equips us to reveal Him now, by bringing His peace into our relationships and communities.

The blessing of seeing God

The promise of this Beatitude - "they will see God" - is both present and future. Even now, purity heightens our awareness of His presence. We see Him in His Word, in His works, and in our daily lives. We experience His nearness in worship and prayer. But this is only a foretaste of the ultimate blessing: the day when we will behold Him face to face, unhindered by sin or imperfection.

John captures this breathtaking hope: "We know that when Christ appears, we shall be like him, for we shall see him as he is. All who have this hope in him purify themselves, just as he is pure." (1 John 3:2-3). The anticipation of seeing God fuels our pursuit of purity now. Every act of confession, every surrender of competing loves, every moment of worship is a preparation for that final vision. Purity of heart is not perfectionism or moral pride - it is a life of continual cleansing, devotion, and longing for God. It is the heart that prays with David, "I seek your face, Lord. Your face, Lord, I will seek." (Psalm 27:8).

As we move to the next Beatitude - "Blessed are the peace-makers" - we see how a pure heart, fixed on God, becomes an instrument of His peace in a world torn by division. Purity does not isolate us from the world; it sends us into it as those who, having seen God, now reflect Him.

8

'BLESSED ARE THE PEACEMAKERS'

Matthew 5:9

*"Blessed are the peacemakers, for they will be
called children of God."*

This Beatitude moves us outward once again, showing how purity of heart naturally leads to peace-making. Those who have been cleansed by God and fixed their hearts on Him are now equipped to carry His peace into a fractured world.

Notice that Jesus does not say *"blessed are the peaceful"* or *"blessed are those who avoid conflict"* but *"blessed are the peacemakers."* This is active, not passive. It is about engaging in the hard work of reconciliation, healing divisions, and bringing the wholeness of God's kingdom into broken relationships and communities.

The Biblical concept of peace

To understand peace-making, we must first grasp the biblical meaning of peace. The Hebrew word for peace, *shalom*, is far richer than simply the absence of conflict. Shalom refers to wholeness, harmony, and flourishing. It is the state of things being as they should be under God's reign.

Isaiah envisioned this peace when he prophesied about the Messiah: *"Of the greatness of his government and peace there will be no end."* (Isaiah 9:7). Peace is not merely ceasing hostilities; it is the presence of righteousness, justice, and reconciliation.

In the New Testament, the Greek word *eirēnē* carries a similar meaning. It is used not just to describe inner calm but also the restored relationship between God and humanity through Christ. Paul declares in Romans 5:1, *"Therefore, since we have been justified through faith, we have peace with God through our Lord Jesus Christ."* This peace is the foundation for all peace-making. Before we bring peace to the world, we must first be reconciled to God.

The God of peace

Peace-making reflects God's character. Throughout Scripture, He is called *"the God of peace"* (Romans 15:33; 1 Thess. 5:23). His mission in Christ is one of reconciliation: *"For God was pleased to have all his fullness dwell in him, and through him to reconcile to himself all things... by making peace through his blood, shed on the cross."* (Colossians 1:19–20). Peace-making is not a secondary matter for God; it is central to His redemptive plan. He takes enemies and makes them friends, restoring what sin has fractured.

When Jesus came, He was announced as the Prince of Peace (Isaiah 9:6). His birth was heralded by angels declaring, *"Glory to God in the highest heaven, and on earth peace to those on whom his favour rests."* (Luke 2:14). Through His life, death, and resurrection, He established peace between God and humanity and commissioned His followers to be instruments of that same peace. In John 20:21, the risen Christ said, *"Peace be with you! As the Father has sent me, I am sending you."* To be a peacemaker is to join God in His reconciling mission.

Peace-making vs. peacekeeping

It is crucial that we distinguish between peace-making and peacekeeping. Peacekeeping often means maintaining the status quo, avoiding conflict, or suppressing tension for the sake of superficial harmony. It can involve sweeping issues under the rug, pretending problems don't exist, or prioritizing comfort over truth. This is not the peace Jesus spoke of. He Himself said, *"Do not suppose that I have come to bring peace to the earth. I did not come to bring peace, but a sword."* (Matthew 10:34). Here, He warns that His message will divide those who receive Him from those who reject Him. His peace is not peace at any cost, but peace built on truth and righteousness.

Peace-making, by contrast, involves addressing conflict honestly and working toward genuine reconciliation. It is not passive but courageous. Peacemakers do not avoid hard conversations; they enter them prayerfully, seeking healing rather than victory.

They confront injustice rather than tolerate it. They labour to dismantle barriers and bring estranged parties together, thereby reflecting the reconciling work of Christ.

Paul captures this active role in 2 Corinthians 5:18–19: *"All this is from God, who reconciled us to himself through Christ and gave us the ministry of reconciliation: that God was reconciling the world to himself in Christ, not counting people's sins against them. And he has committed to us the message of reconciliation."* Peacemakers are ambassadors of this message. They carry the gospel of peace (Ephesians 6:15) and demonstrate it through their actions.

Peace-making in relationships

Peace-making begins close to home - in our families, friendships, and churches. Conflict is inevitable in human relationships, but how we respond reveals whether we are living as peacemakers. Jesus gives clear instructions in Matthew 5:23–24: *"If you are offering your gift at the altar and there remember that your brother or sister has something against you, leave your gift there in front of the altar. First go and be reconciled to them; then come and offer your gift."* Reconciliation takes priority even over worship because it is integral to worship. A pure heart before God requires making peace with others.

Paul echoes this in Romans 12:18: *"If it is possible, as far as it depends on you, live at peace with everyone."* Peacemakers take initiative. They do not wait for others to make the first move but actively seek out reconciliation, even when it is costly. This requires humility, patience, and a willingness to absorb wrongs without retaliation. It means listening carefully, apologizing sincerely, forgiving freely, and choosing relationship over pride.

The cost of peace-making

Peace-making is not easy. It often requires stepping into messy situations, risking rejection, or enduring misunderstanding. It may mean advocating for justice in ways that provoke some opposition. True peace-making is costly because it confronts sin and calls for repentance.

Yet this is precisely what Jesus did for us. He *"made peace through his blood, shed on the cross."* (Colossians 1:20). Our peace with God was purchased at the greatest cost imaginable. As His followers, we should not expect our peace-making to come cheaply.

This costliness is why peacemakers are called *"children of God."* When we engage in peace-making, we resemble our Father. Just as children often bear the likeness of their parents, peacemakers display the family resemblance of God Himself. By bringing reconciliation, we show we belong to the One Who reconciles. We live out our identity as those who have been adopted into His family through Christ (Ephesians 1:5).

Peace-making in the Church

The church is called to be a community that embodies God's peace. Yet, because it is composed of imperfect people, conflict is inevitable. Peace-making within the church is essential for its witness and health. Paul urges believers in Ephesians 4:2–3: *"Be completely humble and gentle; be patient, bearing with one another in love. Make every effort to keep the unity of the Spirit through the bond of peace."* Unity does not mean uniformity; it means maintaining fellowship rooted in Christ even when disagreements arise.

Peace-making in the church involves refusing gossip, slander, and divisive behaviour. Instead, it calls for honest dialogue, mutual forgiveness, and reconciliation. Jesus' instructions in Matthew 18:15–17 provide a model: address conflict privately first, then involve others if needed, always aiming for restoration rather than punishment. When handled in this spirit, conflict can actually strengthen relationships and deepen mutual trust.

Moreover, peace-making in the church will mean embracing diversity. The early church grappled with tensions between Jews and Gentiles, yet Paul proclaimed that Christ *"has made the two groups one and has destroyed the barrier, the dividing wall of hostility."* (Ephesians 2:14). Today, peacemakers in the church work to dismantle divisions of culture, ethnicity, class, and preference, uniting around the gospel rather than secondary issues. A peaceful church is a powerful testimony to a divided world.

Peace-making in society

Peacemakers are not only called to reconcile their personal relationships but also to engage in society as agents of God's peace. This includes working for justice, addressing systemic wrongs, and advocating for those who are not able to speak for themselves. Peace is inseparable from justice; as Isaiah 32:17 declares, *"The fruit of that righteousness will be peace; its effect will be quietness and confidence forever."*

Christian peacemakers are therefore called to confront violence, oppression, and inequality. This might mean mediating disputes in the workplace, volunteering in community reconciliation initiatives, or supporting ministries that heal divisions in neighbourhoods or nations. It can also involve advocating for policies that promote fairness and protect the vulnerable. While these efforts may not solve every societal problem, they reflect the heart of God, who *"upholds the cause of the oppressed and gives food to the hungry."* (Psalm 146:7).

However, biblical peace-making is never divorced from the gospel. While we work to alleviate earthly conflict, we recognize that ultimate peace is found only in Christ. As Paul wrote in Ephesians 2:17, Jesus *"came and preached peace to you who were far away and peace to those who were near."* Social action is important, but our deepest calling as peacemakers is to point people toward reconciliation with God, from which all true peace flows.

Peace-making in hostile situations

Peace-making will often place us in the midst of hostility. Jesus Himself faced constant opposition, yet He responded not with retaliation but with grace. He taught in Matthew 5:44, *"Love your enemies and pray for those who persecute you."* This radical love is at the heart of peace-making.

When we are mistreated or maligned, our instinct is to fight back or withdraw. But peacemakers engage differently. They respond with patience rather than anger, kindness rather than harshness, and forgiveness rather than revenge.

Romans 12:20–21 calls us to this countercultural posture: *"If your enemy is hungry, feed him; if he is thirsty, give him something to drink... Do not be overcome by evil but overcome evil with good."* This is not weakness; it is strength under control, rooted in trust in God's justice. Peacemakers refuse to mirror hostility because they know that vengeance belongs only to God (Romans 12:19). Instead, they disarm hostility with love, modelling Christ, who prayed for His executioners even as He hung on the cross: *"Father, forgive them."* (Luke 23:34). This kind of mercy has the power to break cycles of enmity and open hearts to the gospel.

Practical steps to live as peacemakers

Living as a peacemaker begins with intentional daily choices that reflect God's peace:

1. *Seek reconciliation quickly:* Jesus commands us to make peace promptly (Matthew 5:23–24). Delay allows resentment to fester; swift reconciliation prevents deeper division.

2. *Control our tongues:* James 1:19 teaches, *"Everyone should be quick to listen, slow to speak and slow to become angry."* Careful speech defuses tension, while rash words inflame conflict.

3. *Forgive freely:* Forgiveness is the foundation of peace. Ephesians 4:32 exhorts us, *"Be kind and compassionate to one another, forgiving each other, just as in Christ God forgave you."*

4. *Pray for those in conflict:* Prayer softens our hearts and invites God's wisdom and power into strained situations.

5. *Model humility:* Pride is a root cause of conflict. Peacemakers embrace humility, willing to yield and admit fault when needed (Philippians 2:3).

6. *Be proactive, not passive:* Peace-making requires initiative. Whether in family disputes, church tensions, or social divisions, we take steps to bring people together rather than allowing hostility to harden.

Peacemakers as children of God

Jesus promises that peacemakers *"will be called children of God."* This title is deeply significant. It affirms that peacemakers reflect their heavenly Father's likeness.

God is the ultimate peacemaker, reconciling sinners to Himself and uniting divided humanity in Christ. When we engage in peace-making, we demonstrate our adoption into His family. We bear His image and extend His mission.

Paul captures this identity in Romans 8:14: *"For those who are led by the Spirit of God are the children of God."* The Spirit leads us into peace-making because it aligns us with our Father's heart. As His children, we are to embody His reconciling love, showing the world what He is like. Just as Jesus is the Son who brings peace, so too are we called to walk in His footsteps.

Being called *"children of God"* also carries some eschatological significance. It anticipates the day when God's family will be revealed in glory. Peacemakers will be publicly identified as His true sons and daughters, vindicated before a watching world. This promise strengthens us when peace-making is costly, reminding us that our labour is not in vain.

Peace-making is not optional for followers of Jesus. It is a defining mark of the kingdom and a non-negotiable aspect of our witness. As recipients of God's peace, we are called to be agents of that peace in our homes, churches, communities and beyond.

Persevering in peace-making

Peace-making is noble but rarely easy. It demands perseverance because conflict, pride, and sin are persistent realities in a fallen world. Often, peace-making efforts are misunderstood or even resisted by those entrenched in division. Instead of gratitude, peacemakers may face criticism or hostility from those unwilling to let go of grievances or injustice. Jesus Himself modelled this tension: He came as the Prince of Peace, and yet His ministry provoked anger and opposition from those threatened by His message.

This is why perseverance is so important. Paul exhorts us in Galatians 6:9: *"Let us not become weary in doing good, for at the proper time we will reap a harvest if we do not give up."* Peacemakers must anchor their endurance in the hope of God's promised reward.

They recognize that their labour is not futile because they serve the God who ultimately brings perfect peace. Isaiah offers comfort: *"You will keep in perfect peace those whose minds are steadfast, because they trust in you."* (26:3)

Perseverance in peace-making also means understanding that peace often unfolds gradually. Reconciliation may take time, requiring patience and repeated efforts. Some wounds are deep and heal slowly. Peacemakers commit to the long journey of healing rather than demanding quick results. They trust that even when progress is slow or unseen, God is at work beneath the surface, softening hearts and opening doors.

Peace-making as participation in God's mission

Peace-making is not merely a personal virtue; it is participation in God's cosmic mission to restore all things. Through Christ, God is reconciling the world to Himself and dismantling the effects of sin that fractured His creation. Peacemakers join in this divine work, becoming instruments of His kingdom's advance.

Paul's language in 2 Corinthians 5:18–20 is striking: *"God... reconciled us to himself through Christ and gave us the ministry of reconciliation... We are therefore Christ's ambassadors, as though God were making his appeal through us."* Ambassadors do not represent themselves but their sovereign. In the same way, peacemakers represent the King of Peace, embodying His message and character in the world.

This mission is expansive. It includes proclaiming the gospel, through which people are reconciled to God, as well as living out its implications by reconciling with one another. When believers forgive, serve, and love across barriers, they provide living proof of the gospel's power. Jesus said in John 13:35, *"By this everyone will know that you are my disciples, if you love one another."*

Peace-making is missional: it displays the kingdom's reality and invites others to enter it. Moreover, peace-making anticipates the day when God's peace will saturate all creation.

Revelation 21:4 promises a future with *"no more death or mourning or crying or pain."* Every act of peace-making now is a foretaste of that future. It is a signpost pointing toward the ultimate shalom of the new heavens and new earth, when Christ reigns and every conflict is resolved in His justice and mercy.

The costliness of true peace-making

While peace-making reflects God's heart, it often incurs a cost. It may require relinquishing our right to be vindicated, absorbing insults, or enduring misunderstanding. Jesus Himself warned His followers that living out His kingdom values — including peace-making - would provoke opposition. *"If the world hates you, keep in mind that it hated me first."* (John 15:18).

Sometimes, efforts to bring peace expose deep resistance to truth. Speaking the truth in love can trigger defensiveness or anger in those unwilling to repent or reconcile. Genuine peace-making refuses to settle for false peace built on denial or compromise with sin. It insists on truth as the foundation for lasting peace, even if this means conflict before resolution.

This is why peace-making naturally leads to the next Beatitude: *"Blessed are those who are persecuted because of righteousness."* (Matthew 5:10). Peacemakers often stand in the gap, confronting injustice and urging forgiveness where bitterness reigns. Such actions can provoke backlash. Yet Jesus declares them blessed precisely because they embody the values of His kingdom in a world hostile to those values.

The blessing of being called children of God

The reward for peacemakers - *"they will be called children of God"* - is deeply significant. This title is both present and future. Even now, those who engage in peace-making reflect their Father's likeness and bear His family resemblance. When others see believers reconciling enemies, healing divisions, and embodying forgiveness, they glimpse something of the Father's nature. As Jesus said in Luke 6:35–36, *"Love your enemies, do good to them... Then your reward will be great, and you will be children of the Most High, because he is kind to the ungrateful and wicked. Be merciful, just as your Father is merciful."*

In the future, this identity will be fully revealed. Romans 8:19 tells us, *"The creation waits in eager expectation for the children of God to be revealed."* On that day, peacemakers will be publicly acknowledged as true sons and daughters of God, vindicated as those who reflected His character and participated in His mission. Their efforts, often unseen or unappreciated in this life, will be honoured in eternity.

Peace-making and persecution

The transition from peace-making to persecution may seem to be paradoxical. If peacemakers reflect God's character and work toward harmony, why would they be opposed? The answer lies in the nature of true peace. Because biblical peace is rooted in truth and righteousness, it challenges the false peace maintained by sin and injustice. Peacemakers disrupt the status quo where it resists God's kingdom.

Jesus Himself embodied this tension. He healed, forgave, and reconciled, but He also confronted a lot of hypocrisy, called for repentance, and exposed corruption. His peace-making often provoked those invested in division and power.

Similarly, when we engage in genuine peace-making - calling for forgiveness, dismantling hostility, and confronting injustice - we may face resistance from those unwilling to yield their pride, grudges, or control.

Yet this opposition is itself a mark of fidelity to Christ. As Jesus taught, those persecuted for righteousness' sake are blessed, for theirs is the kingdom of heaven (Matthew 5:10). Peacemakers who endure hostility share in His sufferings and bear witness to His cross-shaped path. Their perseverance testifies that they belong to the King who made peace *"through his blood, shed on the cross."* (Colossians 1:20).

Living as peacemakers today

To live as peacemakers today is to commit ourselves daily to the reconciling way of Jesus. It means forgiving freely, loving sacrificially, speaking truth gently but boldly, and working tirelessly for healing in relationships and communities.

It means praying for those who are in conflict, advocating for those marginalized, and proclaiming the gospel of peace that reconciles sinners to God.

Above all, peace-making requires us to keep our eyes fixed on the One who is our peace. Ephesians 2:14 declares, *"He himself is our peace."* We cannot manufacture peace apart from Him; we can only receive it and then extend it. As we abide in Christ and live out His peace, we become what He calls us to be: blessed peacemakers, known as children of the God of peace.

In the next chapter, we will turn to the final Beatitude: *"Blessed are those who are persecuted because of righteousness."* This Beatitude reminds us that living out the kingdom values of humility, mercy, purity, and peace-making often comes at a cost. Yet it also offers the assurance that those who endure persecution for righteousness will receive the kingdom of heaven in full.

9

'BLESSED ARE THOSE WHO ARE PERSECUTED BECAUSE OF RIGHTEOUSNESS'

Matthew 5:10-12

"Blessed are those who are persecuted because of righteousness, for theirs is the kingdom of heaven. Blessed are you when people insult you, persecute you and falsely say all kinds of evil against you because of me. Rejoice and be glad, because great is your reward in heaven, for in the same way they persecuted the prophets who were before you."

With this final Beatitude, Jesus concludes His description of the blessed life in His kingdom by addressing a sobering reality: following Him will provoke opposition. The Beatitudes have been building progressively: poverty of spirit, mourning over sin, meekness, hunger for righteousness, mercy, purity of heart, and peace-making all lead to a life that stands in stark contrast to the world.

This contrast inevitably invites conflict. Those who embody the values of Christ's eternal kingdom often find themselves at odds with a world that resists them.

Understanding persecution

Persecution, in biblical terms, is not simply limited to violent oppression. It also encompasses any mistreatment, hostility, or slander endured for the sake of righteousness and loyalty to Christ. Jesus specifically includes insults and false accusations alongside outright persecution (Matthew 5:11). This will mean persecution can range from social exclusion and ridicule to legal penalties, discrimination, or even martyrdom.

Importantly, Jesus is not referring to suffering caused by our own wrongdoing or any unwise behaviour. Peter makes this distinction clear: *"If you suffer, it should not be as a murderer or thief or any other kind of criminal, or even as a meddler. However, if you suffer as a Christian, do not be ashamed, but praise God that you bear that name."* (1 Peter 4:15–16).

The blessing Jesus promises is reserved for those persecuted *"because of righteousness"* or *"because of me"* (Matthew 5:10-11). That is, for living faithfully as His disciples and bearing witness to His truth.

Why persecution happens

Jesus' words reveal an unavoidable tension between the values of His kingdom and those of the world. The world is often comfortable with superficial religion or moral compromise but resists the radical righteousness of Christ. He told His disciples plainly in John 15:18-19: *"If the world hates you, keep in mind that it hated me first. If you belonged to the world, it would love you as its own. As it is, you do not belong to the world, but I have chosen you out of the world. That is why the world hates you."*

This is not because Christians seek conflict or impose their beliefs harshly, but because righteousness exposes sin. Jesus said in John 3:19-20, *"Light has come into the world, but people loved darkness instead of light because their deeds were evil. Everyone who does evil hates the light and will not come into the light for fear that their deeds will be exposed."* When we live as salt and light (Matthew 5:13-16), our lives inevitably challenge the darkness around us. This confrontation can provoke anger or hostility from those unwilling to turn to God.

Moreover, the gospel is inherently offensive to human pride. It declares that we are sinners in need of grace, unable to save ourselves, and calls us to repentance and submission to Christ. Paul describes this dynamic in 1 Corinthians 1:18: *"The message of the cross is foolishness to those who are perishing, but to us who are being saved it is the power of God."* Those who embrace this message are reconciled to God, but those who resist it often turn against its messengers.

The righteous are blessed

Despite its difficulty, Jesus pronounces the persecuted *"blessed."* This is striking: persecution is not something we naturally associate with blessing.

Yet in the kingdom of God, suffering for righteousness is not a mark of failure but of faithfulness. It signifies that we are aligned with Christ and His kingdom, sharing in His own rejection by the world.

Jesus roots this blessing in two key realities:

> *Theirs is the kingdom of heaven*: This Beatitude echoes the first one: *"Blessed are the poor in spirit, for theirs is the kingdom of heaven."* (Matthew 5:3). The repetition forms an inclusion, framing the Beatitudes with this promise. It reminds us that those of us who embrace the values of Christ's kingdom - beginning with humility and culminating in suffering for righteousness - are assured of our place in it. Persecution does not strip us of blessing; it confirms that we belong to God's kingdom.

> *Great is your reward in heaven*: Jesus directs our focus forward: *"Rejoice and be glad, because great is your reward in heaven."* (Matthew 5:12). While persecution may bring loss in this life - of reputation, comfort, or even safety - it brings eternal gain. Paul writes in Romans 8:17–18, *"Now if we are children, then we are heirs - heirs of God and co-heirs with Christ, if indeed we share in his sufferings in order that we may also share in his glory. I consider that our present sufferings are not worth comparing with the glory that will be revealed in us."*

The joy Jesus calls us to is not rooted in the pain itself but in the promise that it signals our union with Him and our participation in His kingdom. It is the same joy that enabled the apostles to rejoice after being flogged for preaching Christ: *"The apostles left the Sanhedrin, rejoicing because they had been counted worthy of suffering disgrace for the Name."* (Acts 5:41).

The example of the prophets

In Matthew 5:12, Jesus also places the persecuted in esteemed company: *"For in the same way they persecuted the prophets who were before you."* The prophets of old, like Jeremiah, Elijah, and Isaiah - spoke God's truth boldly and often paid the price for it.

They were mocked, opposed, and in some cases killed for calling people to repentance. Hebrews 11:36–38 recounts their faith: *"Some faced jeers and flogging, and even chains and imprisonment... they were put to death by stoning... the world was not worthy of them."*

By linking His followers with the prophets, Jesus affirms that persecution is not a sign of abandonment but of solidarity with God's messengers throughout history. To be persecuted for righteousness is to stand in the prophetic tradition, bearing witness to God's truth in a resistant world. It is evidence that we are continuing their mission and participating in the story of redemption.

Persecution as confirmation of faith

Persecution also serves as confirmation that our faith is genuine. Paul writes in 2 Timothy 3:12: *"Everyone who wants to live a godly life in Christ Jesus will be persecuted."*

This is not to say that all believers will experience severe persecution, but that opposition is a natural result of faithful living in a fallen world. If we never face resistance, it may indicate that our faith is too comfortable or compromised to challenge the surrounding culture.

Peter encourages believers facing trials: *"These have come so that the proven genuineness of your faith - of greater worth than gold... may result in praise, glory and honour when Jesus Christ is revealed."* (1 Peter 1:7). Persecution therefore refines our faith, stripping away superficiality and forcing us to rely wholly on God. It tests whether we really value Christ above convenience, comfort, or approval.

Enduring persecution with faith

Persecution, whether subtle or severe, tests the strength and sincerity of our faith. Jesus calls His followers not merely to endure it but to endure it faithfully. This endurance comes from anchoring ourselves in His promises and remembering that suffering for His sake is temporary, but glory is eternal.

Paul encourages believers in 2 Corinthians 4:16-18: *"Therefore we do not lose heart. Though outwardly we are wasting away, yet inwardly we are being renewed day by day. For our light and momentary troubles are achieving for us an eternal glory that far outweighs them all. So we fix our eyes not on what is seen, but on what is unseen, since what is seen is temporary, but what is unseen is eternal."*

Here we see the secret to endurance: shifting our gaze from the immediate pain to the eternal perspective. Persecution may press hard upon us, but it is fleeting when viewed in light of eternity. This eternal mindset steels us against despair, reminding us that our suffering is not pointless but purposeful.

Faith in God's sovereignty also fortifies us. When persecuted, it is tempting to feel abandoned or powerless. Yet Scripture assures us that nothing happens outside of God's control. Jesus told His disciples that even the hairs of their heads are numbered (Matthew 10:30) and that not even a sparrow falls without the Father's knowledge (Matthew 10:29). If God's care extends to such details, how much more does He watch over His children in times of trial?

Responding to persecution with grace

Jesus' call to *"rejoice and be glad"* (Matthew 5:12) in the face of persecution may seem impossible. Yet this joy does not come from denying pain but from trusting God's purposes and responding with grace rather than retaliation.

Jesus modelled this perfectly. When reviled, He did not retaliate. When falsely accused, He remained silent before His accusers. Peter reminds us of this example: *"When they hurled their insults at him, he did not retaliate; when he suffered, he made no threats. Instead, he entrusted himself to him who judges justly."* (1 Peter 2:23). Likewise, Stephen, the first Christian martyr, responded with grace even as he was stoned. Acts 7:60 records his final words: *"Lord, do not hold this sin against them."* His prayer mirrors Jesus' own on the cross: *"Father, forgive them"* (Luke 23:34). This radical forgiveness is not humanly natural; it is the fruit of a heart transformed by the Spirit and anchored in Christ's mercy.

To respond with grace is to break the cycle of hatred. It is to choose love in the face of hostility, prayer instead of bitterness, and blessing rather than curse. Paul exhorts believers to: *"Bless those who persecute you; bless and do not curse."* (Romans 12:14).

This posture not only protects our hearts from resentment but also bears powerful witness to the gospel. When we return evil with good, we reflect the mercy of the One who died for His enemies.

The joy of sharing in Christ's sufferings

An extraordinary paradox of the Christian life is that persecution can become a source of joy. Not because suffering itself is pleasant, but because it draws us into deeper fellowship with Christ. Paul expresses this in Philippians 3:10: *"I want to know Christ - yes, to know the power of his resurrection and participation in his sufferings, becoming like him in his death."*

When we suffer for righteousness, we participate in the sufferings of our Savior. We are reminded that He was, *"despised and rejected by mankind"* (Isaiah 53:3) and that our trials identify us with Him.

Peter captures this beautifully: *"Rejoice inasmuch as you participate in the sufferings of Christ, so that you may be overjoyed when his glory is revealed."* (1 Peter 4:13). Persecution is not a sign that God has abandoned us but that we are walking closely enough with Christ to share His rejection.

Moreover, this joy is tied to future glory. The apostles rejoiced after being flogged because they had been *"counted worthy of suffering disgrace for the Name."* (Acts 5:41). Their joy came from knowing that their temporary shame for Christ would give way to eternal honour with Him.

How to stand firm in persecution

When persecution arises, standing firm requires spiritual preparation and discipline. Here are five key principles rooted in Scripture:

1. *Be grounded in God's Word:* When Jesus faced temptation in the wilderness, He responded with Scripture (Matthew 4:4–10). Likewise, when persecution challenges our faith, the Word anchors us. Passages like Romans 8, 1 Peter 4, and Hebrews 12 remind us of God's promises and encourage endurance.

2. *Pray continually:* Prayer strengthens our resolve and keeps our hearts tender. It reminds us that we are not alone and invites God's power into our weakness. Paul's exhortation to *"pray without ceasing"* (1 Thessalonians 5:17) is vital when facing hostility.

3. *Rely on the Holy Spirit:* Jesus assured His disciples that the Spirit would give them words when they were dragged before authorities (Matthew 10:19–20). The same Spirit equips us with courage and wisdom in moments of pressure or fear.

4. *Remember the examples of the faithful*: Hebrews 12:1 urges us to run *"surrounded by such a great cloud of witnesses,"* recalling the perseverance of those who endured before us. Their stories remind us that suffering is not new and that God sustained them - and will sustain us.

5. *Stay connected to the body of Christ:* Fellowship will strengthen resolve. Believers enduring persecution need the encouragement of community. Acts 4 describes how the early church prayed and supported one another under pressure, finding boldness together.

The witness of a joyful response

One of the most powerful testimonies of the early church was its response to persecution. Roman observers were astonished by Christians who faced imprisonment, loss, and even death with composure and joy. This unwavering faith drew many to Christ. Tertullian famously wrote, *"The blood of the martyrs is the seed of the church."* Even today, in regions where believers endure severe persecution, their faith often flourishes because of their resilient witness.

Joy in suffering confounds the logic of the world. It demonstrates that our hope is not anchored in comfort, reputation, or safety but in Christ alone. When we rejoice under trial, we reveal the surpassing worth of knowing Him (Philippians 3:8).

Living with eternal perspective

Ultimately, Jesus calls us to rejoice not in the pain of persecution but in the certainty of our heavenly reward: *"Great is your reward in heaven."* (Matthew 5:12). This lifts our gaze beyond the present.

Paul describes this heavenly focus in Colossians 3:1–2: *"Since, then, you have been raised with Christ, set your hearts on things above... Set your minds on things above, not on earthly things."*

This eternal perspective frees us from fear and bitterness. It reminds us that persecution, though painful, cannot touch our inheritance in Christ (1 Peter 1:4). No insult, slander, or suffering can diminish the glory that awaits those who endure.

Jesus assures us that every act of faithfulness, every insult borne for His name, will be remembered and rewarded in His kingdom.

Persecution, then, is not merely a burden to bear but an opportunity to glorify God, deepen our faith, and proclaim the worth of Christ. In the next section, we will explore how believers can actively prepare for persecution, cultivate resilience, and respond in ways that honour Christ and display His gospel to the watching world.

Preparing for persecution

While many believers around the world face severe persecution, others may experience subtler forms - mockery, exclusion, or social rejection.

Regardless of its form, Jesus warns that persecution is not a remote possibility but an inevitable reality for His followers. *"Everyone who wants to live a godly life in Christ Jesus will be persecuted."* (2 Timothy 3:12).

Preparation is therefore essential:

1. *Deepen your roots in Christ:* Jesus spoke of those who "receive the word with joy" but *"fall away when trouble or persecution comes because of the word."* (Mark 4:16–17). Surface-level faith cannot withstand pressure. We must cultivate deep roots through consistent prayer, Scripture meditation, and communion with God so that when storms come, we remain anchored in Him.

2. *Expect it without surprise:* Peter wrote, *"Dear friends, do not be surprised at the fiery ordeal that has come on you to test you, as though something strange were happening to you."* (1 Peter 4:12). Knowing that persecution is part of discipleship helps prevent disillusionment. Jesus warned His followers in advance: *"If they persecuted me, they will persecute you also."* (John 15:20).

3. *Resolve to stand firm:* Before persecution arises, we must decide whom we will serve. Daniel *"resolved not to defile himself."* (Daniel 1:8) long before he faced the lions' den. Similarly, we must settle in our hearts that we will remain faithful, even when it costs us. This pre-decided loyalty gives strength in moments of testing.

4. *Pray for courage and wisdom:* The early church prayed not for escape but for boldness. In Acts 4:29, after Peter and John were threatened, they prayed: *"Lord… enable your servants to speak your word with great boldness."* God answered by filling them with the Holy Spirit and granting courage. We too must ask God for wisdom to respond rightly and boldness to endure.

5. *Strengthen your community ties:* Persecution often isolates. Believers need the support of a faithful community. Hebrews 10:24–25 urges us to *"spur one another on toward love and good deeds… encouraging one another - and all the more as you see the Day approaching."* A good faith community provides prayer, accountability, and comfort in suffering.

Encouragement for modern believers

For those living in societies with relative religious freedom, this Beatitude still applies. Though we may not face imprisonment or violence, following Christ faithfully is still going to provoke opposition. Standing firm on biblical convictions in a culture that celebrates relativism, and moral autonomy often invites criticism or exclusion.

Examples abound: a student mocked for upholding biblical ethics; an employee pressured to compromise integrity; a believer ridiculed online for sharing their faith. These moments, while not as extreme as martyrdom, are still forms of persecution *"because of righteousness."* They test our allegiance to Christ over comfort or approval.

In such situations, Jesus' words bring perspective and comfort. First, they remind us that opposition is normal for those who belong to Him. We are not alone or abnormal in facing hostility for our faith.

Second, they remind us of the eternal reward that outweighs temporary loss. As the great Apostle Paul declared, *"I consider everything a loss because of the surpassing worth of knowing Christ Jesus my Lord."* (Philippians 3:8).

Moreover, we must not allow fear of persecution to silence our witness. Jesus warned, *"Whoever is ashamed of me and my words, the Son of Man will be ashamed of them."* (Luke 9:26). Instead, we must emulate the apostles, who declared, *"We must obey God rather than human beings!"* (Acts 5:29). Even if our culture grows more hostile to Christian truth, we are called to proclaim Christ with humility, courage, and love.

Responding with love and grace

Perhaps the greatest challenge in persecution is maintaining a posture of love toward those who oppose us. Yet this is precisely what Jesus commands: *"Love your enemies and pray for those who persecute you."* (Matthew 5:44). Such love is not sentimental but deliberate - choosing always to seek their good, pray for their repentance, and refuse bitterness.

This is not weakness but strength. It reflects the heart of Christ, who bore insults silently and prayed for His executioners. When we respond to hostility with grace, we disarm our opponents and bear witness to a love that transcends retaliation. Paul urges in Romans 12:21: *"Do not be overcome by evil, but overcome evil with good."*

History is full of examples of this transforming love. Many persecutors of Christians throughout the centuries have been won to faith by the grace, patience, and forgiveness shown by those they opposed. The gospel is most compelling when it is embodied under fire.

The completion of the beatitudes

This final Beatitude brings the sequence full circle. It begins where it started - with *"the kingdom of heaven"* (Matthew 5:3, 10). The poor in spirit enter the kingdom of heaven through humble dependence on God, and the persecuted inherit it as proof of their loyalty to Him.

The progression of the Beatitudes shows us the path of discipleship: humility leads to repentance, which produces meekness, hunger for righteousness, mercy, purity, peace-making, and ultimately persecution. This last step now reminds us that living out the preceding virtues will inevitably put us at odds with the world.

Yet this Beatitude also assures us that such opposition is not defeat but victory. Persecution reveals that we are truly living as kingdom citizens. It identifies us with Christ, aligns us with the prophets, and secures for us the reward of eternal glory. Thus, Jesus can command: *"Rejoice and be glad."* What the world calls loss, He calls blessedness.

Looking ahead: Courage for today, hope for tomorrow

As we conclude the Beatitudes, we see how countercultural the values of Christ's kingdom truly are. Poverty of spirit, mourning, meekness, mercy, purity, peace-making, and persecution do not describe worldly success, yet they mark the truly blessed.

They form a portrait of the kingdom life that Jesus both modelled and invites us to embrace. So for those facing persecution today, take heart: you are in the company of the prophets, the apostles, and Christ Himself. Your suffering is not wasted but woven into the grand story of redemption. And for those who live with relative ease, this Beatitude calls us to boldness - to live so faithfully for Christ that, should opposition arise, we would stand firm.

Paul's words in Romans 8:35-37 offer a fitting conclusion: *"Who shall separate us from the love of Christ? Shall trouble or hardship or persecution or famine or nakedness or danger or sword?... No, in all these things we are more than conquerors through him who loved us."* Persecution is not the end of the story; glory is.

The kingdom of heaven belongs to those who follow Christ even in suffering, knowing that joy unspeakable and eternal awaits. This is why Jesus can declare the persecuted blessed: because in losing the world, they gain Him.

10

SALT AND LIGHT: THE INFLUENCE OF KINGDOM PEOPLE

Matthew 5:13–16

"You are the salt of the earth. But if the salt loses its saltiness, how can it be made salty again? It is no longer good for anything, except to be thrown out and trampled underfoot. You are the light of the world. A town built on a hill cannot be hidden. Neither do people light a lamp and put it under a bowl. Instead, they put it on its stand, and it gives light to everyone in the house. In the same way, let your light shine before others, that they may see your good deeds and glorify your Father in heaven."

Having just outlined the character of those who belong to God's kingdom in the Beatitudes, Jesus now turns to their influence. The Beatitudes describe what kingdom citizens are; these verses describe what they do. They are not merely passive recipients of grace - they are agents of transformation. Jesus uses two vivid metaphors (salt and light) to describe the calling of His followers to engage the world in a way that preserves, illuminates, and draws others to God.

Salt of the earth: preserving and purifying

Salt was highly valued in the ancient world. It served many purposes, including: preserving food, enhancing flavour, and even purifying wounds. To call His disciples *"the salt of the earth"* was both an honour and a charge. Just as salt prevents decay and brings taste to otherwise bland food, so believers are called to preserve what is good and add vitality to a world marred by sin.

1. Salt as preserver

In Jesus' time, without refrigeration, salt was essential for preventing food from spoiling. This imagery speaks to the moral decay of the world. Left unchecked, sin corrupts and destroys. Through their holy lives and godly influence, Christians act as a preservative, slowing society's moral deterioration.

Paul's warning in 2 Timothy 3:1–5 paints a sobering picture of a world spiralling into selfishness and godlessness, but it is precisely into such a world that God sends His people as salt - to hold back the rot. This preservative role is not fulfilled by withdrawal but by presence. Salt must come into contact with food to preserve it; likewise, believers must engage the world, not retreat from it. Jesus does not envision His disciples forming isolated enclaves of holiness detached from society but rather permeating it with the distinctiveness of His kingdom.

2. Salt as flavour

Salt also enhances taste. Without it, food is bland and lifeless. In the same way, Christians are to bring a distinctiveness, a vibrancy, to the world around them. Paul uses similar imagery in Colossians 4:6: *"Let your conversation be always full of grace, seasoned with salt, so that you may know how to answer everyone."* Our presence should make life richer, not because of us but because we carry the joy, hope, and grace of Christ.

This means that Christians should be known not merely for what they oppose but for the beauty and goodness they bring: kindness, integrity, compassion, and joy. A salty life is attractive because it offers an alternative to the emptiness and cynicism so prevalent in the world.

3. Salt as purifier

Salt also has antiseptic qualities. It was used in ancient times to cleanse wounds and prevent infection. In this sense, believers are called to confront sin and bring healing where there is brokenness. This involves speaking the truth in love (Ephesians 4:15) and offering the redemptive hope of the gospel to those enslaved by sin. Our role is not merely to lament the world's condition but to bring the cleansing power of Christ into it.

The warning: Losing saltiness

Jesus issues a stark warning: *"But if the salt loses its saltiness, how can it be made salty again? It is no longer good for anything."* (Matthew 5:13).

While pure sodium chloride does not chemically lose its saltiness, the salt used in Palestine often contained impurities. Over time, exposure to moisture or mixing with other substances could render it tasteless and useless.

This metaphor warns against compromise. When believers blend so fully with the world that they become indistinguishable from it, they lose their preserving and purifying influence. A Christian who hides their distinctiveness is like salt that has lost its flavour: ineffective and irrelevant. Jesus calls His disciples to remain *in* the world but not be *of* the world (John 17:15–16), maintaining their sharpness and distinctiveness in a culture that pressures them toward conformity.

Light of the world: illuminating truth

Jesus' second metaphor is equally striking: *"You are the light of the world."* Light dispels darkness, guides, and reveals what is hidden. Throughout Scripture, light is associated with God and His truth. Psalm 27:1 declares, *"The Lord is my light and my salvation,"* while John 8:12 records Jesus' own words: *"I am the light of the world. Whoever follows me will never walk in darkness but will have the light of life."*

Here, Jesus extends this identity to His followers. As His disciples, we are not light in and of ourselves but reflect His light, much like the moon reflects the sun. Just as Jesus is the source of light, we become its bearers, shining His truth into a darkened world.

1. Light reveals and exposes

Light exposes what is hidden. Darkness will conceal, but light makes visible. Paul writes in Ephesians 5:11–13: *"Have nothing to do with the fruitless deeds of darkness but rather expose them… everything exposed by the light becomes visible."* By living according to God's truth, believers expose sin for what it is - not through self-righteous condemnation, but by embodying a different way of life. When we live with honesty, purity, and integrity, our lives reveal the emptiness of deception and corruption.

Our conduct itself becomes a quiet but powerful rebuke to the darkness. This is why Jesus warned in John 3:20 that *"everyone who does evil hates the light."* A faithful Christian presence can provoke resistance because it exposes what many would prefer remain hidden.

2. Light guides

Light not only exposes; it also guides. A lamp or torch in ancient times provided direction in the darkness. Similarly, Christians are called to live in a way that points others to God's truth. Psalm 119:105 says, *"Your word is a lamp for my feet, a light on my path."* As we follow Christ, our lives become signposts directing others toward Him.

This guidance is especially vital in a world marked by moral confusion and spiritual blindness. Jesus calls His followers to live with such clarity and distinctiveness that others are drawn out of darkness and toward His light.

3. Light attracts

Light naturally draws people. A city on a hill cannot be hidden because its light is visible from miles away. In the same way, Christians are to live openly and visibly as followers of Christ. Jesus explicitly rejects secrecy: *"Neither do people light a lamp and put it under a bowl."* (Matthew 5:15). Our faith is not meant to be hidden but displayed so that others *"may see your good deeds and glorify your Father in heaven"* (Matthew 5:16).

The purpose: God's glory

The ultimate goal of being salt and light is not our recognition but God's glory. Jesus says our good deeds should lead others to *"glorify your Father in heaven."* Our influence is not about showcasing our morality but pointing to Him. When people see lives transformed by grace, they are compelled to consider the One who made it possible. This emphasis on visible good works is not contrary to grace but flows from it. Ephesians 2:10 reminds us: *"For we are God's handiwork, created in Christ Jesus to do good works, which God prepared in advance for us to do."*

These works, lived out before a watching world, then become windows through which others glimpse God's character.

Living as salt and light today

The metaphors of salt and light are timeless, but they take on fresh relevance in every generation. In a world that is morally confused and spiritually dark, Jesus' call remains urgent. To live as salt and light is to live visibly distinct lives that point others to God's reality. This is not optional for followers of Christ - it is an integral part of discipleship.

Here are some practical ways to embody these metaphors in our modern context:

1. Maintain integrity and holiness

Integrity is the *"saltiness"* that preserves and flavours society. In workplaces where dishonesty is normalized, in industries driven by greed, or in cultures dominated by compromise, Christians stand out by refusing to cut corners or manipulate. Paul urges all believers in Philippians 2:15 to *"become blameless and pure, 'children of God without fault in a warped and crooked generation.' Then you will shine among them like stars in the sky."*

Holiness does not mean isolation but distinctiveness. It means living transparently before God, letting our character and decisions reflect His standards rather than society's shifting norms. This quiet, consistent faithfulness has a preserving effect, restraining corruption and pointing people toward a better way.

2. Demonstrate love in action

Salt adds flavour, and light draws attention - our faith becomes visible when expressed through tangible love. Jesus said, *"By this everyone will know that you are my disciples, if you love one another."* (John 13:35). Acts of compassion, generosity, and service flavour the world with God's grace and draw others toward Him. This might include mentoring someone in need, visiting the sick, providing for the poor, or advocating for justice. Small, everyday acts of kindness often shine most brightly in dark settings.

When believers respond with grace where others may retaliate, forgive where others hold grudges, and give where others hoard, they embody the distinctiveness of Christ's kingdom.

3. Speak truth graciously

Light not only shines through actions but also through words. To be salt and light always includes speaking God's truth with humility and courage. In an age where moral relativism prevails, graciously articulating biblical convictions is vital.

Colossians 4:6 instructs, *"Let your conversation be always full of grace, seasoned with salt, so that you may know how to answer everyone."* Our words should both preserve truth and attract hearers. This requires wisdom: not harsh condemnation, but gentle, reasoned explanations of why we believe what we believe. Such speech invites dialogue rather than defensiveness.

4. Engage culture without compromise

Being salt and light does not mean retreating from culture but engaging it faithfully. This involves participating in workplaces, schools, communities, and in public life while maintaining a distinctive Christian identity. Jesus prayed not for His followers to be taken out of the world but to be protected from the evil one while remaining in it (John 17:15).

Engaging culture faithfully might include pursuing excellence in our vocations, contributing to civic life, and influencing systems for good. However, it also means resisting conformity. Romans 12:2 warns: *"Do not conform to the pattern of this world, but be transformed by the renewing of your mind."* Salt must retain its flavour, and light must not be hidden by fear or compromise.

5. Resist the temptation to hide

Jesus warns against hiding our light *"under a bowl."* Fear often tempts believers to conceal their faith to avoid ridicule or rejection. Yet hiding our light defeats its purpose. Faith is meant to be visible - not ostentatiously displayed for self-glory, but naturally evident through words, actions, and priorities.

Practical ways to avoid hiding include speaking openly about our faith when opportunities arise, praying in public without embarrassment, and letting our ethical decisions reflect biblical values even when costly. Our lives should provoke curiosity in those around us, leading them to *"see your good deeds and glorify your Father in heaven."* (v. 16).

Resisting the loss of saltiness

Jesus' warning about salt losing its saltiness is a sober reminder. While chemically speaking salt does not lose flavour, it can be contaminated or diluted until it becomes useless. Spiritually, this happens easily when believers compromise with sin, lose their distinctiveness, or blend so thoroughly with the world that they no longer stand out.

Common ways this happens include:

> *Moral compromise:* Adopting the attitudes or behaviours of our culture that contradict Scripture.

> *Spiritual apathy:* Losing zeal for God and neglecting prayer, Scripture, and fellowship, resulting in weakened witness.

> *Fear of man:* Prioritizing human approval over God's call, leading to silence when truth must be spoken.

The antidote is ongoing renewal in Christ. We remain *"salty"* by staying close to our God through daily prayer, immersion in Scripture, regular and ongoing repentance, and fellowship with other believers who encourage us to live boldly. The writer of Hebrews calls us to *"spur one another on toward love and good deeds... encouraging one another - and all the more as you see the Day approaching."* (Hebrews 10:24–25)

Salt and light as missional identity

These metaphors are not only descriptive; they are missional. Jesus does not command His followers merely to be salt and light privately but to influence the world actively. This connects directly to His Great Commission: *"Go and make disciples of all nations."* (Matthew 28:19).

Salt permeates food; light penetrates darkness. In the same way, believers are to permeate the world with the gospel and shine into its darkest corners. This missional identity means that every believer, not just pastors or missionaries, is called to impact their sphere of influence for Christ. Whether in homes, workplaces, neighbourhoods, or nations, we are sent as agents of God's kingdom. Our everyday faithfulness becomes part of His larger mission to redeem the world.

Paul ties this calling directly to the gospel in Philippians 2:15–16: *"You… shine among them like stars in the sky as you hold firmly to the word of life."* Our good deeds and faithful witness point to the *"word of life"* - the message of Christ that brings salvation. Salt and light are not ends in themselves; they serve the greater purpose of making God known.

Salt and light in discipleship

Discipleship involves learning not only who Jesus is but how to live like Him in the world. These metaphors frame discipleship as both inward transformation and outward witness.

The Beatitudes described the inward character of a disciple: humility, mercy, purity, and righteousness. Now, Jesus turns outward: disciples live distinctively so that others see and are drawn to the Father.

This dual focus prevents extremes. Discipleship is not mere private piety disconnected from the world, nor is it social activism devoid of spiritual foundation. Salt and light integrate the two: deep inner transformation leads to outward influence grounded in the gospel.

For churches, this means equipping believers not only to grow spiritually but also to live missionally. Corporate worship, small groups, and teaching should all aim to prepare God's people to be salt and light in their daily contexts. The gathered church fuels the scattered church, sending believers back into the world as witnesses.

The result: Glory to the Father

The ultimate purpose of being salt and light is encapsulated in Matthew 5:16: *"that they may see your good deeds and glorify your Father in heaven."* Our lives are not meant to point to ourselves but to God. When unbelievers observe Christians living with integrity, love, and courage, they are prompted to consider the One who makes such lives possible.

Peter echoes this in 1 Peter 2:12: *"Live such good lives among the pagans that, though they accuse you of doing wrong, they may see your good deeds and glorify God on the day he visits us."* Even in contexts of misunderstanding or hostility, faithful witness can lead others to salvation and ultimately to glorify God.

The challenges of living as salt and light

While Jesus' call to be salt and light is clear, living it out in a resistant culture is challenging. Darkness resists light, and a decaying world resists the preserving influence of salt. Those who live distinctively will face misunderstanding, ridicule, or even hostility. This is why Jesus places this passage immediately after the Beatitude on persecution.

To shine in darkness and to preserve what is good inevitably puts us at odds with those who prefer concealment or moral compromise.

1. The pressure of conformity

Modern culture often prizes tolerance over truth and celebrates individual autonomy above moral absolutes. In such a context, believers may feel pressured to downplay their convictions to avoid offending others. There is a temptation to blend in, hiding our light under a bowl (Matthew 5:15) rather than risking the disapproval of others.

But Jesus calls His disciples to resist conformity. Paul's exhortation is striking: *"Do not conform to the pattern of this world, but be transformed by the renewing of your mind."* (Romans 12:2). Transformation precedes influence. Only by remaining distinct can we fulfil our calling as salt and light.

2. The risk of isolation

In response to the world's hostility, some Christians withdraw altogether, retreating into safe enclaves where they avoid contact with unbelievers. While this may feel protective, it contradicts Jesus' intent. Salt does no good sealed away in a container; it must be scattered. Light is useless hidden under a covering; it must shine where darkness is thickest.

Jesus deliberately sends His followers into the world (John 17:18) not to imitate it but to transform it. Peace-making, mercy, and evangelism all require presence among those who do not yet know Christ.

3. The danger of hypocrisy

Few things undermine our witness more than hypocrisy. When our lives fail to match our words, our salt loses its flavour, and our light is dimmed. Jesus later warns of those who *"do not practice what they preach."* (Matthew 23:3). Integrity is essential.

We cannot call others to towards repentance while harbouring unrepentant sin ourselves. This is why Jesus' metaphors rest on the foundation of the Beatitudes: only those transformed from within - poor in spirit, pure in heart, merciful, hungry for righteousness - can truly influence the world for Christ.

Practical encouragement for being salt and light

Though challenging, living as salt and light is both possible and deeply rewarding when rooted in God's grace. Here are practical ways to remain faithful:

1. Stay close to Christ

We shine because we reflect His light. As Jesus said, *"I am the light of the world."* (John 8:12). Our influence depends on intimacy with Him. Through daily prayer, Scripture reading, and worship, we draw near to the source of light and are renewed to radiate Him to others. Like Moses, whose face shone after being in God's presence (Exodus 34:29), time with Christ transforms us and equips us to shine.

2. Rely on the Holy Spirit

We cannot live out this calling in our own strength. The Spirit empowers us to display Christ's character and grants boldness in witness. Acts 1:8 promises: *"You will receive power when the Holy Spirit comes on you; and you will be my witnesses."* This power is not merely for dramatic moments of evangelism but for daily faithfulness in ordinary life - patient endurance, gracious speech, sacrificial love.

3. Practice consistent faithfulness

Influence is not usually dramatic or instant. It grows through consistent, everyday acts of obedience. Quiet integrity in your workplace, patient kindness in your home, and humble service in your community are all ways God uses His people to flavour and illumine their surroundings. Often, our most powerful witness may come not through speeches but through steady, unpretentious faithfulness that catches others' attention.

4. Embrace small acts of light

Darkness is dispelled by even the smallest light. You don't have to be a preacher or public figure to make an impact. A kind word, an honest apology, or an invitation to pray for someone can pierce the gloom of discouragement or confusion. Jesus' teaching here is profoundly democratic: *"You are the light of the world."* applies to every disciple, regardless of gifting or position.

Salt and light in the face of opposition

Living as salt and light often provokes resistance. The light exposes what darkness prefers to hide, and salt stings when applied to wounds. Jesus warns that those who live this way will sometimes be maligned or persecuted (Matthew 5:11–12). Yet even opposition can amplify our witness.

In 1 Peter 2:12, suffering believers are encouraged to: *"Keep your conduct among the Gentiles honourable, so that when they speak against you as evildoers, they may see your good deeds and glorify God."* A gracious response to criticism often speaks louder than words.

When believers choose to endure insult or mistreatment without retaliation, it compels observers to reconsider their assumptions about God. History shows that opposition often strengthens rather than weakens the church. The early Christians, despite facing severe persecution, transformed the Roman Empire not through power but through their distinctiveness - caring for the sick, rescuing abandoned infants, forgiving enemies, and joyfully enduring hardship. Their salt and light turned the world upside down (Acts 17:6).

Salt, light, and mission

Jesus' teaching here is missional. Salt and light are outward-facing metaphors. They exist for the benefit of what surrounds them. Salt does not flavour itself; light does not shine merely for its own sake. Likewise, our faith is not meant to be privatized or self-contained. We are called to bless and influence everyone around us.

This outward orientation aligns with God's covenantal plan from the beginning. Israel was chosen not merely for its own sake but to be *"a light for the Gentiles"* (Isaiah 49:6). Jesus now applies this vocation to His followers. The church is God's instrument to bring His light to the nations. Our daily lives - our words, actions, and priorities - are meant to be missionary in nature, pointing others toward Him.

Missional living does not always mean formal evangelism. It means living in such a way that the reality of God's kingdom becomes visible. Our integrity in business, our patience in suffering, our generosity with time and resources - all of these make the gospel credible and attractive.

Transition: Salt, light, and the law

This call to influence naturally raises questions about the standard of righteousness that fuels it. What kind of life truly preserves and illumines? Jesus immediately addresses this in the next section of the Sermon on the Mount: *"Do not think that I have come to abolish the Law or the Prophets."* (Matthew 5:17).

Here, He clarifies that kingdom living is not lawless but fulfils God's original intent for righteousness. The shift from salt and light to His teaching on the Law is deliberate. Jesus first describes the outward impact of kingdom citizens, then explains the inner righteousness that undergirds that impact. Influence flows not from superficial religiosity but from a deep transformation of heart and obedience rooted in love for God.

As we move into this next section, we will see Jesus redefine righteousness - not as mere external conformity, but as the kind of inward purity and devotion that surpasses even the strictest legalism of His day. Only such righteousness can sustain a life that truly shines and preserves.

Conclusion: The call to visible faith

Jesus' words about salt and light challenge every believer to consider: Does my life make a noticeable difference? Am I distinct enough to preserve goodness and illuminate truth? Or has my saltiness diminished, my light dimmed under fear or compromise?

This is not a call to self-reliance but to dependence on Christ. He is the true Light (John 8:12) and the one who flavours the world through His Spirit in us. As we abide in Him, our influence is not forced but natural. Our lives become living testimonies, drawing others to *"glorify your Father in heaven."* (Matthew 5:16).

In a dark and decaying world, even a small amount of salt preserves. Even the faintest light shines. If we remain faithful, Christ's presence in us will accomplish what He promised: through ordinary disciples living extraordinary lives of grace, truth, and love, the world will glimpse the reality of the kingdom of God.

- 11 -

CHRIST AND THE FULFILMENT OF THE LAW

Matthew 5:17–20

"Do not think that I have come to abolish the Law or the Prophets; I have not come to abolish them but to fulfil them. For truly I tell you, until heaven and earth disappear, not the smallest letter, not the least stroke of a pen, will by any means disappear from the Law until everything is accomplished. Therefore, anyone who sets aside one of the least of these commands and teaches others accordingly will be called least in the kingdom of heaven, but whoever practices and teaches these commands will be called great in the kingdom of heaven. For I tell you that unless your righteousness surpasses that of the Pharisees and the teachers of the law, you will certainly not enter the kingdom of heaven."

Having described the character and influence of His disciples in the Beatitudes and the call to be salt and light, Jesus now turns to address the foundation of kingdom righteousness. His words here are crucial for understanding not only His teaching in the Sermon on the Mount but also His entire ministry. How does Jesus relate to the Law of Moses and the Scriptures of the Old Testament? What kind of righteousness does He require of His followers? And how is this righteousness achieved?

The Law and the Prophets

The phrase *"the Law or the Prophets"* refers to the entire Hebrew Scriptures, what we now call the Old Testament. The Law (Torah) was given through Moses, containing God's commands and instructions for Israel. The Prophets encompassed those books that applied and interpreted the Law, calling God's people back to covenant faithfulness. Together, this phrase summarizes the written Word of God available to Jesus' listeners. Many of Jesus' contemporaries totally misunderstood His ministry. His bold teaching, His challenges to traditional interpretations, and His radical calls for heart-level obedience led some to suspect that He sought to overturn the Law altogether.

Jesus anticipates this objection and denies it emphatically: *"Do not think that I have come to abolish the Law or the Prophets."* Instead, He declares, *"I have not come to abolish them but to fulfil them."* This statement is monumental. Jesus positions Himself not against the Scriptures but as their fulfilment. He is not introducing a new standard disconnected from the old; rather, He is bringing God's purposes in the Law and Prophets to their intended goal.

What does it mean to "fulfil" the Law?

To "fulfil" (Greek *plēroō*) means to bring to completion or to bring to its intended purpose. Jesus fulfills the Law and the Prophets in several interconnected ways:

1. Fulfilment through His life and obedience

Jesus perfectly obeyed the Law, succeeding where all others failed. Israel repeatedly broke the covenant, and yet Jesus kept it flawlessly. His obedience was comprehensive - not only external compliance but perfect heart alignment with God's will.

He could declare truthfully in John 8:29, *"I always do what pleases him."* In His life, Jesus embodied the righteousness the Law required but humanity could not achieve.

2. Fulfilment through His teaching

In the Sermon on the Mount, Jesus deepens and clarifies the Law's meaning, stripping away distortions and superficial interpretations. He does not relax the Law; He intensifies it, pressing it inward to address motives, desires, and the heart (as we will see in His teaching on anger, lust, and oaths). His words reveal the Law's ultimate intention: not merely to regulate behaviour but to transform the inner person.

3. Fulfilment through His death and resurrection

Jesus also fulfils the Law sacrificially. The old covenant sacrificial system pointed forward to Him. The blood of bulls and goats could never truly take away sins (Hebrews 10:4), but they foreshadowed His perfect, once-for-all sacrifice.

On the cross, Jesus bore the curse of the Law (Galatians 3:13), satisfying its demands and opening the way for sinners to be justified apart from works of the Law (Romans 3:21–22).

4. Fulfilment through His person

Finally, Jesus fulfils the Law and Prophets by actually being their ultimate subject. The Scriptures all point to Him. After His resurrection, He explained to His disciples, *"what was said in all the Scriptures concerning himself."* (Luke 24:27).

He is the true and better Moses, leading His people out of bondage to sin; the true and better David, reigning over God's kingdom; the suffering servant foretold by Isaiah and the ultimate prophet whom Moses promised (Deuteronomy 18:15). All of Scripture finds its *"yes"* in Him (2 Corinthians 1:20).

The permanence of God's Word

Jesus underscores the enduring authority of Scripture: *"Until heaven and earth disappear, not the smallest letter, not the least stroke of a pen, will by any means disappear from the Law until everything is accomplished."* (Matthew 5:18).

Here He affirms that God's Word is unchanging and reliable, down to the tiniest detail. The *"smallest letter"* refers to the Hebrew *yod*, the tiniest character, and the *"least stroke"* refers to a minute mark distinguishing similar letters.

This declaration reinforces that Jesus is not dismantling Scripture but honouring it. The Law will remain in force *"until everything is accomplished,"* that is, until God's redemptive purposes are fully realized. This includes both the fulfilment of its prophecies in Christ and the consummation of His kingdom at His return.

For Jesus, Scripture is inviolable. His teaching does not nullify it but reveals its true meaning and goal. This challenges any notion that His message is detached from or opposed to the Old Testament. Rather, He calls His disciples to a deep reverence for God's Word and to a righteousness rooted in it.

Practicing and teaching the commands

Jesus continues: *"Anyone who sets aside one of the least of these commands and teaches others accordingly will be called least in the kingdom of heaven, but whoever practices and teaches these commands will be called great in the kingdom of heaven."* (Matthew 5:19). Here, Jesus connects greatness in His eternal kingdom not to status or influence but to obedience and faithful teaching.

This verse warns against two main errors: neglecting obedience ourselves and also leading others into laxity. Even the *"least"* commands matter because they reflect God's character and will. Jesus calls His followers to a life of integrity where practice and teaching align. We must not merely affirm Scripture theoretically but embody it practically.

Greatness in the kingdom is tied to both living and transmitting God's Word faithfully. This includes parents teaching children, mentors guiding younger believers, and pastors instructing congregations. Yet teaching is not limited to formal roles. Every Christian influences others - by example, conversation, or counsel. How we handle God's commands either strengthens or undermines their authority in the eyes of those around us.

Surpassing the righteousness of the Pharisees

Jesus climaxes this section with a startling statement: *"For I tell you that unless your righteousness surpasses that of the Pharisees and the teachers of the law, you will certainly not enter the kingdom of heaven."* (Matthew 5:20). To His hearers, this would have been shocking. The Pharisees were renowned for their scrupulous devotion to the Law of God, meticulously observing rituals and regulations. If their righteousness was insufficient, what hope was there for everyone else?

Jesus is not demanding more of the same kind of righteousness - He is contrasting two fundamentally different approaches. Pharisaic righteousness was always external, focused on visible behaviour and legal compliance. Jesus calls for a righteousness that is internal and transformative, flowing from a heart renewed by God.

This anticipates the contrasts that follow in the Sermon: anger versus murder, lust versus adultery, love for enemies versus hatred. Jesus drives beyond surface-level observance to the heart-level holiness God desires. True righteousness is not about appearing good but about being made good from within by God's Spirit.

The nature of surpassing righteousness

When Jesus calls His followers to a righteousness that *"surpasses that of the Pharisees,"* He is not calling them to outdo the Pharisees at their own game, i.e. more rules, stricter observance, longer prayers etc. Instead, He is redefining righteousness altogether. Pharisaic righteousness was primarily external: it focused on behaviour, ritual precision, and public appearance. Jesus calls for an inward, heart-based righteousness rooted in love for God and transformed desires.

The Pharisees excelled at rule-keeping, but their righteousness was superficial. Jesus later rebukes them in Matthew 23:27–28: *"You are like whitewashed tombs, which look beautiful on the outside but on the inside are full of the bones of the dead and everything unclean. In the same way, on the outside you appear to people as righteous but on the inside, you are full of hypocrisy and wickedness."* Their problem was not that they cared too much about the Law but that they misunderstood its purpose.

True righteousness goes beyond mere conformity to external standards. It is about the heart. This is why Jesus later deepens the Law's commands: anger is equated with murder, lust with adultery. He is showing that sin begins not in our actions but in our desires, motives, and attitudes. Surpassing righteousness penetrates the surface to the source of our conduct: the heart.

Righteousness as an inner transformation

The righteousness Jesus demands is not something we can achieve by human effort. Left to ourselves, we are incapable of it. Romans 3:10 declares, *"There is no one righteous, not even one."* The Law exposes our failure rather than resolving it.

As Paul explains in Romans 3:20: *"Through the law we become conscious of our sin."* This is why Jesus' teaching here drives us to grace. The demand for surpassing righteousness is not meant to crush us into despair but to awaken us to our need for Him. Jesus alone fulfils the Law perfectly. Jesus alone will provide the righteousness we lack. Through faith in Him, we receive what we call *imputed righteousness* - His perfect record is credited to us. Paul rejoices in this exchange: *"This righteousness is given through faith in Jesus Christ to all who believe."* (Romans 3:22).

Yet Jesus' words also speak about *imparted righteousness* - the transforming work of the Spirit that makes us holy in practice. Salvation is not merely about forgiveness; it is about renewal. Through the new covenant promised in Ezekiel 36:26-27, God gives us a new heart and puts His Spirit within us, empowering us to obey from love rather than mere duty.

This is the surpassing righteousness Jesus envisions: not self-produced morality but Spirit-enabled holiness flowing from a transformed heart.

The Law as a guide and a pointer to Christ

Far from abolishing the Law, Jesus reveals its ultimate purpose: to point us to Him. Paul calls the Law *"our guardian until Christ came that we might be justified by faith."* (Galatians 3:24). The Law shows us God's holiness and our sin, driving us to seek mercy. Once we are united to Christ by faith, the Law is fulfilled in us - not by external compulsion but by internal transformation.

Romans 8:4 explains that God sent His Son, *"in order that the righteous requirement of the law might be fully met in us, who do not live according to the flesh but according to the Spirit."*

Thus, obedience under the new covenant is not a matter of legalistic box-checking but Spirit-empowered delight in God's will. David captures this heart posture in Psalm 40:8: *"I desire to do your will, my God; your law is within my heart."* This is the kind of righteousness Jesus commends - an obedience that always flows from love.

The Pharisees' error: Externalism without transformation

To clearly understand the sharpness of Jesus' strong statement in Matthew 5:20, we must first grasp the Pharisees' mindset. They believed righteousness was measured by meticulous adherence to rules - tithing even herbs (Matthew 23:23), ritual washings, Sabbath restrictions — but neglected *"the more important matters of the law — justice, mercy and faithfulness."* Their focus on external compliance bred pride, hypocrisy, and spiritual blindness.

By contrast, Jesus calls His disciples to internal integrity. He does not relax God's standards but deepens them, requiring not just outward conformity but inward purity. This is why He later says in Matthew 6:1, *"Be careful not to practice your righteousness in front of others to be seen by them."* True righteousness is never about performance for human approval, it always about us living transparently before God.

This is the surpassing righteousness Jesus demands: it is deeper, truer, and more holistic. It addresses the root rather than just the fruit of sin.

Grace and the call to righteousness

How, then, do we reconcile this high standard with the gospel of grace? Does Jesus' demand here for surpassing righteousness contradict salvation by faith alone? Not at all. Grace does not nullify righteousness; it produces it. As Titus 2:11–12 explains: *"For the grace of God has appeared that offers salvation to all people. It teaches us to say 'No' to ungodliness and worldly passions, and to live self-controlled, upright and godly lives in this present age."*

Grace saves us apart from works but also transforms us for good works. It is both pardon and power. We are justified by faith alone, but the faith that justifies is never alone - it bears the fruit of obedience.

This is why Jesus insists that those who enter His kingdom will be marked by a righteousness that exceeds external legalism. Not because they earn salvation by it, but because the new birth inevitably produces it.

The Kingdom and righteousness

Jesus' statement also connects righteousness to our ability to embrace the reality of God's kingdom. Jesus said, *"Unless your righteousness surpasses that of the Pharisees... you will certainly not enter the kingdom of heaven."* (Matthew 5:20). Entrance into the kingdom is inseparable from transformation. Those who belong to Christ are not only forgiven but remade. This is why the write of Hebrews urges: *"Make every effort to live in peace with everyone and to be holy; without holiness no one will see the Lord."* (12:14)

This holiness is not flawless perfection in this life, but it is real and clearly observable. It flows from the Spirit's sanctifying work. This is not our human achievement. Kingdom citizens display this righteousness not to gain acceptance but because they have been accepted already by God, in Christ. Their lives become evidence of their new identity.

Righteousness that glorifies God

Ultimately, surpassing righteousness is God-centred rather than man-centred. The Pharisees sought righteousness for self-exaltation. Jesus calls His disciples to righteousness that glorifies God. This echoes His earlier words about shining light so that others *"may see your good deeds and glorify your Father in heaven."* (Matthew 5:16).

This is why Jesus firmly roots His teaching in the heart. Only righteousness that springs from love for God and flows outward in love for others fulfils the Law's essence. When asked which commandment was greatest, Jesus summarized the Law in Matthew 22:37–39: *"Love the Lord your God with all your heart and with all your soul and with all your mind... and love your neighbour as yourself."* This is the righteousness which Jesus demands - a Spirit-imparted righteousness of love.

This section prepares us for what follows in Matthew 5:21–48, where Jesus gives six examples contrasting superficial, Pharisaic interpretations of the Law with His much deeper, heart-focused teaching: anger, lust, divorce, oaths, retaliation, and love for enemies.

Each example illustrates what surpassing righteousness looks like in practice. By framing His teaching with this statement about fulfilling the Law and surpassing Pharisaic righteousness, Jesus makes clear that He is not lowering the bar but raising it, pointing to a standard that can only be met by those transformed by His grace and indwelt by His Spirit.

From Law to Gospel to transformation

Jesus' relationship to the Law is not one of abolition but fulfilment. He fulfils it as the obedient Son, the perfect Teacher, the sacrificial Lamb, and the promised Messiah. In Him, the Law's demands are met and its purposes realized. And for those who belong to Him, the Law is no longer an external code condemning us, but an internal reality written on our hearts by His Spirit.

This is the surpassing righteousness Jesus calls us all to embrace: a righteousness rooted in Him, empowered by His Spirit, and displayed in lives that reflect His kingdom. As we move into His next teachings, we will see this righteousness applied to the most ordinary and challenging aspects of daily life.

Obedience in light of fulfilment

Jesus' declaration that He came to fulfil the Law and the Prophets reshapes how we must view obedience. Under the old covenant, obedience was largely framed in terms of external compliance: do this, avoid that.

But in Christ, obedience is elevated and transformed. It is no longer driven by fear of punishment or a desire for self-righteousness but springs from gratitude for grace and love for the One Who fulfilled the Law on our behalf.

Paul captures this dynamic in Romans 6:17–18: *"Thanks be to God that, though you used to be slaves to sin, you have come to obey from your heart the pattern of teaching that has now claimed your allegiance. You have been set free from sin and have become slaves to righteousness."* Note the shift here: obedience is now *"from your heart,"* it is born out of inward renewal rather than mere outward restraint.

This is the kind of obedience which Jesus calls for - a joyful, wholehearted alignment with God's will that flows from the transformed heart promised a long time ago in the new covenant (Jeremiah 31:33; Ezekiel 36:26–27). Rather than lowering God's standards, grace makes them attainable by changing the very desires of those who believe.

The role of Scripture in kingdom living

Jesus' words in Matthew 5:18 affirm the enduring authority of Scripture: *"Not the smallest letter, not the least stroke of a pen, will by any means disappear from the Law until everything is accomplished."* For the disciples of Jesus, Scripture remains the unshakable foundation for faith and practice.

This means that kingdom living is inseparable from Scripture. Far from dismissing the Old Testament as irrelevant, Jesus teaches His followers to see it through the lens of His fulfilment. The Law and the Prophets are not discarded but reinterpreted and brought to completion in Him. As Paul writes, *"All Scripture is God-breathed and is useful for teaching, rebuking, correcting and training in righteousness."* (2 Timothy 3:16–17)

Thus, we approach the Old Testament not as a discarded relic but as a vital testimony pointing us to Christ. The sacrificial system, for instance, finds its fulfilment in His atoning death (Hebrews 10:1–14). The moral commands reveal God's holiness, which the Spirit now writes on our hearts. Even the ceremonial and civil aspects of the Law, though no longer binding in their original form, instruct us in God's character and wisdom. In the kingdom, Scripture is both fulfilled and foundational. Jesus upholds its authority while redirecting us to its ultimate purpose: to lead us to Him and shape us into His likeness.

The danger of relaxing God's commands

Jesus warns in Matthew 5:19 against *"setting aside"* even *"the least of these commands"* or teaching others to do likewise. This is a sober caution against diluting God's standards to accommodate cultural pressures or personal preferences.

Kingdom greatness is linked not to popularity or influence but to faithfulness in both practicing and teaching God's commands. This principle applies broadly today. There is a temptation to soften difficult teachings - on holiness, forgiveness, sexuality, generosity, or love for enemies - to make them more palatable.

Yet Jesus insists that we must not minimize God's Word. Even the *"least"* commands reveal His character and matter deeply to Him. To disregard them is to erode our witness and misrepresent our King.

By contrast, those who *"practice and teach"* God's commands - living them out and instructing others faithfully - are called *"great in the kingdom of heaven."* This is not greatness as the world defines it but greatness in God's eyes, marked by humility, faithfulness, and integrity. It is the greatness of those who live under the Word's authority and help others do the same.

Surpassing righteousness: Heart over appearance

The climactic statement in verse 20 - *"unless your righteousness surpasses that of the Pharisees and the teachers of the law"* – now summarizes Jesus' entire approach to righteousness. His concern is not more rules but deeper transformation. He calls all of His followers to move beyond appearances to authenticity, beyond externalism to inward devotion.

This surpassing righteousness cannot be manufactured. It comes only through union with Christ and the work of the Spirit. Paul contrasts law-based righteousness with the righteousness of faith in Philippians 3:9: *"Not having a righteousness of my own that comes from the law, but that which is through faith in Christ - the righteousness that comes from God on the basis of faith."* Justification is by faith, but sanctification - the growth in holy living - is the inevitable result of that faith.

Surpassing righteousness, therefore, is not a human achievement but a divine gift. It is both imputed (credited to us in Christ) and imparted (worked out in us by the Spirit). It touches not only what we do but who we are - our thoughts, motives, and loves.

This is why Jesus will soon address issues like anger, lust, retaliation, and love for enemies. He is moving from principle to practice, showing what Spirit-wrought righteousness looks like in everyday life.

Fulfilment and the kingdom ethic

This passage bridges the Beatitudes' description of kingdom character with Jesus' forthcoming ethical instructions. It roots His moral teaching in His identity as the fulfiller of the Law and Prophets. His disciples are not to live by legalistic rule-keeping but by Spirit-enabled conformity to God's heart as revealed in Christ.

In this sense, the 'kingdom ethic' is Christ-centred rather than law-centred. Jesus does not discard God's commands; He internalizes them. He reframes obedience as relational rather than merely regulatory. The Law showed what righteousness looked like in commands; Jesus embodies it in His person. As we follow Him, His life becomes the template for ours.

Thus, righteousness in the kingdom is not merely *"not breaking rules"* but actively imitating Christ's love, mercy, humility, and holiness. As Paul urges in Ephesians 5:1–2: *"Follow God's example, therefore, as dearly loved children and walk in the way of love, just as Christ loved us."*

Anticipating Jesus' six illustrations

Verses 21–48, which immediately follow, serve as practical case studies of this surpassing righteousness. Jesus will take six familiar commands or teachings and intensify them:

1. *Anger and Reconciliation (v. 21–26):* Moving beyond prohibiting murder to addressing anger and contempt.
2. *Lust and Purity (v. 27–30):* Going beyond the prohibition of adultery to root out lustful desires.
3. *Divorce and Faithfulness (v. 31–32):* Upholding covenant faithfulness in marriage.

4. *Oaths and Truthfulness (v. 33–37):* Calling for radical honesty without evasions or manipulations.

5. *Retaliation and Generosity (v. 38–42):* Rejecting revenge and embracing self-giving responses.

6. *Love for Enemies (v. 43–48):* Extending love even to adversaries, reflecting God's perfect love.

Each of these builds on the foundation laid in Matthew 5:17–20. Jesus is not discarding the Law but revealing its heart-level intent. He is calling His disciples to embody a righteousness that flows from grace and mirrors God's own character.

Scripture, fulfilment, and transformation

As Jesus links the authority of Scripture to inner transformation of His followers, He provides a holistic vision for discipleship. His words affirm that Scripture is not obsolete; rather, it is fulfilled and deepened in Him. Kingdom obedience is neither lawlessness nor legalism but a grace-driven conformity to Christ. This vision also guards against two opposite errors:

➢ *Legalism:* Seeking to earn righteousness by external compliance.

➢ *Antinomianism:* Treating grace as license to disregard God's commands.

Jesus rejects both of these. He fulfils the Law, freeing us from its condemning power, while also empowering us to live out its true intent through His Spirit.

From fulfilment to formation

Matthew 5:17–20 is pivotal. It anchors Jesus' ethical teaching in His fulfilment of Scripture and sets the stage for His radical redefinition of righteousness. In Him, the Law's demands are both satisfied and transformed into a living reality for those who belong to His kingdom.

As we turn to His six illustrations of deepened righteousness, we will see this principle applied concretely to real-life situations.

Jesus will move from the foundation - Scripture fulfilled in Him - to the formation of His disciples, showing how their lives must be reshaped from the inside out.

In this way, Christ does not abolish the Law but fulfils it and, through His Spirit, fulfils it in us. The result is a people whose obedience is not superficial or forced but heartfelt and radiant, shining as salt and light in the world.

- 12 -

A RIGHTEOUSNESS OF THE HEART: ANGER AND RECONCILIATION

Matthew 5:21–26

"You have heard that it was said to the people long ago, 'You shall not murder, and anyone who murders will be subject to judgment.' But I tell you that anyone who is angry with a brother or sister will be subject to judgment. Again, anyone who says to a brother or sister, 'Raca,' is answerable to the court. And anyone who says, 'You fool!' will be in danger of the fire of hell.

Therefore, if you are offering your gift at the altar and there remember that your brother or sister has something against you, leave your gift there in front of the altar. First go and be reconciled to them; then come and offer your gift.

Settle matters quickly with your adversary who is taking you to court. Do it while you are still together on the way, or your adversary may hand you over to the judge, and the judge may hand you over to the officer, and you may be thrown into prison. Truly I tell you, you will not get out until you have paid the last penny."

From murder to anger: The deeper intent of the Law

Jesus begins His series of six contrasts with the very familiar command, *"You shall not murder."* (Exodus 20:13). All of those listening at the time would have agreed with this law. Murder was universally condemned, and to most, it seemed the ultimate moral boundary. Yet Jesus presses down beyond the surface. He declares that harbouring anger or contempt is subject to the same divine judgment as the act of murder itself.

This is startling. By equating anger with murder in principle, Jesus is not saying they are identical in consequence or civil penalty, but He is exposing the root from which murder grows. Murder always begins in the heart - with resentment, hatred, and hostility. By addressing anger, Jesus confronts sin at its source.

In doing so, He redefines righteousness. It is not enough to avoid committing murder physically. Kingdom righteousness requires uprooting the inner hostility that gives rise to it. Jesus' teaching goes beneath the surface behaviour to the heart's condition. This reflects His consistent emphasis throughout the Sermon on the Mount: sin is not merely what we do outwardly but what we cultivate inwardly.

The heart-level danger of anger

Anger is not always sinful. Scripture acknowledges righteous anger - anger at injustice or evil - that reflects God's own holy indignation (Ephesians 4:26). Jesus Himself displayed righteous anger when He cleansed the temple (John 2:13-17). However, most human anger is not righteous. It is self-centred, rooted in wounded pride, frustration, or hostility toward others. Such anger is destructive, corrosive, and incompatible with the love Jesus commands.

Uncontrolled anger leads to contemptuous words and actions. Jesus references insults like *"Raca"* (an Aramaic term of derision meaning *"empty-headed"*) and *"You fool!"* - words that demean and devalue others. Such speech flows from a heart of disdain and reveals a disposition contrary to the love of neighbour central to God's law (Leviticus 19:18).

Jesus warns that such anger invites judgment as serious as that for murder because it violates the same principle: treating others not as image-bearers of God but as objects of scorn. The progression is abundantly clear: anger leads to insult, insult to dehumanization, and dehumanization can lead to violence.

Anger and the image of God

Why does Jesus treat anger so seriously? Because every person bears the image of God (Genesis 1:27). To harbour anger or contempt toward someone is, in effect, to despise one who reflects God's likeness. James highlights this contradiction: *"With the tongue we praise our Lord and Father, and with it we curse human beings, who have been made in God's likeness"* (James 3:9).

Kingdom righteousness requires that we see others as God sees them. When we allow anger and contempt to take root, we not only violate our neighbour but also offend the God who created them. Jesus' teaching confronts us with this reality: reconciliation with God cannot be separated from reconciliation with others.

The urgency of reconciliation

Jesus illustrates this with a striking scenario: a person offering a gift at the altar - engaged in worship - suddenly remembers that someone has something against them. His command is radical: *"Leave your gift there... First go and be reconciled to them; then come and offer your gift."* (Matthew 5:23–24).

In Jewish culture, offering a gift at the altar was a sacred act performed in the temple at Jerusalem, often after a long journey. Yet Jesus insists that reconciliation takes precedence even over worship. Why? Because broken relationships will very often hinder our communion and intimacy with God. Worship offered while harbouring unresolved conflict is compromised. Isaiah records God's rebuke: *"When you spread out your hands in prayer, I hide my eyes from you... your hands are full of blood!"* (1:15)

Jesus' point is very clear: we cannot separate love for God from love for others. As 1 John 4:20 declares, *"For whoever does not love their brother and sister, whom they have seen, cannot love God, whom they have not seen."* Thus, before we approach God in worship, we must seek peace with those we have wronged or who have a grievance against us. This does not mean we can control others' responses or always achieve full reconciliation, but it does mean we take initiative. Paul echoes this in Romans 12:18: *"If it is possible, as far as it depends on you, live at peace with everyone."*

Reconciliation as kingdom priority

By placing reconciliation above ritual, Jesus overturns the empty religiosity that prioritizes external acts over relational integrity. In the kingdom, restored relationships are part of true worship. This aligns with Hosea 6:6: *"For I desire mercy, not sacrifice, and acknowledgment of God rather than burnt offerings."*

Jesus calls His disciples to embody this mercy. The priority is not mere ritual observance but love – a love expressed by seeking forgiveness, humbling ourselves, and making amends where possible. Worship flows from hearts cleansed not only vertically before God but also horizontally with others.

Settling matters quickly

Jesus then gives another illustration: *"Settle matters quickly with your adversary who is taking you to court."* (Matthew 5:25). His point is practical and spiritual. Delaying reconciliation allows conflict to escalate and harden. What begins as a dispute can spiral into judgment, imprisonment, and lasting consequences. The imagery of court and debt underscores the seriousness of unresolved conflict. Jesus likens it to imprisonment from which escape is impossible *"until you have paid the last penny."* (v. 26). This serves as both practical wisdom and spiritual metaphor: harbouring anger and refusing reconciliation traps us, enslaving us in bitterness and guilt.

Paul similarly urges urgency in Ephesians 4:26–27: *"Do not let the sun go down while you are still angry, and do not give the devil a foothold."* Anger unresolved becomes fertile ground for division and spiritual harm. The kingdom ethic calls for swift action to mend relationships, preventing seeds of hostility from taking root.

A new standard of righteousness

Through this teaching, Jesus exposes the insufficiency of superficial righteousness. The Pharisees could say, *"I have never murdered,"* but Jesus presses deeper: *"Have you harboured anger? Have you insulted or devalued another? Have you failed to seek reconciliation?"*

This is surpassing righteousness - righteousness that flows from a transformed heart. It is not content merely to avoid harm but actively pursues peace. It is proactive, not reactive. It seeks to root out anger before it bears fruit in words or deeds. This is why reconciliation is so central in the kingdom: it reflects God's reconciling nature.

As Paul writes in 2 Corinthians 5:18, *"All this is from God, who reconciled us to himself through Christ and gave us the ministry of reconciliation."* Those reconciled to God become reconcilers, extending His peace to others.

Overcoming anger: Practical steps

Anger is one of the most common struggles we face. It can flare suddenly or just simmer quietly beneath the surface, eroding relationships and poisoning our hearts. Jesus calls His followers to deal with anger at its root. Here are some biblical steps to overcome it:

1. Recognize and admit your anger

Anger often disguises itself. We downplay it as "frustration" or "irritation," but until we honestly name it, we cannot confront it. James 1:19–20 advises, *"Everyone should be quick to listen, slow to speak and slow to become angry, because human anger does not produce the righteousness that God desires."* Acknowledging anger allows us to examine its cause and surrender it to God.

2. Examine its source

Ask yourself: What is fuelling this anger? Is it wounded pride, unmet expectations, jealousy, or genuine injustice? Righteous anger is rare and directed at sin itself, not personal offense. Most anger reveals our true self-centredness or deep desire for control. Identifying its source helps us address the heart issues behind it.

3. Submit your anger to God in prayer

Prayer is crucial for disarming anger. Pour out your feelings honestly to God, asking Him to replace resentment with His peace. Psalm 37:8 warns, *"Refrain from anger and turn from wrath; do not fret - it leads only to evil."* Bringing anger into the presence of God invites His Holy Spirit to transform it and gives us perspective on what truly matters.

4. Seek the Spirit's Power

Self-discipline alone cannot uproot deep-seated anger. The fruit of the Spirit – *love, joy, peace, forbearance, kindness,* is the antidote.

As we walk by the Spirit, He reshapes our reactions, giving us patience where we once lashed out and compassion where we once condemned.

5. Resolve conflicts quickly

Jesus' command to *"settle matters quickly"* (Matthew 5:25) reflects the wisdom of dealing with anger before it festers. Unresolved grievances harden into bitterness. Paul echoes this urgency: *"Do not let the sun go down while you are still angry."* (Ephesians 4:26). Addressing issues early prevents small offenses from escalating into deep wounds.

6. Speak words that heal

Instead of lashing out, Scripture calls us to *"speak the truth in love."* (Ephesians 4:15). Anger often erupts in harsh words that wound. Proverbs 15:1 reminds us: *"A gentle answer turns away wrath, but a harsh word stirs up anger."* Choosing gentle, grace-filled speech helps de-escalate conflict and fosters reconciliation.

7. Choose forgiveness

Forgiveness is the ultimate release valve for anger. It does not excuse wrongdoing but frees us from being enslaved to it. Jesus ties forgiveness directly to our relationship with God: *"For if you forgive other people when they sin against you, your heavenly Father will also forgive you."* (Matthew 6:14). Holding onto anger will imprison us; forgiving will liberate us.

The spiritual discipline of forgiveness

Forgiveness is not optional in the kingdom - it is foundational. Jesus modelled it supremely on the cross, praying, *"Father, forgive them, for they do not know what they are doing."* (Luke 23:34). His followers are called to extend the same mercy they have received.

1. Forgiveness mirrors God's grace

Paul commands in Ephesians 4:31–32: *"Get rid of all bitterness, rage and anger… Be kind and compassionate to one another, forgiving each other, just as in Christ God forgave you."*

Forgiveness is grounded in our experience of God's grace. We forgive not because others deserve it but because we ourselves have been forgiven an infinite debt.

2. Forgiveness breaks the cycle of retaliation

Left unchecked, anger perpetuates serious cycles of retaliation. Forgiveness interrupts this pattern, replacing vengeance with mercy. Romans 12:19 reminds us, *"Do not take revenge… but leave room for God's wrath."* When we forgive, we entrust justice to God and release the burden of trying to exact it ourselves.

3. Forgiveness heals relationships

Forgiveness is essential for reconciliation. It opens the door for estranged relationships to be restored. Jesus links forgiveness to reconciliation in this passage: if we know someone who has a grievance against us, we are to seek peace. Forgiveness is the soil in which reconciliation can take root.

4. Forgiveness is both a decision and a process

Forgiveness begins as an act of the will: choosing to release someone from their debt to us. Yet the emotional aftermath often lingers, requiring ongoing surrender. Each time resentment resurfaces, we reaffirm our choice to forgive, asking God to align our hearts with His.

Reconciliation as a reflection of God's character

Jesus' emphasis on reconciliation reveals its deep theological roots. The kingdom of God is, at its core, about reconciliation - God reconciling sinners to Himself and then reconciling people to one another.

God's reconciling work

Paul writes in Colossians 1:21–22: *"Once you were alienated from God and were enemies in your minds… But now he has reconciled you by Christ's physical body through death to present you holy in his sight."* Reconciliation is central to the gospel. God took the initiative, sending Christ to bridge the chasm caused by our sin.

Our ministry of reconciliation

Because we have been reconciled, we are entrusted with extending reconciliation to others. *"All this is from God... who gave us the ministry of reconciliation."* (2 Corinthians 5:18). This ministry is not limited to proclaiming the gospel but includes embodying it in our relationships - pursuing peace, humbling ourselves, and seeking restoration.

When we reconcile, we display God's heart to the world. Each act of forgiveness and each step toward peace becomes a small picture of the gospel, demonstrating that God's grace has power not only to heal our relationship with Him but also to transform how we relate to others.

The urgency of Jesus' command

Notice the immediacy in Jesus' words: *"Leave your gift there... first go and be reconciled."* (Matthew 5:23-24). Worship is interrupted because reconciliation cannot wait. Broken relationships poison our spiritual lives. We can't compartmentalize them and imagine we can draw near to God unaffected.

Jesus' call to urgency confronts our tendency to delay those hard conversations or nurse grudges. The longer we wait, the more entrenched anger becomes. Kingdom righteousness requires courage: courage to apologize, to admit fault, to forgive, and to seek peace - even when it is uncomfortable or humbling.

Anger, worship, and the Kingdom

Jesus' teaching ties relational integrity directly to worship. We cannot authentically love God while refusing to love those He made in His image. True worship integrates both. Micah 6:6-8 captures this balance: *"What does the Lord require of you? To act justly and to love mercy and to walk humbly with your God."* Justice, mercy, and humility before God are inseparable. This is why reconciliation is not an optional add-on to the Christian life but a core expression of kingdom living. Worship that pleases God flows from reconciled hearts - hearts that reflect His mercy and His passion for peace.

Kingdom citizens as peacemakers

Of course this teaching echoes the Beatitude: *"Blessed are the peacemakers, for they will be called children of God."* (Matthew 5:9). Anger divides, but reconciliation unites. In seeking peace, we reflect the nature of our Father, who made peace with us through Christ's blood (Colossians 1:20). When we take initiative to reconcile - whether apologizing for harsh words, forgiving long-held grievances, or pursuing dialogue with those estranged - we live out our identity as God's children. Peace-making is costly, requiring humility and patience, but it is also Christlike.

Having addressed anger and reconciliation, Jesus will next turn to lust and purity (Matthew 5:27–30), showing how kingdom righteousness penetrates even deeper into the heart. Just as anger violates the spirit of the command against murder, lust violates the spirit of the command against adultery. In both cases, Jesus calls His followers to holiness that begins within, transforming desires as well as deeds.

The depth of reconciliation in the kingdom

Jesus' teaching on anger and reconciliation is not simply about conflict resolution; it is about embodying the heart of God in our relationships. In His kingdom, reconciliation is not peripheral but central, because it flows directly from the gospel itself. When we seek reconciliation, we enact the very grace that God has extended to us in Christ.

Reconciliation goes beyond avoiding harm

Many people believe righteousness consists of avoiding obvious wrongdoing: *"I haven't killed anyone,"* or *"I haven't done anything terrible."* But Jesus dismantles this superficial view. Kingdom righteousness is not measured by what we refrain from doing but by what we actively pursue.

It is not enough to avoid hatred or physical harm; we are called upon to also be reconcilers, peacemakers, and restorers of broken relationships. This is far more demanding because it requires humility, intentionality, and love that mirrors God's own.

It is one thing to avoid striking out in anger; it is another to humble oneself, seek forgiveness, and mend what is broken. This is the kind of righteousness that surpasses that of the Pharisees (Matthew 5:20) - a righteousness rooted in transformed hearts, not merely restrained hands.

Barriers to reconciliation

Despite Jesus' command, reconciliation is often difficult. Pride, fear, and pain stand in the way. Recognizing these barriers helps us confront them in light of the gospel.

> ➢ *Pride:* We resist admitting we were wrong or making the first move. Pride whispers, *"They should come to me,"* but Jesus says, *"Go to them first."* (Matthew 5:24). The humility required for reconciliation reflects the humility of Christ Himself (Philippians 2:5–8).

> ➢ *Fear of Rejection:* What if the other person refuses reconciliation? While this is possible, our responsibility is obedience, not results. Paul reassures us in Romans 12:18: *"If it is possible, as far as it depends on you, live at peace with everyone."* God calls us to faithfulness, leaving the outcome in His hands.

> ➢ *Bitterness and Unforgiveness:* Long-standing hurts can harden our hearts. But holding on to bitterness enslaves us, not the other person. Forgiveness, even when reconciliation is incomplete, frees us from anger's grip and aligns our hearts with God's mercy.

The practice of reconciliation

Reconciliation is both theological and practical. It involves specific actions rooted in spiritual truths. Here are steps to help embody Jesus' call:

1. Take initiative promptly

Jesus' instruction is urgent: *"Leave your gift there... First go"* (Matthew 5:23–24). Waiting prolongs division. The longer conflict lingers, the more entrenched it becomes.

Taking initiative - whether by writing a note, making a call, or arranging a meeting - demonstrates a kingdom-first mindset that values restored fellowship over personal pride.

2. Approach with humility

Reconciliation begins not with demands but with humility. Even if you believe you were mostly right, acknowledge your part in the conflict. Jesus teaches us to remove the plank from our own eye before addressing another's speck (Matthew 7:5). Humility disarms defensiveness and creates space for dialogue.

3. Listen actively

James 1:19 reminds us to be *"quick to listen, slow to speak."* So genuine listening always conveys respect and opens the door to understanding. Often, conflict escalates because neither side feels heard. Peace-making requires hearing not just words but emotions and perspectives, even when they differ from ours.

4. Speak truth with grace

Reconciliation does not ignore real issues. Instead, it involves honest yet gentle speech. Ephesians 4:15 urges us to *"speak the truth in love."* Confronting sin or misunderstanding is necessary, but grace-filled words ensure our aim is always restoration, not vindication.

5. Extend and receive forgiveness

True reconciliation hinges on forgiveness. This means releasing resentment, even if apologies are incomplete. Forgiveness does not erase consequences or condone wrongdoing, but it mirrors Christ's love and prevents anger from festering. Colossians 3:13 exhorts: *"Bear with each other and forgive one another... Forgive as the Lord forgave you."*

6. Seek ongoing peace

Reconciliation is not always instantaneous. Some wounds heal gradually. Building trust may take time, requiring consistent patience, humility, and prayer. As peacemakers, we persevere, reflecting the steadfast love of our reconciling God.

Reconciliation as worship

Jesus links reconciliation to worship. Leaving a gift at the altar to be reconciled is not only about resolving disputes; it is also about approaching God with integrity. Our vertical relationship with God is intertwined with our horizontal relationships with others.

In Matthew 22:37–40, Jesus summarizes the Law with two clear commands: love God and love your neighbour. These two are inseparable. When we neglect reconciliation, we undermine both. Worship without reconciliation is incomplete because it ignores the relational nature of God's kingdom. This connection explains why unresolved anger so deeply hinders spiritual vitality. It blocks intimacy with God because it contradicts His very character. As we reconcile with others, we reflect His heart and clear the path for unhindered fellowship with Him.

The witness of reconciliation

When we practice reconciliation, we bear a powerful witness to the world. In a culture that's marked by division and vengeance, forgiveness and restoration are radical. Jesus said, *"By this everyone will know that you are my disciples, if you love one another."* (John 13:35).

Reconciliation demonstrates that the gospel is transformative. It shows that grace has power not just to save but to heal. The church becomes a living testimony of God's reconciling work, inviting outsiders to encounter the God who reconciles sinners to Himself. Historically, some of the most compelling Christian witnesses have come through reconciliation: enemies embracing in forgiveness, fractured communities restored, estranged families reunited through Christ's grace. Such acts of peace shine brightly in a world accustomed to hostility.

The eschatological dimension of reconciliation

Reconciliation in the present also anticipates the future. The ultimate vision of God's kingdom is one of perfect harmony: *"He will wipe every tear from their eyes. There will be no more death or mourning or crying or pain."* (Revelation 21:4).

Every act of reconciliation here is a foretaste of that final peace. When we forgive and pursue restored relationships now, we live out the future reality of God's kingdom in the present. Our peace-making signals that the reign of Christ has already begun and points forward to the day when His peace will cover the earth fully.

Preparing for Jesus' teaching on lust and purity

This section on anger and reconciliation naturally leads to Jesus' next teaching on lust (Matthew 5:27–30). Just as He moves from murder to anger - addressing the heart behind the act - He will move from adultery to lust, thus exposing sin at its root. Both examples illustrate how surpassing righteousness penetrates beneath external actions to internal desires.

By first addressing anger and reconciliation, Jesus establishes a principle: righteousness in the kingdom is not satisfied with superficial compliance. It demands transformation of the heart, shaping how we view others - not as objects of contempt or desire, but as image-bearers worthy of love and respect.

A Kingdom shaped by peace

Jesus' teaching on anger and reconciliation confronts us with the radical nature of His kingdom. The kingdom of heaven is where relationships matter profoundly, where worship cannot be separated from love, where peace is pursued urgently, and where hearts are transformed from bitterness to mercy.

Kingdom citizens do not merely avoid outward violence; they uproot anger and cultivate reconciliation. They take initiative, forgive freely, and reflect the reconciling heart of their King. In doing so, they reveal the righteousness that surpasses that of the Pharisees - a righteousness not of mere avoidance but of active, Christlike love. As we turn to Jesus' teaching on lust and purity, we will see this pattern continue. The kingdom calls us not only to external obedience but to inner holiness - a life reshaped from the inside out by the grace of God.

- 13 -

PURITY OF HEART: LUST AND HOLINESS

Matthew 5:27–30

"You have heard that it was said, 'You shall not commit adultery.' But I tell you that anyone who looks at a woman lustfully has already committed adultery with her in his heart. If your right eye causes you to stumble, gouge it out and throw it away. It is better for you to lose one part of your body than for your whole body to be thrown into hell. And if your right hand causes you to stumble, cut it off and throw it away. It is better for you to lose one part of your body than for your whole body to go into hell."

From adultery to lust: The heart of the matter

In this passage, Jesus follows the same pattern He used when addressing anger. He begins with the very familiar command taken from the Ten Commandments: *"You shall not commit adultery."* (Exodus 20:14). For most listeners, obedience to this law seemed straightforward: avoid physical unfaithfulness in marriage. But Jesus presses deeper, declaring that lustful intent is itself adulterous at the heart level.

This is radical. Jesus redefines adultery not merely as a physical act but as a matter of internal desire. The kingdom standard is not just external fidelity but purity of heart. By equating lust with adultery, Jesus exposes the root issue: sin begins in the heart, long before it manifests outwardly.

This aligns with His later teaching in Matthew 15:19: *"For out of the heart come evil thoughts - murder, adultery, sexual immorality…"* Jesus' point is not to trivialize adultery but to show that God's standard is far higher than avoiding external acts. The Law was always intended to point to this deeper righteousness.

Adultery violates marital faithfulness; lust undermines it from within, corrupting the heart and eroding love, trust, and covenant commitment.

What is lust?

Lust is more than just noticing physical beauty or experiencing natural attraction - it is a wilful, cultivated desire that objectifies another person for selfish pleasure. It reduces someone made in God's image to an instrument of gratification. Lust treats others not as persons to be honoured but as objects to be consumed.

Jesus' wording, *"looks at a woman lustfully,"* implies an intentional gaze, not a passing glance. The issue is not seeing but looking with desire, dwelling on it in the imagination. Lust turns the mind into a stage where sin rehearses itself in private long before it ever reaches action.

By addressing lust, Jesus is calling His followers to a radically different way of seeing other people. Jesus is insisting that righteousness is not merely about restraining behaviour but transforming perception: seeing people not as objects of desire but as image-bearers of God, worthy of dignity and respect.

Purity of heart and kingdom holiness

This teaching echoes the sixth Beatitude: *"Blessed are the pure in heart, for they will see God."* (Matthew 5:8). Purity of heart means undivided devotion to God and integrity in thought and desire. It is not merely abstaining from sin outwardly but inwardly aligning the heart with God's holiness.

Purity is central to kingdom life because God Himself is holy. To be citizens of His kingdom mean reflecting His character. Jesus' words dismantle any illusion that we can compartmentalize our faith: holiness is inward transformation, not external formality. A heart corrupted by lust is incompatible with the kingdom's call to love and integrity.

The radical imagery of self-denial

Jesus intensifies His warning with shocking language: *"If your right eye causes you to stumble, gouge it out... If your right hand causes you to stumble, cut it off."* (Matthew 5:29–30).

These words are not literal commands for self-mutilation but vivid hyperbole to emphasize the seriousness of sin and the urgency of decisive action against it. The right eye and right hand represented what was most valuable or powerful to a person in that culture. Jesus is saying, *"Remove anything - even what seems essential - if it leads you into sin."* His point is clear: nothing is worth jeopardizing your eternal soul. Sin must be dealt with ruthlessly and decisively.

This echoes Paul's strong exhortation in Romans 8:13: *"If you live according to the flesh, you will die; but if by the Spirit you put to death the misdeeds of the body, you will live."* Kingdom living requires active, Spirit-empowered resistance to sin - not casual tolerance of it.

The consequences of unchecked lust

Jesus connects lust directly to judgment: *"It is better... than for your whole body to be thrown into hell."* This very stark warning underscores that lust is not harmless fantasy but spiritually deadly. Left unchecked, it will warp our desires, enslave our minds, damage relationships, and distance us from God.

Scripture consistently warns of sexual sin's destructive power. Proverbs 6:25–29 cautions against lust, likening it to playing with fire: *"Can a man scoop fire into his lap without his clothes being burned?"* Paul likewise exhorts believers in 1 Corinthians 6:18: *"Flee from sexual immorality... he who sins sexually sins against his own body."* Sexual sin uniquely binds body and soul, leaving deep scars if unrepented. Jesus' warning is sobering but loving. He confronts lust not to shame but to save—to draw His followers away from sin's path toward death and onto the narrow road of life.

Lust and the objectification of others

Lust is inherently dehumanizing. It strips away personhood, reducing someone to their physical attributes. This violates the second great commandment: *"Love your neighbour as yourself"* (Matthew 22:39). True love honours and protects others; lust exploits and consumes.

In our own culture, which is saturated with sexual imagery and commodification, lust is constantly normalized. Advertising, entertainment, and media often treat people as objects to sell products or fantasies. Jesus' teaching confronts this head-on, calling His followers to resist cultural currents and reclaim a kingdom vision of human dignity. To see others as God sees them requires the renewing of our minds (Romans 12:2). It means reshaping our imagination to view people not through lenses of desire or comparison but as fellow image-bearers deserving of respect and purity.

Guarding the heart and mind

Because lust begins internally, combating it requires guarding both heart and mind. Proverbs 4:23 instructs: *"Above all else, guard your heart, for everything you do flows from it."* Practical measures include:

➤ *Filtering inputs:* Being vigilant about what we watch, read, and consume.

➤ *Taking thoughts captive:* 2 Corinthians 10:5 urges us to *"take captive every thought to make it obedient to Christ."* Redirecting the mind quickly prevents sinful desires from taking root.

➤ *Cultivating gratitude and contentment*: Lust thrives on dissatisfaction. Learning to be content (Philippians 4:11) helps quench its fuel.

➤ *Focusing on God's presence:* Filling our minds with Scripture, worship, and prayer redirects our desires toward what is holy and satisfying.

Holiness is not only defensive; it is proactive. As we fix our eyes on Christ, we replace distorted desires with pure ones. Jesus calls us to purity not merely by suppression but by transformation - reshaping what we love until our hearts reflect His heart.

Cultivating purity: Practical strategies for kingdom living

Jesus' radical teaching on lust demands an equally radical response. Purity of heart is not achieved passively but requires intentional, Spirit-empowered effort.

1. Guarding what we see and hear

Since Jesus pinpoints the *"look"* of lust, we must be vigilant about what we expose ourselves to visually and mentally. The psalmist declares, *"I will not look with approval on anything that is vile."* (Psalm 101:3). In a culture which is saturated with sexually charged imagery, this means exercising discernment with media, entertainment, social media, and even casual browsing.

Job put this really well when he said: *"I made a covenant with my eyes not to look lustfully at a young woman."* (Job 31:1). This kind of pre-determined resolve helps us avoid temptation rather than reacting in the moment. It is far easier to prevent lust's entry than to uproot it once it has taken hold.

2. Renewing the mind

Paul urges believers: *"Do not conform to the pattern of this world, but be transformed by the renewing of your mind."* (Romans 12:2). Lust thrives on mental images and fantasy; countering it requires replacing these with truth. Immersing ourselves in Scripture fills our minds with God's perspective, reshaping how we see others and ourselves. Meditation on passages such as Philippians 4:8 (*"whatever is true, whatever is noble, whatever is right, whatever is pure… think about such things"*) shifts our mental focus. This is not only avoiding bad thoughts but actively cultivating godly ones.

3. Practicing spiritual disciplines

Spiritual disciplines such as prayer, fasting, and Scripture memorization deepen our dependence on God. Fasting, in particular, trains us to deny immediate appetites for a higher satisfaction in God. Prayer brings our struggles into His presence, asking for deliverance and strength. These practices reinforce that victory over lust is not willpower alone but Spirit-enabled.

4. Establishing boundaries

Boundaries are not legalism but wisdom. That is why Joseph fled from Potiphar's wife (Genesis 39:12) rather than reason with temptation.

Likewise, we should create protective measures: avoiding settings that may invite compromise, setting clear lines in our relationships, and using appropriate tools like internet filters or accountability software. Such steps are not signs of weakness but of humility - recognizing our vulnerability and depending on God's grace.

5. Pursuing accountability

Lust thrives in secrecy. James 5:16 calls us to *"confess your sins to each other and pray for each other so that you may be healed."* Accountability breaks the isolation of sin. Having trusted fellow believers to whom we confess struggles and from whom we receive prayer support and encouragement, helps guard against temptation and fosters growth. Accountability is not about shaming but about mutual support in the pursuit of holiness. The church should be a safe place where believers help each other battle against sin while resting in the grace of the gospel.

The role of the Holy Spirit in purity

Purity is ultimately not a human achievement but a work of the Holy Spirit. Left to ourselves, we are powerless against sin's pull. But Romans 8:13 assures us: *"If by the Spirit you put to death the misdeeds of the body, you will live."* The Spirit convicts, empowers, and reshapes our desires. When we walk by the Spirit, we are promised that we *"will not gratify the desires of the flesh."* This does not mean we never feel temptation, but it means we are no longer slaves to it. The Spirit produces new fruit in us - self-control, purity, and love - that replaces the destructive patterns of sin. This transformation is gradual but real. Over time, our tastes change. What once enticed us begins to lose its grip as our hearts delight more in God's beauty than in counterfeit pleasures.

Lust's impact on relationships and intimacy

Jesus' teaching also reveals how lust corrupts relationships. By equating lust with adultery, He shows that it's not merely private or harmless but relationally destructive. Lust undermines trust, erodes intimacy, and distorts God's design for sexuality.

1. Lust corrupts marriage

Even if not acted upon physically, lust violates the exclusivity of marital intimacy. Jesus frames lust as *"adultery of the heart"* because it betrays covenant fidelity. Spouses wounded by lust often feel betrayed, as though affection has been shared with another - even if only in thought.

Paul's teaching in Ephesians 5:25–28 highlights the contrast here: husbands are to love their wives *"just as Christ loved the church,"* nourishing and cherishing them. Lust replaces this sacrificial love with self-centred desire. It turns intimacy, meant to be mutual and covenantal, into consumption.

2. Lust distorts singleness

For the unmarried, lust can warp perspectives on relationships and sexuality, fostering unrealistic expectations or unhealthy fantasies. Instead of seeing others as whole persons, lust will fragment them into appealing parts. This warped mindset makes genuine friendship and future marital intimacy difficult because it teaches us to view people as means to an end rather than as fellow image-bearers.

3. Lust fuels exploitation

Unchecked lust contributes to systemic issues like pornography, sexual exploitation, and eventually human trafficking. Behind these industries lies a culture of objectification that feeds on and perpetuates sinful desire. Every lustful glance, though seemingly private, connects to larger patterns of dehumanization that oppose God's kingdom ethic of love and dignity.

Redeeming vision: Seeing people as God sees them

The antidote to lust is not merely repression but redeemed vision. Jesus invites us to see others through kingdom eyes - not as objects of desire but as beloved creations of God. This requires a heart purified by grace. David prayed, *"Create in me a pure heart, O God, and renew a steadfast spirit within me."* (Psalm 51:10).

This prayer reflects the kind of transformation Jesus demands. Purity is not simply the absence of lust but the presence of love rightly ordered: love for God that reshapes how we see and treat others. When our vision is redeemed, we learn to honour others in thought as well as deed. Men and women are no longer reduced to mere physicality but seen as brothers and sisters in Christ, worthy of respect and care.

The eternal stakes of purity

Jesus concludes His teaching with sobering language about hell (Matthew 5:29–30). This underscores that holiness is never optional. Unrepented lust signals a heart unreconciled to God. While believers stumble and always find forgiveness in Christ, persistent, unchecked sin reveals a life not submitted to His lordship.

Paul echoes this warning in 1 Thessalonians 4:3–5: *"It is God's will that you should be sanctified: that you should avoid sexual immorality... not in passionate lust like the pagans, who do not know God."* Lust is incompatible with knowing God because it opposes His holiness and love.

Yet the good news is that Jesus not only warns but redeems. Through His cross, He forgives adulterous hearts. Through His Spirit, He renews impure desires. Through His kingdom, He forms a people who delight in holiness. His call to radical purity is matched by His power to bring it about in us.

Looking ahead: Holiness in all relationships

This teaching naturally leads to Jesus' next teaching on marriage, divorce, and faithfulness (Matthew 5:31–32). Purity of heart lays the foundation for covenantal fidelity. As Jesus moves from lust to marriage, He reinforces that kingdom righteousness is relational and holistic, transforming both desire and commitment. Before addressing external issues like divorce, Jesus begins inwardly, purifying hearts from lust. Only then can we understand His vision for faithfulness and intimacy rooted in covenant love.

The beauty of holiness

Jesus' teaching on lust is both challenging and liberating. It confronts our deepest struggles, but it also offers hope: purity is possible because of Him. The kingdom offers freedom not only from outward sin but from the inward chains that enslave us. Holiness is not restrictive but freeing. It restores relationships, renews intimacy, and refocuses our desires on God's glory. When we pursue purity, we discover that true joy and beauty are found not in lust's fleeting shadows but in the light of God's presence: *"Blessed are the pure in heart, for they will see God."* (Matthew 5:8).

Restoration for the heart ensnared by lust

Jesus' teaching on lust is searching and convicting. It strips away our defences and exposes the hidden struggles of the heart. Yet while His words are sharp, they are not meant to crush us but to call us to healing. The same Jesus who declares that lust is adultery of the heart - also came, *"to seek and to save the lost."* (Luke 19:10). For those ensnared by lust, there is hope in His grace and power to restore.

1. Confession and repentance

Restoration begins with confession. We must bring our hidden struggles into the light. Proverbs 28:13 says, *"Whoever conceals their sins does not prosper, but the one who confesses and renounces them finds mercy."* Confession involves both acknowledging sin before God and, where appropriate, seeking accountability with trusted believers. Repentance is not mere regret but a turning - a decisive change of direction. It involves forsaking sinful habits, cutting off all sources of temptation (as Jesus vividly commands), and then embracing new patterns of holiness. This turning is not done in isolation but with the Spirit's enabling.

2. Receiving God's forgiveness

Shame often keeps people trapped in cycles of lust. They feel unworthy to approach God or too defiled to be cleansed. Yet the gospel speaks directly to this.

In 1 John 1:9 we are assured: *"If we confess our sins, he is faithful and just and will forgive us our sins and purify us from all unrighteousness."* God not only forgives; He purifies. David, after his own grievous sexual sin, prayed: *"Wash me, and I will be whiter than snow."* (Psalm 51:7). His experience reminds us that no sin is beyond God's cleansing grace. Christ's blood covers even adulterous hearts and renews them.

3. The transforming power of grace

Grace does not simply pardon; it actually transforms. *"The grace of God… teaches us to say 'No' to ungodliness and worldly passions, and to live self-controlled, upright and godly lives."* Titus 2:11–12. Through grace, desires that once enslaved are replaced by new desires for holiness and intimacy with God.

This transformation is gradual but real. As we daily surrender to the Spirit, He reshapes what we love. We learn to delight in God more than in fleeting pleasures. Lust's grip loosens as our hearts become captivated by something greater: the beauty of Christ Himself.

The role of the church in restoration

Purity is not pursued in isolation. God has given us the church as a community of grace and accountability. Unfortunately, many avoid sharing their struggles for fear of judgment. Yet the church is called to be a place where broken sinners find healing, not condemnation.

1. Creating a culture of grace

Galatians 6:1 instructs, *"Brothers and sisters, if someone is caught in a sin, you who live by the Spirit should restore that person gently."* This requires gentleness, not harshness. Those who fall into lust need both truth and compassion: truth to confront sin, compassion to offer hope. Churches must resist the extremes of permissiveness (minimizing sin) or harshness (crushing the sinner). Instead, they must hold out both the seriousness of Jesus' words and the sufficiency of His cross.

2. Accountability and support

Believers need trusted relationships where they can confess struggles without fear and receive prayer, encouragement, and practical help. James 5:16 says, *"Confess your sins to each other and pray for each other so that you may be healed."* Healing comes when sin loses its secrecy and is met with gospel-centred support. Mentorship, accountability partnerships and small groups help provide this environment. In these settings, believers can be honest about temptation, celebrate victories, and be reminded that they are not alone in their pursuit of holiness.

3. Discipling in a hyper-sexualized culture

Because our culture constantly bombards us with sexualized messages, churches must equip believers with biblical wisdom about sexuality. Teaching should affirm God's good design for sex within marriage, expose cultural lies, and provide practical tools for guarding the heart and mind. When the church fails to disciple in this area, believers often absorb their views on sexuality from the world. Jesus' teaching here is a clarion call for the church to reclaim a vision of purity that is both realistic about temptation and hopeful about transformation.

Purity as a witness in the world

In a culture enslaved to lust, purity shines brightly. Jesus calls His followers to be salt and light (Matthew 5:13–16). Few things display the countercultural power of the gospel more clearly than lives marked by sexual integrity and inner purity.

Paul exhorts believers in Philippians 2:14–15: *"Do everything without grumbling or arguing, so that you may become blameless and pure... Then you will shine among them like stars in the sky."* Purity, far from being restrictive, is luminous - it points to a better kingdom where love is untainted, relationships are whole, and intimacy is rightly ordered under God's reign. When Christians model purity in both heart and conduct, they offer a stark alternative to a world marred by objectification and brokenness. They embody a wholeness that invites others to seek the source of such transformation.

The link between lust and covenant faithfulness

Jesus' teaching on lust naturally transitions to His next words about marriage and divorce (Matthew 5:31–32). The connection is profound: inner purity safeguards outer fidelity. Lust erodes trust, poisons intimacy, and undermines covenant commitment, whereas purity strengthens and sustains it.

Marriage is designed to reflect God's covenant love - faithful, exclusive, enduring. When hearts are corrupted by lust, this covenant imagery is distorted. Jesus therefore addresses the heart before He addresses the covenant itself. Purity of desire is foundational for the covenantal faithfulness He will soon demand.

The hope of redemption

For those who have stumbled deeply - whether through habitual lust, pornography, infidelity, or broken relationships - Jesus offers redemption. He restores what sin has marred.

Joel 2:25 contains a precious promise: *"I will repay you for the years the locusts have eaten."* God can heal marriages fractured by lust, renew minds scarred by impurity, and give hope where shame once ruled.

Peter's story offers reassurance. He denied Jesus three times yet was restored and became a pillar of the church. Likewise, even grievous sins can be forgiven, and repentant sinners can be renewed. In Christ, failure is never final. His blood is sufficient not only to cleanse but also to transform and recommission.

Preparing for Jesus' teaching on marriage and divorce

As we move to Jesus' next words on marriage and divorce (Matthew 5:31–32), we see the logical flow of Jesus' teaching. Having now addressed anger and reconciliation (relationships strained by hostility) and also lust (relationships corrupted by desire), He now addresses covenant fidelity directly. Marriage is the arena where love, purity, and faithfulness converge.

Jesus' high view of marriage builds upon His high view of the heart: only those transformed inwardly by grace can live out the covenantal faithfulness He envisions. This underscores again that kingdom righteousness is holistic: it transforms desire, thought, word, and deed.

Purity as the path to seeing God

Purity is not merely about denial but about greater vision. Jesus promises, *"Blessed are the pure in heart, for they will see God."* (Matthew 5:8). Lust clouds our vision and darkens our hearts; purity clears our sight and draws us nearer to His presence.

When we fight lust and pursue holiness, we are not simply avoiding sin; we are seeking God. We exchange counterfeit pleasures for the true delight of intimacy with Him. In the end, Jesus' teaching on lust is not merely a prohibition - it is also an invitation: to a life of freedom, wholeness, and abundant joy in His kingdom.

– 14 –

FAITHFULNESS IN COVENANT: MARRIAGE AND DIVORCE

Matthew 5:31–32

"It has been said, 'Anyone who divorces his wife must give her a certificate of divorce.' But I tell you that anyone who divorces his wife, except for sexual immorality, makes her the victim of adultery, and anyone who marries a divorced woman commits adultery."

The context of Jesus' teaching

In these verses, Jesus continues His pattern of contrasting the prevailing interpretations of the Law with His own authoritative teaching. He addresses a sensitive and deeply personal subject: marriage and divorce. His words would have been striking to His audience, who lived in a culture where divorce, while regulated, was relatively common and often treated lightly.

Under Mosaic Law, divorce was permitted but it was controlled. Deuteronomy 24:1–4 allowed a man to divorce his wife if he *"found something indecent about her,"* provided he gave her a formal certificate of divorce. This regulation was not seen as an endorsement of divorce but a safeguard for women, ensuring legal recognition and protection in a patriarchal society. By Jesus' time, however, rabbinic debates had emerged over what *"something indecent"* meant. Two schools of thought existed:

➢ *The Hillel school:* Interpreted it broadly, allowing divorce for almost any reason, even trivial matters such as a poorly cooked meal.

➢ *The Shammai school*: Interpreted it narrowly, restricting divorce to cases of sexual immorality.

Against this backdrop, Jesus raises the bar dramatically. Rather than entering the debate over acceptable grounds, He reframes the issue entirely. He shifts the focus from legal permissions to God's original intent for marriage and calls His followers to covenantal faithfulness.

God's design for marriage

To understand Jesus' teaching, we must first grasp the biblical foundation of marriage. In Matthew 19:4–6, when He is pressed further on this issue, Jesus refers back to Genesis: *"Haven't you read,"* he replied, *"that at the beginning the Creator made them male and female,"* and said, *"For this reason a man will leave his father and mother and be united to his wife, and the two will become one flesh"? So they are no longer two, but one flesh. Therefore, what God has joined together, let no one separate.'"*

Here, Jesus anchors marriage not in human law but in creation itself. Marriage is not just a social contract or legal arrangement; it is a divine covenant. God Himself joins husband and wife into a unique *"one flesh"* union, reflecting His design for permanence, intimacy, and fidelity.

This *"one flesh"* union is quite profound. It is physical, emotional, spiritual, and covenantal. It actually mirrors God's covenantal faithfulness to His people. Throughout Scripture, marriage is used as a metaphor for God's relationship with His people (Isaiah 54:5; Hosea 2:19–20; Ephesians 5:25–32). Thus, to break marriage lightly is to misrepresent the steadfast, covenant-keeping nature of God Himself.

Divorce as a concession, not an ideal

Jesus' statement in Matthew 5:31–32 challenges the prevailing attitude that divorce was simply a matter of paperwork. By pointing to the heart behind divorce, He reveals that it violates God's design for covenantal permanence.

Elsewhere, Jesus clarifies that Moses permitted divorce *"because your hearts were hard."* (Matthew 19:8). It was a concession in a fallen world, intended to regulate sin and protect the vulnerable, not an expression of God's ideal. God's heart for marriage is expressed plainly in Malachi 2:16: *"I hate divorce,"* says the Lord. His hatred is not arbitrary but rooted in His love for what marriage signifies and His compassion for the pain that divorce will bring.

Jesus' teaching restores marriage to its covenantal purpose, calling His followers to faithfulness that reflects God's own. His exception clause - *"except for sexual immorality"* - acknowledges that marital unfaithfulness can so violate the covenant that it may actually warrant divorce. Yet even here, the focus is on the seriousness of the covenant breach, not on legitimizing easy exit.

The weight of Jesus' words

Jesus intensifies the matter by declaring that wrongful divorce results in adultery: *"Anyone who divorces his wife, except for sexual immorality, makes her the victim of adultery, and anyone who marries a divorced woman commits adultery."* (Matthew 5:32). Why such strong language?

In Jewish culture, a divorced woman would often remarry for economic survival. If her divorce was not valid in God's eyes, her subsequent marriage would be adulterous. Thus, a man who divorced his wife for trivial reasons effectively forced her into adultery by putting her in a position where remarriage was then necessary.

This reveals to us how deeply Jesus values marriage fidelity. He exposes the casual attitude toward divorce as not only socially harmful but spiritually devastating. His teaching confronts both the initiator of wrongful divorce and those who disregard the covenantal nature of remarriage.

Marriage as covenant, not contract

The difference between a covenant and a contract is key to understanding Jesus' view of marriage. A contract is based on mutual benefit and can be broken if one party fails to uphold their end. A covenant, by contrast, is a solemn vow rooted in faithfulness regardless of the other's performance. It is a binding, lifelong commitment made before God.

Marriage, in Jesus' view, is covenantal. It is not conditioned on perpetual satisfaction or convenience. It is a reflection of God's unwavering covenant with His people, who often fail Him, yet whom He continues to love.

Ephesians 5:25 calls husbands to love their wives *".. just as Christ loved the church and gave himself up for her."* This sacrificial love is steadfast, enduring even in difficulty. By framing marriage this way, Jesus calls His followers to mirror God's covenantal love. Divorce, while permitted in cases of grievous sin like adultery, is not to be pursued lightly or casually. The kingdom ethic elevates marriage beyond human legalism to divine faithfulness.

The heart of the matter

As with anger and lust, Jesus' teaching on divorce ultimately addresses the heart. The Pharisees were just content with legal compliance: issuing proper certificates and observing all the formalities. Jesus, however, looks deeper. He exposes the self-centeredness and hardness of heart that seek escape from covenant obligations rather than working for reconciliation.

Kingdom righteousness calls for transformed hearts that honour God's design even when it is very costly. This means nurturing marriages through forgiveness, patience, and sacrificial love. It means resisting the cultural mindset that views marriage as disposable and instead embracing it as sacred. Jesus' standard is high because it reflects His kingdom's values. His followers are called to live differently - not shaped by convenience or cultural norms but by God's original intention for marriage.

The hope for broken marriages

While Jesus' teaching is uncompromising, it is not devoid of grace. Many have experienced the pain of divorce, whether through their own sin, the betrayal of a spouse, or circumstances beyond their control. The gospel offers hope for healing and renewal.

Psalm 34:18 declares: *"The Lord is close to the broken-hearted and saves those who are crushed in spirit."* For those wounded by divorce, Jesus extends comfort and restoration. For those who have sinned, there is forgiveness through repentance and faith. His words call us not to despair over past failures but to embrace His transforming grace for the future.

Forgiveness and restoration in broken marriages

Even in the face of betrayal or failure, the gospel holds out the possibility of redemption and renewal. Jesus' words on marriage and divorce confront the hardness of human hearts but also point to the transforming power of God's grace.

1. The call to forgive

In marriage, forgiveness is not optional - it is essential. When Jesus commands His followers to forgive *"seventy-seven times"* (Matthew 18:22), He establishes that forgiveness is to be ongoing and unconditional. While this does not mean ignoring sin or enabling destructive behaviour, it does mean refusing to hold onto bitterness or repay wrong with wrong.

Forgiveness is not weakness; it is strength rooted in the cross. Ephesians 4:32 exhorts: *"Be kind and compassionate to one another, forgiving each other, just as in Christ God forgave you."* In marriage, forgiveness mirrors the covenant love of God, who continues to love His unfaithful people and calls them back to Himself.

2. Restoring trust through repentance

In cases of marital betrayal, such as infidelity, trust is shattered. While forgiveness is immediate and unconditional in principle, rebuilding trust is often a slow process requiring true repentance and patient restoration. This involves confession, accountability, and tangible change over time.

James 5:16 encourages confession and prayer: *"Confess your sins to each other and pray for each other so that you may be healed."* Healing in marriage after sin is not instant but progressive, requiring both partners to lean on God's grace and the support of His people.

3. The power of reconciliation

God's desire is always for reconciliation where possible. Paul writes in 2 Corinthians 5:18 that God *"reconciled us to himself through Christ and gave us the ministry of reconciliation."*

This ministry extends to marriages fractured by sin or conflict. While some situations, particularly serious abuse or persistent unrepentant sin, require separation for safety or righteousness, many marriages have experienced a miraculous restoration through God's intervention and grace.

Nurturing covenant faithfulness in marriage

Faithfulness in marriage is not automatic; it must be cultivated intentionally. Jesus' teaching calls His followers not only to avoid divorce but to actively nurture marriages that reflect His kingdom values. Here are biblical practices that strengthen covenant faithfulness:

1. Prioritize spiritual unity

A Christ-centred marriage is anchored in shared faith. Couples grow closer to each other as they grow closer to God. Regular prayer together, reading Scripture, and participating in worship cultivate spiritual intimacy that sustains marriage through trials. Ecclesiastes 4:12 captures this beautifully: *"A cord of three strands is not quickly broken."*

2. Practice sacrificial love

Ephesians 5:25 commands husbands to *"love your wives, just as Christ loved the church and gave himself up for her."* This sacrificial love applies equally to wives and husbands. It means putting your spouse's needs above your own, serving rather than demanding, and embodying the self-giving love of Christ. In practical terms, this might mean acts of kindness, patience in conflict, and a willingness to lay down pride for the sake of unity. Covenant faithfulness will only thrive when both partners are committed to giving rather than taking.

3. Communicate with grace and honesty

Many marital conflicts arise not from major sins but from poor communication. James 1:19 offers timeless wisdom: *"Everyone should be quick to listen, slow to speak and slow to become angry."* Healthy marriages cultivate open, honest dialogue marked by respect and empathy rather than defensiveness or hostility.

Regularly checking in with one another emotionally, resolving misunderstandings quickly, and addressing issues before they fester all contribute to long-term faithfulness.

4. Guard against temptation

Faithfulness also requires vigilance. Temptation often enters subtly through complacency, unresolved conflict, or emotional disconnection. Proverbs 4:23 warns: *"Above all else, guard your heart, for everything you do flows from it."* Guarding the heart means avoiding situations that compromise integrity, setting wise boundaries, and being transparent with one another.

Marriage as a witness to the kingdom

Jesus' teaching elevates marriage beyond private relationship to public witness. A marriage rooted in covenant faithfulness testifies to God's steadfast love. When spouses forgive, persevere through hardship, and remain faithful, they display the gospel in tangible form.

Paul links marriage explicitly to Christ and the church in Ephesians 5:31–32: *"For this reason a man will leave his father and mother and be united to his wife... This is a profound mystery – but I am talking about Christ and the church."*

Marital faithfulness preaches to the world about Christ's unwavering love for His people. Conversely, casual divorce distorts this beautiful image, misrepresenting God's nature.

Kingdom citizens, therefore, view marriage as more than personal fulfilment – it is a vocation to display God's covenantal faithfulness in a fallen world.

Divorce and the reality of brokenness

Even with Jesus' high standard, we live in a world marred by sin. Divorce is a painful reality for many, often stemming from betrayal, abuse, abandonment, or deep incompatibility. Jesus' words do not deny this brokenness but confront it with truth and grace.

For those who have experienced divorce, the gospel brings hope rather than condemnation. Romans 8:1 promises: *"Therefore, there is now no condemnation for those who are in Christ Jesus."* Past failures or wounds do not define a believer's standing in God's kingdom. His grace meets us in our brokenness and offers renewal.

Church communities must extend compassion to those who are wounded by divorce, helping them experience healing, avoid shame, and find restoration in Christ. The kingdom ethic is not legalistic rigidity but transformative grace that calls people forward into holiness and hope.

How this teaching fits the kingdom ethic

Jesus' instruction on marriage and divorce fits seamlessly into His broader kingdom vision. In the Sermon on the Mount, Jesus consistently moves from outward compliance to inward transformation, from minimal legal obligations to wholehearted devotion.

- *Anger:* Not merely avoiding murder, but reconciling relationships.
- *Lust:* Not merely avoiding adultery but cultivating purity of heart.
- *Marriage:* Not merely following legal divorce procedures but living out covenantal faithfulness.

In each case, Jesus calls His followers to a righteousness that surpasses the Pharisees - not in quantity of rules kept but in quality of heart transformation. Kingdom righteousness flows from grace, empowering believers to reflect God's character in all of life, including marriage.

The intersection of law and grace

Jesus' words on divorce remind us of the interplay between law and grace. His standard reveals our inability: left to ourselves, we fail in anger, lust, and covenant faithfulness. But His grace meets us in that failure, forgives us, and empowers us by His Spirit to live out a higher calling.

The law exposes sin; grace redeems sinners and transforms them into saints who embody the very holiness the law pointed toward. This is why Jesus came not to abolish the Law but to fulfil it (Matthew 5:17). His teaching on marriage is not a legalistic burden but a pathway to freedom — the freedom to love faithfully, forgive radically, and reflect God's covenantal nature.

Discipleship and marriage: Building covenant faithfulness

Marriage, like all aspects of Christian life, requires intentional discipleship. Healthy, Christ-centred marriages do not happen by accident - they are cultivated through spiritual growth, daily commitment, and reliance on God's Word and Spirit.

1. Discipling married couples

Churches play a vital role in equipping couples to live out their marriage vows faithfully. Practical discipleship for marriage involves:

➢ *Premarital preparation:* Teaching couples the biblical vision of marriage as covenant, not contract, and preparing them for realistic expectations and lifelong commitment.

➢ *Ongoing support:* Offering marriage enrichment classes, counselling, and mentorship for couples.

➢ *Rooting marriages in the Gospel:* Ensuring couples understand that marriage is not sustained by willpower alone but by grace. The same gospel that reconciles sinners to God also reconciles spouses to one another.

Discipleship in marriage helps believers see that all the daily sacrifices, acts of service, and perseverance required in marriage are not drudgery but opportunities to display Christlike love.

2. Fostering community among couples

Christian marriages will flourish in the context of community. Couples need fellowship with believers who will encourage them, pray for them, and hold them accountable. Small groups, couples' ministries, and intergenerational mentorship pairings allow for wisdom-sharing between older, seasoned couples and those newly married.

Proverbs 27:17 reminds us: *"As iron sharpens iron, so one person sharpens another."* Married believers sharpen each other not only in faith but in practical wisdom about communication, conflict resolution, and perseverance.

Pastoral sensitivity in divorce and remarriage

Jesus' words on divorce carry weight, but they must be applied pastorally and sensitively, recognizing the pain, complexity, and brokenness surrounding this issue.

1. Ministering to the divorced

Divorce often brings deep shame, regret, and feelings of failure. The church must be a place where divorced believers encounter grace rather than stigma. Pastors and leaders should:

> ➤ *Affirm God's forgiveness:* Emphasize that those in Christ are not defined by divorce but by His righteousness (2 Corinthians 5:21).

> ➤ *Provide counselling and healing:* Offer biblically grounded counselling to address grief, identity, and restoration after divorce.

> ➤ *Encourage healthy community:* Help those who are divorced integrate fully into church life, countering isolation with fellowship.

The goal is not to minimize sin where it has occurred but to magnify Christ's mercy and provide a path forward toward healing and holiness.

2. Guidance on remarriage

Jesus' words about remarriage as adulterous (Matthew 5:32) have prompted much debate over the years. In pastoral application, discernment is always needed. Scripture permits remarriage in some cases (e.g., where divorce was due to sexual immorality, or where an unbelieving spouse may depart— 1 Corinthians 7:15). Each situation requires prayerful wisdom, always balancing truth with grace.

Pastors must approach such situations not as legal adjudicators but as shepherds, leading believers toward repentance where needed and offering restoration rooted in God's Word.

The heart of pastoral care

When dealing with marriage and divorce, pastoral care must reflect Jesus' balance of truth and grace. He neither trivialized marriage nor condemned broken people beyond hope. To the woman at the well, who had five previous husbands, Jesus spoke both truth (*"The fact is, you have had five husbands..."*) and grace (*"I... am he,"* revealing Himself as Messiah; John 4:17–26).

This balance should characterize how the church addresses marriage breakdown. Upholding Jesus' high view of marriage must be coupled with extending His compassionate invitation to those wounded by relational sin and failure.

Practical steps for covenant faithfulness

For married couples seeking to embody Jesus' teaching, several disciplines can help nurture covenant faithfulness:

1. Daily prayer together

Praying as a couple strengthens spiritual intimacy and unites hearts around God's purposes. Even brief prayers reinforce dependence on Him and remind couples that marriage is a threefold cord with God at its centre (Ecclesiastes 4:12).

2. Intentional quality time

Busyness always erodes closeness. Regularly setting aside time for conversation, shared activities, and emotional connection prevents distance and fosters intimacy.

3. Quick reconciliation

Ephesians 4:26 urges, *"Do not let the sun go down while you are still angry."* Couples who are committed to quick forgiveness and reconciliation prevent resentment from festering and maintain relational health.

4. Continual learning

Reading Scripture, attending marriage seminars, or studying Christian books on marriage can provide fresh insight and practical tools for communication and problem-solving.

Marriage and the kingdom vision

Marriage in the kingdom is not merely private fulfilment; it is a public display of God's covenantal love. By calling His followers to covenant faithfulness, Jesus lifts marriage above cultural norms and embeds it within His redemptive mission. When marriages reflect this vision, they stand as living testimonies of the gospel:

➢ They demonstrate that love can endure hardship because it is grounded in grace.

➢ They show that forgiveness is possible because Christ has forgiven us.

➢ They embody the steadfastness of God Himself, who will never abandon His bride, the church.

Such marriages shine light into a world where commitment is fragile and covenant is often discarded. They proclaim that in Christ, faithfulness is not only possible but beautiful.

Preparing for Jesus' teaching on oaths and truthfulness

Following His teaching on marriage and divorce, Jesus addresses oaths and truthfulness (Matthew 5:33–37). The connection is profound: just as marriage demands covenant fidelity, so too truthfulness demands integrity in our speech. Both involve honouring one's word and reflecting God's faithful character. Jesus moves naturally from fidelity in the covenant of marriage to fidelity in everyday speech. Both stem from the same heart of righteousness He is forming in His disciples - a heart that mirrors God's truth and steadfastness.

Covenant faithfulness as kingdom living

Jesus' words on marriage and divorce call His followers back to God's original intent: which is a lifelong covenant reflecting His unchanging love.

In a culture where marriage is often treated lightly, the kingdom ethic restores its sacredness. Faithfulness in marriage is not burdensome; it is a joyful participation in God's covenantal love story. For those who are married, His teaching is a summons to deeper commitment and sacrificial love.

For those who are divorced or broken-hearted, it is an invitation to healing and grace. For all His disciples, it is a reminder that the righteousness He requires is not self-generated but Spirit-empowered, rooted in the transforming work of His kingdom.

As we turn next to Jesus' teaching on oaths, we will see this same principle continue: kingdom living is marked by integrity of heart - whether in our covenants, in our words, or in our relationships.

INTEGRITY IN SPEECH:
OATHS AND TRUTHFULNESS

Matthew 5:33–37

"Again, you have heard that it was said to the people long ago, 'Do not break your oath, but fulfil to the Lord the vows you have made.' But I tell you, do not swear an oath at all: either by heaven, for it is God's throne; or by the earth, for it is his footstool; or by Jerusalem, for it is the city of the Great King. And do not swear by your head, for you cannot make even one hair white or black. All you need to say is simply 'Yes' or 'No'; anything beyond this comes from the evil one."

The context of oaths in Jesus' time

In first-century Jewish culture, oaths were a common part of daily life. People invoked oaths to guarantee the truthfulness of their words, often swearing *"by heaven,"* *"by the earth,"* or *"by Jerusalem."*

Such practices stemmed from those Old Testament commands about vow-keeping, such as Leviticus 19:12: *"Do not swear falsely by my name and so profane the name of your God."*

Oaths were originally intended to underscore truthfulness and invoke God as witness to one's word. However, by Jesus' day, they had been misused. Rabbinic traditions had developed elaborate distinctions between binding and non-binding oaths.

For example, swearing *"by Jerusalem"* was considered non-binding, but swearing *"toward Jerusalem"* was binding. This view created loopholes, allowing people to technically avoid lying while still being deceitful.

Jesus confronts this misuse. He moves beyond regulating oaths to addressing the deeper issue: integrity. His teaching cuts through the legalism of vow-making to call His followers to simple, honest speech rooted in truth.

From external compliance to internal integrity

As with anger, lust, and divorce, Jesus shifts the focus from outward observance to inward transformation. The command against false oaths was never just about formulas of speech; it was about truthfulness. Instead of relying on complex oaths to authenticate their words, Jesus calls His disciples to be people whose speech is inherently trustworthy.

"All you need to say is simply 'Yes' or 'No'" (Matthew 5:37). Kingdom citizens should be known for such integrity that their bare word is enough. They do not need to pile up assurances or invoke sacred things in order to prove their honesty because their character backs up their speech. This reflects God's own nature. Scripture repeatedly affirms that God is faithful and true. Numbers 23:19 declares: *"God is not human, that he should lie... Does he speak and then not act? Does he promise and not fulfil?"* As His children, we are called to reflect His truthfulness in every word we speak.

Why does Jesus forbid oaths?

When Jesus says, *"Do not swear an oath at all,"* is He prohibiting all forms of oath-taking, even in legal or formal settings? Some Christian traditions, such as the Quakers, have interpreted His words literally, refusing even court oaths. Others see Jesus as targeting the manipulative oath practices of His day, rather than formal oaths required by law.

The key here lies in His underlying point: integrity should be so characteristic of His disciples that oaths become unnecessary. Jesus is not primarily addressing official legal settings but everyday speech, where oaths had become tools for evasion rather than truth. In essence, He says: *"Be so truthful that you don't need oaths to back up your words."*

James 5:12 echoes Jesus' teaching almost verbatim: *"Above all, my brothers and sisters, do not swear - not by heaven or by earth or by anything else. All you need to say is a simple 'Yes' or 'No.' Otherwise you will be condemned."* Both passages affirm that honesty should be habitual, not situational.

The heart behind oath-making

The Pharisaic system of oaths had two major flaws:

➤ *It encouraged deceit:* People could technically avoid lying by making "non-binding" oaths they never intended to keep.

➤ *It diminished God's authority:* By swearing by heaven, earth, or Jerusalem instead of God's name, people tried to distance themselves from invoking Him directly, as if that made their words less accountable.

Jesus dismantles this thinking by reminding His hearers that all such things - heaven, earth, Jerusalem, even their own heads - belong to God. There is no speech outside His jurisdiction. To swear by any created thing is still to implicate God, for He is Lord of all.

Thus, Jesus calls His disciples away from gamesmanship in speech toward wholehearted honesty. The issue is not merely swearing falsely but having a duplicitous heart. Oath-making was a symptom of a deeper problem: a culture where words could not be trusted without added guarantees. Jesus insists His followers must be different.

The simplicity of "Yes" and "No"

Jesus' antidote to oath-laden speech is radical simplicity: *"All you need to say is simply 'Yes' or 'No'"* (v. 37). This reflects a life of such integrity that promises are kept, statements are reliable, and no extra assurances are needed. When a disciple says *"yes,"* it is as good as done; when they say *"no,"* it is final.

This simplicity does not mean being blunt or unkind but being consistent and truthful. It excludes exaggeration, half-truths, manipulative language, and verbal hedging. It reflects an undivided heart - what Jesus earlier described as being *"pure in heart."* (Matthew 5:8) - where inner reality and outer words align. In contrast, speech that requires embellishment or oaths suggests unreliability. Jesus warns that such speech *"comes from the evil one"* (v. 37), for Satan is the *"father of lies"* (John 8:44). To twist truth or speak dishonestly is to echo his nature rather than God's.

Integrity as a kingdom value

Truthfulness is foundational to life in God's kingdom. Without it, relationships fracture, trust erodes, and communities crumble. Proverbs 12:22 states: *"The Lord detests lying lips, but he delights in people who are trustworthy."* In a world where deception is now commonplace - whether in politics, advertising, business, or personal relationships - Jesus' call to simple honesty is radically countercultural.

Kingdom integrity means that our words are dependable, our promises kept, and our speech marked by consistency. It flows from a transformed heart, not from fear of being caught. It seeks to honour God, not manipulate others.

The connection between words and character

Jesus' teaching here echoes His later words in Matthew 12:34: *"The mouth speaks what the heart is full of."* Speech reveals character. A person who habitually lies or manipulates shows a disordered heart. Conversely, those whose words are steady and truthful demonstrate inner righteousness.

This is why Jesus addresses oaths within the broader context of the Sermon on the Mount: He is forming disciples whose hearts and lives align with God's will. Just as anger is murder of the heart and lust is adultery of the heart, so deceit is falsehood of the heart. Integrity begins inwardly, transforming not only what we say but who we are.

Everyday applications of Jesus' teaching

What does *"let your yes be yes"* look like in practice? It applies broadly:

> ➤ *In promises:* Keep commitments, even when inconvenient (Psalm 15:4 praises those *"who keep an oath even when it hurts"*).
> ➤ *In business:* Be transparent and fair, avoiding deceptive practices or misleading claims.

- ➤ *In relationships:* Speak honestly without manipulation or passive-aggression.
- ➤ *In casual speech:* Avoid exaggeration or empty assurances (*"I swear I'll do it!"*), instead cultivating straightforward reliability.

Kingdom citizens do not need to invoke elaborate guarantees; their character is their guarantee.

Integrity and the formation of disciples

Jesus' call to straightforward honesty is more than a rule about speech - it is about forming whole people whose lives are characterized by truth. Integrity means wholeness, consistency, and alignment between our inner reality and our outward words and actions. It is not merely about avoiding lies but about cultivating a truthful character.

This is why Jesus places this teaching in the Sermon on the Mount. He is describing the kind of person who belongs to His kingdom: not merely those who avoid obvious sins but those whose hearts have been transformed. As in the earlier teachings on anger, lust, and marriage, Jesus moves beyond surface-level obedience to inner righteousness.

Discipleship, then, involves cultivating this integrity. It is about becoming people who are trustworthy, consistent, and reliable. This transformation cannot be achieved by mere willpower. It flows from the gospel: from being so shaped by God's truth and so indwelt by His Spirit that deceit becomes incompatible with who we are.

Integrity and God's character

Truthfulness is central to God's nature. Scripture repeatedly affirms that God is the God of truth:

- ➤ **Numbers 23:19**: *"God is not human, that he should lie... Does he promise and not fulfil?"*

- ➤ **Psalm 31:5**: *"Into your hands I commit my spirit; deliver me, Lord, my faithful God."*
- ➤ **John 14:6**: Jesus declares, *"I am the way and the truth and the life."*

Because God is always perfectly truthful, His words are utterly trustworthy. His promises never fail. When His people speak truthfully, they reflect His full character. When they lie or manipulate, they distort His image.

Integrity is thus a theological issue, not just an ethical one. To be people of truth is to bear witness to the One who is Truth. This is why Jesus says anything beyond simple honesty *"comes from the evil one."* (Matthew 5:37). Falsehood aligns us with Satan, whose nature is deceit (John 8:44), while truthfulness always aligns us with God.

Truthfulness and community

Integrity does more than reflect God's nature - it also builds strong, healthy communities. Lies fracture trust. Once truth is compromised, relationships suffer, and suspicion grows. But when words can be trusted, relationships flourish. The church, as a kingdom community, is called to be marked by this kind of integrity.

Paul underscores this in Ephesians 4:25: *"Therefore each of you must put off falsehood and speak truthfully to your neighbour, for we are all members of one body."* Truth-telling is not optional because the body depends on trust. Just as physical members of the body must coordinate and communicate reliably, so must believers in Christ's body.

When believers speak truthfully, they create an environment where people feel safe, respected, and valued. Honesty nurtures accountability and encourages confession, healing, and growth. It strengthens marriages, friendships, and fellowship. Without integrity in speech, the church cannot function as the family God intends it to be.

The freedom of simple honesty

Oath-making, in its manipulative form, implies a world where words are unreliable, where trust must be propped up with extra assurances. Jesus liberates His followers from this duplicity. He calls them to the freedom of simple honesty, where speech is unadorned, promises are kept, and there is no need for elaborate guarantees.

This freedom flows from security in God. Because we rest in His approval, we are not driven by fear of being exposed or the need to impress others. We can speak plainly without embellishment. We do not need to *"swear"* to convince because our lives bear consistent testimony to our truthfulness.

Everyday integrity in action

Living out this teaching requires attentiveness in ordinary speech:

> ➤ *Avoiding exaggeration:* Casual overstatements (*"I've told you a thousand times…"*) can erode credibility.
> ➤ *Keeping commitments:* Following through on even small promises builds trustworthiness.
> ➤ *Resisting manipulation:* Words should not be used to pressure, flatter insincerely, or mislead.
> ➤ *Owning mistakes:* When we fail, admitting wrong rather than covering it up demonstrates integrity.

These practices, though seemingly simple, bear powerful witness. In a world accustomed to broken promises, half-truths, and deceptive speech, straightforward honesty is striking.

Integrity in professional and public life

Jesus' teaching also extends to our various roles in society. In workplaces, business dealings, and civic life, truthfulness is essential for credibility and witness. Christians who conduct business honestly, who speak plainly rather than misleading customers or colleagues, embody the kingdom ethic in tangible ways.

Proverbs 11:1 says: *"The Lord detests dishonest scales, but accurate weights find favour with him."* God's concern for integrity includes fairness in economic dealings and honesty in professional conduct. When believers live this out, they demonstrate that their loyalty is not to profit or image but to Christ.

The cost and reward of integrity

Integrity can be costly. Speaking the truth may invite conflict, refusing to participate in deception can jeopardize advancement, and being honest might expose vulnerabilities. Yet Jesus calls His disciples to bear this cost, trusting God's reward.

In Matthew 10:32, He promises: *"Whoever acknowledges me before others, I will also acknowledge before my Father in heaven."* To live truthfully is to acknowledge Christ not only in words but in character. Integrity is not merely about avoiding sin; it is about aligning every part of life with His kingdom.

This cost, however, is matched by reward. Integrity brings peace of conscience, freedom from duplicity, and credibility in witness. It builds strong relationships and deepens fellowship with God, who *"desires truth in the inner parts."* (Psalm 51:6).

Truthfulness as an act of worship

Ultimately, integrity in speech is an act of worship. It honours God as the God of truth. When we speak honestly, keep our word, and resist deceit, we are offering Him obedience that delights His heart.

Psalm 15 paints a picture of the person who may dwell in God's presence: *"Lord, who may dwell in your sacred tent? Who may live on your holy mountain? The one whose walk is blameless, who does what is righteous, who speaks the truth from their heart... who keeps an oath even when it hurts..."* (Psalm 15:1–4)

Integrity is not simply ethical behaviour; it is also covenantal faithfulness; a reflection of life lived before God.

Preparing for Jesus' teaching on retaliation and generosity

This teaching on oaths flows naturally into what follows: Jesus' instruction on retaliation and generosity (Matthew 5:38–42). Integrity in speech lays the foundation for integrity in action. Just as disciples are called to truthful words, they are called to gracious deeds - even toward those who wrong them.

Truthfulness, generosity, and non-retaliation share a common root: a heart transformed by God's character. In the next section, Jesus will extend His kingdom ethic even further, showing how disciples respond to injustice not with revenge but with self-giving love.

The kingdom of uncomplicated honesty

Jesus' call to *"let your yes be yes"* is breathtakingly simple but profoundly transformative. It invites us into a way of life free from duplicity, manipulation, and posturing. It forms a people whose words are as dependable as their deeds because both spring from the same Spirit-renewed heart.

In the kingdom, honesty is not a legal requirement but a natural expression of grace-filled lives. It is not forced but flows from alignment with God's truth. To be truthful, then, is to live as a citizen of His reign - a living testimony that the God who cannot lie has made us new.

Habits that sustain integrity

Integrity is not cultivated overnight. It is the fruit of consistent choices, small daily acts of honesty, and a heart anchored in Christ. To develop integrity in speech, we must nurture habits that shape our words and align them with truth.

1. Regular self-examination

Psalm 139:23–24 provides a model prayer: *"Search me, God, and know my heart… See if there is any offensive way in me and lead me in the way everlasting."* Periodically reflecting on our words and motives invites the Spirit's conviction where dishonesty has crept in - whether through exaggeration, broken promises, or careless speech.

Self-examination is not morbid introspection but a pathway to growth. It helps us identify patterns that undermine integrity and bring them into the light of God's transforming grace.

2. Confession and accountability

When we fail, confession is essential. James 5:16 urges, *"Confess your sins to each other and pray for each other so that you may be healed." Sharing* struggles with trusted friends or mentors builds accountability and reinforces our commitment to truthful living. Accountability is not a sign of weakness but of humility and dependence on God's community for support.

3. Slow, thoughtful speech

Proverbs 10:19 warns: *"Sin is not ended by multiplying words, but the prudent hold their tongues."* Speaking less hastily helps guard against careless promises or half-truths. Pausing before speaking gives space to ensure our words align with truth and grace.

4. Scripture memorization

Filling our minds with God's Word equips us to combat dishonesty. Verses like Ephesians 4:25 *("put off falsehood and speak truthfully")* or Matthew 12:36 *("everyone will have to give account on the day of judgment for every empty word they have spoken")* remind us of the weight of our words and root us in truth.

Integrity in modern contexts

In today's world, speech is no longer limited to spoken words. Our communication spans texts, emails, social media posts, and digital platforms. Jesus' call to integrity applies as much online as offline.

1. Digital honesty

The anonymity and distance of digital communication often embolden people to misrepresent themselves, exaggerate, or speak harshly. Kingdom integrity rejects this. Whether crafting a social media post, responding to an email, or participating in online forums, disciples of Jesus are called to truth and grace.

Colossians 4:6 instructs: *"Let your conversation be always full of grace, seasoned with salt."* This includes digital speech, which should reflect kindness, accuracy, and sincerity.

2. Avoiding clickbait and misinformation

Sharing unverified information, sensational headlines, or misleading content violates the spirit of Jesus' teaching. Integrity requires diligence: checking facts, resisting gossip, and ensuring that what we pass on is true. Proverbs 12:22 reminds us: *"The Lord detests lying lips, but he delights in people who are trustworthy."*

3. Transparency in professional communication

In workplaces, digital tools often blur lines between efficiency and ethics. Cutting corners on reports, misrepresenting data, or over-promising in emails all erode credibility. Living out Matthew 5:37 means ensuring even our written "yes" and "no" are reliable, building trust with colleagues and clients alike.

Words as instruments of healing or harm

Integrity in speech is not merely about avoiding falsehood; it is about using words to build rather than destroy. Proverbs 18:21 declares that: *"The tongue has the power of life and death."* Honest, gracious words breathe life - encouraging, strengthening, and comforting others. False or careless words wound and divide. The Apostle Paul urges believers in Ephesians 4:29: *"Do not let any unwholesome talk come out of your mouths, but only what is helpful for building others up according to their needs."* This frames our speech not merely in terms of truthfulness but also in terms of purpose: our words should edify and reflect God's love.

Integrity demands that our speech be consistent with our identity in Christ. A *"yes"* rooted in integrity not only affirms truth but also serves the good of the listener, aligning our words with God's redemptive purposes.

Integrity and trust in relationships

Personal relationships thrive on trust, and trust is built on truthful words. In friendships, in marriages, in families, and in communities, integrity of speech fosters security and intimacy.

When people know they can rely on our words, relationships deepen. Conversely, dishonesty corrodes trust. Even 'small' lies - broken promises, withheld truths, misleading assurances - chip away at relational stability. Jesus' command to let our *"yes"* be yes protects relationships by rooting them in reliability.

For example:

> *In marriage:* Keeping vows and speaking truth nurtures intimacy and stability.
> *In parenting:* Consistent honesty builds credibility with children, teaching them by example.
> *In friendships:* Transparency fosters vulnerability and mutual support.

Kingdom relationships are anchored in truth because they reflect the God who is truth.

The link between truthfulness and justice

Integrity in speech also plays a vital role in justice. False testimony, slander, or misrepresentation harms the vulnerable and perpetuates injustice. The Old Testament repeatedly warns against false witness (Exodus 20:16), recognizing that untruth corrodes not only personal relationships but societal structures.

Jesus' command pushes His disciples toward a life where honesty safeguards fairness, where words protect rather than exploit. Truthfulness therefore becomes part of the kingdom's restorative mission, working against the lies that oppress and destroy.

Integrity and spiritual warfare

Jesus' closing remark - *"anything beyond this comes from the evil one."* (Matthew 5:37) - frames dishonesty as a spiritual battle. Satan is called *"the father of lies."* (John 8:44).

Deceit aligns us with his destructive work. Every falsehood, however small, reflects his influence rather than God's kingdom. Conversely, integrity resists the devil's schemes.

Truth-telling is part of the spiritual armour Paul describes in Ephesians 6:14: *"Stand firm then, with the belt of truth buckled around your waist."* To live truthfully is to stand against Satan's tactics, anchoring ourselves in Christ, who is Truth personified.

Integrity as preparation for radical generosity

Jesus' teaching on integrity prepares us for what follows: His instruction on retaliation and generosity (Matthew 5:38–42). Both require trust in God's justice and a relinquishing of manipulation or self-protection. Just as integrity renounces dishonest speech to control outcomes, radical generosity renounces retaliation to control justice.

Kingdom living involves surrendering our perceived 'rights' to assert ourselves - whether by swearing some elaborate oaths or demanding retribution. Integrity of speech lays the groundwork for integrity of action, freeing us to live honestly and generously in a world accustomed to deception and self-interest.

A kingdom of truthful people

Jesus' teaching on oaths is not merely about word formulas - it is about becoming truthful people whose lives reflect God's truth. In His kingdom, speech is simple and reliable because hearts are pure and aligned with His character.

This vision is deeply countercultural. In a world riddled with spin, exaggeration, and manipulation, disciples of Jesus stand out by their unvarnished honesty. Their *"yes"* means yes. Their *"no"* means no. Their speech, whether in person or online, builds trust and bears witness to the God who is faithful and true.

As we move next to Jesus' teaching on retaliation and generosity, we will see this trajectory continue: integrity in speech gives way to integrity in action, as disciples embody a righteousness that reflects God's own nature in every aspect of life.

- 16 -

RADICAL GENEROSITY AND GRACE

Matthew 5:38-42

"You have heard that it was said, 'Eye for eye, and tooth for tooth.' But I tell you, do not resist an evil person. If anyone slaps you on the right cheek, turn to them the other cheek also. And if anyone wants to sue you and take your shirt, hand over your coat as well. If anyone forces you to go one mile, go with them two miles. Give to the one who asks you, and do not turn away from the one who wants to borrow from you."

The Old Testament principle of justice: *"Eye for Eye"*

Jesus begins by quoting the familiar legal maxim: *"Eye for eye, and tooth for tooth."* (Exodus 21:24; Leviticus 24:20; Deuteronomy 19:21). This principle, which is known as *lex talionis* (the law of retaliation), was part of Israel's legal system. Its purpose was not to promote vengeance but to limit it. It established proportional justice: punishment should fit the offense, neither exceeding it nor falling short. In its original context, this law protected against escalating cycles of revenge. In the ancient world, personal retaliation often spiralled out of control - an injury could lead to a feud, and a feud to bloodshed. By embedding *lex talionis* within judicial processes, Israel's law restrained vengeance and ensured fairness through courts, not personal vendettas.

However, by Jesus' day, this principle had been misapplied to personal relationships. Instead of serving as a judicial guideline, it had become a justification for private retaliation. People used it to defend their right to strike back, to settle scores, and to demand satisfaction. Jesus challenges this distortion and calls His followers to a radically different ethic.

Jesus' radical call: Do not retaliate

"But I tell you," Jesus says, *"do not resist an evil person"* (5:39). His words are startling. He is not merely asking His disciples to refrain from vengeance; He commands them to relinquish even the instinct for self-assertion.

The kingdom ethic goes beyond restraining retaliation - it rejects it altogether. This does not mean passive submission to evil or indifference to injustice. Rather, Jesus calls His followers to always respond to wrongdoing not with equal force but with transformative grace. Instead of mirroring evil, they are to overcome it with good (Romans 12:21). His examples illustrate this principle vividly.

Turning the other cheek

"If anyone slaps you on the right cheek, turn to them the other cheek also." (v. 39). A slap on the right cheek in that culture was not primarily an act of violence but of insult - a backhanded blow symbolizing contempt. Jesus' instruction is not about enduring physical assault but about refusing to retaliate against personal offense or humiliation. To *"turn the other cheek"* is to reject the cycle of insult and revenge. It is to absorb wrong without escalating it, demonstrating that one's dignity rests not on retaliation but on identity in God's kingdom. It is a powerful act of nonviolent resistance, stripping the offender of their power to provoke and asserting moral strength through grace.

Giving more than demanded

Jesus continues: *"If anyone wants to sue you and take your shirt, hand over your coat as well."* (v. 40). Under Jewish law, a person's coat (outer garment) was protected from permanent seizure because it served as both clothing and bedding. By suggesting His disciples willingly offer even this essential item, Jesus teaches voluntary generosity in the face of legal exploitation. Rather than clinging to rights or possessions, kingdom citizens respond with open-handed grace. They value people over property and hold to a higher allegiance than personal entitlement. This is not about enabling injustice but about disarming it through unexpected generosity.

Going the extra mile

"If anyone forces you to go one mile, go with them two miles." (v. 41). This refers to the Roman practice of conscription, where soldiers could compel civilians to carry their equipment for one mile.

It was a hated symbol of occupation and oppression. Yet Jesus calls His followers to exceed even this coerced demand. To *"go the second mile"* is to transform compulsion into voluntary service. It denies resentment its hold and replaces it with grace.

By doing more than required, disciples demonstrate freedom from bitterness and showcase a kingdom ethic that transcends retaliation. They bear witness that their loyalty is to God, not merely to human authorities.

Radical generosity to those in need

Finally, Jesus says: *"Give to the one who asks you, and do not turn away from the one who wants to borrow from you."* (v. 42). Here, He broadens the principle from responding to wrongs to proactive generosity. Kingdom living is not defensive but abundantly gracious, open to meeting needs even when inconvenient.

This is not some call to reckless giving or ignoring wisdom (cf. 2 Thessalonians 3:10), but to a posture of generosity that reflects God's own. It pushes back against self-protective instincts and invites trust in God's provision.

The kingdom ethic of non-retaliation

In all these examples, Jesus overturns the popular principle of proportional justice with the principle of gracious self-giving. His followers are called to relinquish personal vengeance, forego asserting their rights, and respond to evil not with resistance but with redemptive love.

This is not natural. It cuts against our instinct for self-defence and fairness. Yet it embodies the very character of Christ, who *"when they hurled their insults at him, he did not retaliate; when he suffered, he made no threats. Instead, he entrusted himself to him who judges justly."* (1 Peter 2:23).

By rejecting retaliation and embracing generosity, disciples reflect their King. They bear witness to a kingdom where justice is ultimately God's and where love has the power to break cycles of hostility.

Misunderstandings to avoid

It is important to clarify what Jesus is not teaching:

➤ He is not advocating the toleration of abuse or injustice without recourse to legal or protective measures. His teaching is about personal retaliation, not the role of courts or governments (Romans 13:1–4).

➤ He is not prohibiting self-defence in situations of danger or harm.

➤ He is not calling for passivity but for active, non-retaliatory engagement that mirrors God's grace.

Jesus' ethic is not weakness but strength: the strength to relinquish vengeance, to trust God with justice, and to respond to evil in a way that confounds it.

The transformative power of grace

When disciples reject retaliation, they break the chain of escalating harm. Instead of mirroring evil, they bear witness to a greater reality: the grace of God's kingdom. Such responses are disarming, revealing a freedom that confounds worldly logic.

Paul captures this in Romans 12:17–21: *"Do not repay anyone evil for evil... Do not be overcome by evil, but overcome evil with good."* This is precisely what Jesus calls His followers to embody - a radical generosity that confronts evil not by matching it but by surpassing it with grace.

Practical applications of non-retaliation

Jesus' teaching is challenging because it confronts our instinctive desire for fairness and self-preservation. Living it out requires wisdom, humility, and deep dependence on God's Spirit. Here are practical ways this principle applies in daily life:

1. Responding to insults with grace

When insulted, our natural reflex is to retaliate - whether with harsh words, sarcasm, or cold withdrawal. Yet Jesus calls us to respond differently: to *"turn the other cheek."*

This means refusing to mirror contempt and instead choosing gentleness. Proverbs 15:1 affirms: *"A gentle answer turns away wrath, but a harsh word stirs up anger."* In practice, this might involve staying calm in conflict, speaking respectfully even when wronged, or walking away from arguments that fuel anger. Such restraint is not weakness, but strength rooted in self-control and trust in God.

2. Yielding rights for the sake of peace

Jesus' example of surrendering one's coat teaches the principle of releasing personal rights rather than demanding them in every situation. This might involve letting go of minor grievances in relationships, defusing tension by conceding small disputes, or choosing harmony over vindication. Paul illustrates this well in 1 Corinthians 6:7, rebuking believers who sue one another: *"The very fact that you have lawsuits among you means you have been completely defeated already. Why not rather be wronged? Why not rather be cheated?"* He underscores that kingdom values prioritize peace and witness over winning at all costs.

3. Serving those who burden us

"Going the extra mile" calls for exceeding even unfair demands with generosity. In modern terms, this could mean:

➢ Helping a difficult colleague beyond what is required.
➢ Volunteering extra time to assist someone who imposes on us.
➢ Responding to unreasonable requests not with resentment but with grace.

Such acts demonstrate freedom from bitterness and reflect Christ's own servanthood.

4. Practicing generosity toward need

Jesus' command to *"give to the one who asks"* invites us to cultivate a posture of open-handedness. This includes practical charity - meeting financial needs, offering hospitality, or lending time and resources without expecting repayment.

Generosity dismantles the hold of materialism and fear. It reflects confidence in God's provision and mirrors His lavish grace: *"Freely you have received; freely give."* (Matthew 10:8).

Reflecting Christ's example

Jesus' own life perfectly embodies this ethic. Throughout His ministry, He absorbed hostility without retaliation, choosing grace over vengeance. At His arrest, He rebuked Peter's violent defence: *"Put your sword back in its place... for all who draw the sword will die by the sword."* (Matthew 26:52). He then healed the ear of the man who came to seize Him (Luke 22:51), modelling non-retaliatory love even in crisis.

Most profoundly, on the cross, Jesus fulfilled His own teaching. He endured injustice silently, mocked and beaten, yet prayed: *"Father, forgive them, for they do not know what they are doing."* (Luke 23:34). He entrusted Himself to the Father's judgment, as Peter writes: "When they hurled their insults at him, he did not retaliate... Instead, he entrusted himself to him who judges justly" (1 Peter 2:23). In this, Jesus reveals that rejecting retaliation is not passive submission but active trust in God. His silence was not weakness but the strength of divine love, breaking the cycle of vengeance and securing salvation.

Trusting God's justice

Central to this teaching is the conviction that God Himself will vindicate His people. Romans 12:19 declares: *"Do not take revenge... but leave room for God's wrath, for it is written: 'It is mine to avenge; I will repay,' says the Lord."* When we refuse to retaliate, we are not denying justice; we are deferring it to God. We relinquish our claim to personal vengeance, trusting that His judgment is wiser and more perfect than ours.

This perspective frees us from the consuming burden of payback and anchors us in hope. Faith in God's justice liberates us to respond with grace rather than retaliation. We can endure wrongs without being overcome by bitterness because we know that evil will not ultimately triumph.

Non-retaliation as kingdom witness

When Christians practice non-retaliation, they bear compelling witness to the world. Such responses defy human instinct and worldly logic, drawing attention to the transforming power of the gospel. Imagine:

> A believer forgiving a public insult rather than retaliating online.

> A Christian employee serving a hostile boss with excellence rather than spite.

> A follower of Christ responding to exploitation with surprising generosity.

These actions raise questions: *"Why would you respond that way?"* The answer points to Christ. Non-retaliation shines light on His kingdom, where grace reigns and vengeance belongs to God alone.

Non-retaliation and inner freedom

Choosing not to retaliate also frees us internally. Retaliation chains us to the wrong done against us, keeping us entangled in anger and resentment. But grace releases us. When we refuse to repay evil, we step out of its orbit. We refuse to let it define us. Paul's exhortation in Romans 12:21 captures this liberation: *"Do not be overcome by evil, but overcome evil with good."*

Evil is overcome not when we match its force but when we transcend it with love. This is the paradox of the kingdom: true victory comes not through asserting ourselves but through yielding to God's higher way.

Boundaries and wisdom in applying Jesus' teaching

While Jesus' words call for radical grace, they do not negate prudence or boundaries. Refusing retaliation is not the same as enabling harm. For example:

> Victims of abuse are not required to remain in unsafe situations; seeking help and legal protection is consistent with biblical wisdom.

> Lending to the needy does not mean fuelling destructive habits; discernment must accompany generosity.

Kingdom living requires both grace and wisdom. Jesus Himself sometimes withdrew from danger (John 10:39) and confronted wrong directly (John 18:23). His teaching is not simplistic passivity but Spirit-led discernment that prioritizes love without compromising righteousness.

Practical habits for cultivating grace over retaliation

To embody the command of Jesus, we must cultivate habits that prepare our hearts to respond with grace:

> *Pray for enemies:* As Jesus will teach later (Matthew 5:44), praying for those who wrong us softens our hearts and aligns us with God's mercy.
> *Practice restraint:* Train yourself to pause before reacting — whether in speech, email, or action — allowing space for prayerful reflection.
> *Meditate on Christ's example:* Regularly reflect on passages like 1 Peter 2:21–23, where Jesus' endurance of suffering inspires our own.
> *Entrust wrongs to God:* Consciously surrender injustices to His judgment, reminding yourself that vengeance belongs to Him.

These disciplines shape us over time, enabling Spirit-formed responses rather than instinct-driven reactions.

Preparing for love of enemies

This teaching naturally leads to Jesus' next and even more challenging command: *"Love your enemies and pray for those who persecute you."* (Matthew 5:44). Non-retaliation is the first step; active love for enemies is its completion.

Turning the other cheek is restraint; loving enemies is redemptive initiative. By rejecting retaliation, we lay down the weapons of self-defence. By loving our enemies, we take up the tools of God's kingdom - mercy, forgiveness, and grace.

This progression reflects the heart of the gospel itself: God did not merely refrain from punishing sinners; He actively loved them, sending His Son to save them.

Grace that overcomes

Jesus' command to reject retaliation is radical because it calls us to entrust justice to God and embody grace toward those who wrong us. It is a call to mirror Christ, who bore injustice without retaliation and conquered evil not through force but through sacrificial love.

This teaching invites us into the freedom of God's kingdom - a freedom from vengeance, from bitterness, and also from the relentless demand to defend ourselves. It calls us to trust God so deeply that we can respond to evil with generosity, breaking cycles of hostility with the surprising power of grace.

Practical examples of radical generosity

Jesus' teaching does not merely call for restraint from revenge; it pushes further, urging active, grace-filled generosity even in the face of injustice or demand. This radical generosity flows from hearts transformed by God's love and anchored in His provision.

1. Generosity in personal relationships

We encounter countless small opportunities to live out this principle daily:

> *Overlooking minor offenses:* Instead of retaliating for harsh words or petty slights, we can choose gracious silence or a kind response.
> *Offering help to those who wrong us:* Lending aid to someone who has mistreated us is one of the clearest ways to "go the second mile."
> *Absorbing inconvenience joyfully:* Yielding our schedule, preferences, or comfort to serve others - even those who do not appreciate it - reflects Christ's self-giving spirit.

Such actions seem small but testify powerfully that we live by a different standard than the world's.

2. Generosity in material terms

Jesus' command to *"give to the one who asks"* challenges our grip on possessions. Radical generosity might involve:

> Giving financially to someone in genuine need, even when repayment is uncertain.

> Offering hospitality without expectation of return (Luke 14:12–14).

> Sharing resources freely with neighbours or community members, modelling open-handed trust in God's provision.

This echoes Acts 2:44–45, where early believers *"sold property and possessions to give to anyone who had need."* Their radical generosity reflected their confidence in God's care and deepened their witness to the watching world.

3. Generosity in forgiveness

Forgiveness is a form of generosity. It cancels a relational "debt" owed to us and refuses to demand payback. When we forgive freely - even without apology - we are mirroring God's mercy: *"Be kind and compassionate to one another, forgiving each other, just as in Christ God forgave you."* (Ephesians 4:32). In this sense, forgiveness can be seen as the ultimate act of *"turning the other cheek."* It breaks chains of resentment and creates space for healing and reconciliation.

Historical illustrations of non-retaliation

Throughout history, followers of Jesus have embodied His call to radical grace, often at great cost. Their examples inspire and challenge us to live out this ethic in our own contexts.

1. Martin Luther King Jr. and nonviolent resistance

During the American civil rights movement, Dr. Martin Luther King Jr. championed nonviolence grounded explicitly in Jesus' teaching from the Sermon on the Mount. Facing brutal injustice, he urged followers to resist evil not with violence but with love, declaring: *"We shall meet your physical force with soul force. Do to us what you will, and we shall continue to love you... We will wear you down by our capacity to suffer."*

This approach was not passivity, it was a powerful witness. It exposed the moral bankruptcy of oppression and echoed Christ's example, demonstrating that grace is stronger than vengeance.

2. The early church and persecution

In the first centuries, Christians endured waves of persecution from Roman authorities. Yet historical records show their refusal to retaliate. Instead, they prayed for their persecutors, served their communities, and even provided aid to those who hated them. Tertullian wrote that the blood of martyrs became *"the seed of the church"* precisely because their gracious endurance pointed unmistakably to Christ.

3. Corrie ten Boom and forgiveness after the holocaust

Corrie ten Boom was a Dutch Christian who survived a Nazi concentration camp, who later forgave one of her former captors who sought her pardon. She described the moment she extended her hand in forgiveness despite feeling no emotional warmth: *"The will can function regardless of the temperature of the heart. Jesus, help me!"*

Her obedience unleashed a flood of grace, illustrating that forgiveness and non-retaliation depend not on feelings but on faith in Christ's power.

The role of trust in God's provision

Radical generosity and non-retaliation are impossible if we cling to our own security, rights, or sense of justice. They require surrender - entrusting our needs and vindication entirely to God.

➤ *Trust in His justice:* When we refuse vengeance, we rest in His promise: *"It is mine to avenge; I will repay."* (Romans 12:19).

➤ *Trust in His provision:* When we give generously or yield possessions, we believe Jesus' words in Matthew 6:33: *"Seek first his kingdom and his righteousness, and all these things will be given to you as well."*

> *Trust in His sovereignty:* When wronged, we affirm that He is sovereign, able to redeem even injustice for His purposes, as seen in Joseph's words: *"You intended to harm me, but God intended it for good."* (Genesis 50:20).

This trust then frees us from the fear that drives retaliation or hoarding. It enables us to live open-handedly, confident that God Himself upholds and defends His children.

Preparing for love of enemies

Jesus' teaching on non-retaliation naturally builds toward His climactic command in the Sermon on the Mount: *"Love your enemies and pray for those who persecute you."* (Matthew 5:44). Turning the other cheek is the foundation; loving enemies is the fulfilment.

Non-retaliation halts the cycle of harm; love actively transforms it. In the next section, Jesus moves beyond restraint to proactive compassion, calling His followers not just to endure enemies but to bless them. This is the pinnacle of kingdom ethics: imitating the indiscriminate, lavish love of the Father.

Radical generosity as a foretaste of the kingdom

When we turn the other cheek, give freely, and serve without retaliation, we offer glimpses of the kingdom breaking into this world. Our actions become signs pointing to a new reality where grace reigns over vengeance and love triumphs over hatred.

These choices are not natural - they are supernatural. They testify that God has changed our hearts. They confront a world bound by payback logic with a different economy: one rooted in mercy, generosity, and unshakable trust in the King who provides and vindicates.

Conclusion: Living the second mile life

Jesus' call to reject retaliation and embrace generosity is not merely moral advice; it is an invitation to share His own life. He is the One who turned the other cheek, who yielded His rights, who carried our burdens farther than we could imagine, and who gave not just His cloak but His very life for our redemption.

To live this way is to walk in His footsteps. It is to embody His kingdom, where victory comes through sacrifice, and greatness is measured by servanthood, and where evil is overcome not by force but by self-giving love.

As we turn to Jesus' next teaching on loving our enemies, we will see this ethic reach its highest point: the command to extend to our enemies the very love we ourselves have received from God.

17

LOVING YOUR ENEMIES: REFLECTING THE FATHER'S PERFECT LOVE

Matthew 5:43-48

"You have heard that it was said, 'Love your neighbour and hate your enemy.' But I tell you, love your enemies and pray for those who persecute you, that you may be children of your Father in heaven. He causes his sun to rise on the evil and the good and sends rain on the righteous and the unrighteous. If you love those who love you, what reward will you get? Are not even the tax collectors doing that? And if you greet only your own people, what are you doing more than others? Do not even pagans do that? Be perfect, therefore, as your heavenly Father is perfect."

The common assumption: Love friends, hate enemies

Jesus begins by exposing a familiar cultural ethic: *"Love your neighbour and hate your enemy."* (v. 43). While the command to love one's neighbour comes directly from Leviticus 19:18 (*"love your neighbour as yourself"*), the phrase *"hate your enemy"* is found nowhere in Scripture. It reflects a distortion of God's law.

In Jesus' time, some Jewish groups, such as the Zealots, saw hatred of enemies - particularly Roman oppressors - as not only natural but virtuous.

The Qumran sect (associated with the Dead Sea Scrolls) even codified this in their community rule: *"Love all the sons of light... and hate all the sons of darkness."*

Over time, neighbour love had been narrowed to apply only to one's own group, while enemies - whether political, social, or personal - were excluded.

Jesus overturns this mindset entirely. His kingdom does not operate by tribal loyalty or reciprocal affection. Instead, He commands His disciples to extend love even to those who oppose, harm, or despise them.

The radical command: Love your enemies

Jesus' words are startling: *"But I tell you, love your enemies and pray for those who persecute you."* (v. 44). This is not mere tolerance or avoidance; it is proactive, redemptive love. It calls for benevolence, compassion, and even intercession on behalf of those who wrong us.

This love is *agape* – which is self-giving, unconditional, and not contingent on the recipient's worthiness or response. It is the love God Himself shows to a rebellious world. Jesus' command pushes us beyond instinct and comfort into the supernatural realm of grace.

Consider the context: many of His hearers lived under Roman occupation, subject to harsh taxes, military coercion, and social humiliation. To love such enemies was humanly unthinkable. Yet Jesus calls for precisely this because His kingdom is not of this world (John 18:36). It operates by a different logic - one rooted in the character of God.

Praying for persecutors

Jesus not only commands love for enemies but specifically calls us to pray for those who persecute us. Prayer transforms both our hearts and our perspective. When we bring our enemies before God, we begin to see them as He does: not merely as threats or adversaries but as lost people in need of redemption. Prayer for enemies disarms resentment.

It shifts us from wishing harm upon them to desiring their good. It aligns us with Jesus' own example: on the cross, He prayed, *"Father, forgive them, for they do not know what they are doing."* (Luke 23:34). Stephen, the first Christian martyr, echoed this as he was stoned: *"Lord, do not hold this sin against them."* (Acts 7:60).

Such prayers are not easy. They often begin through gritted teeth, as an act of obedience rather than feeling. Yet as we persist, God softens our hearts, freeing us from hatred's grip and filling us with His love.

Why love enemies? To reflect the Father

Jesus roots this command in our identity as God's children: *"that you may be children of your Father in heaven."* (v. 45). To love enemies is to display the family resemblance of our heavenly Father. He *"causes his sun to rise on the evil and the good and sends rain on the righteous and the unrighteous."* His common grace blesses even those who deny or defy Him.

God's love is not selective or transactional. He does not bless only the obedient or favour His friends. He gives generously to all because love is His nature. When we love enemies, we mirror this indiscriminate, generous love, demonstrating that we truly belong to His kingdom.

The insufficiency of reciprocal love

Jesus contrasts enemy-love with the world's standard: *"If you love those who love you, what reward will you get? Are not even the tax collectors doing that?"* (v. 46). Reciprocal love - kindness toward those who are first kind to us - is natural, but it is not uniquely Christian. Even the despised tax collectors - collaborators with Rome - and pagans (those outside the covenant community) love within their circles.

Kingdom love goes much further. It exceeds all cultural norms and human instinct. It does *"more than others"* (v. 47). It crosses boundaries, dissolves hostility, and embodies a love that cannot be explained apart from God Himself.

The call to perfection

Jesus concludes: *"Be perfect, therefore, as your heavenly Father is perfect."* (v. 48). This verse can feel overwhelming. Does Jesus expect sinless moral flawlessness? The Greek word for *"perfect"* (*teleios*) here means *"complete," "mature,"* or *"whole."*

He is calling His disciples to be fully formed in love, reflecting the wholeness of the Father's character. This echoes Leviticus 19:2: *"Be holy because I, the Lord your God, am holy."* Holiness is not merely separation from sin but likeness to God.

In context, Jesus' command calls us to maturity in love that embraces even enemies - love that is indiscriminate, sacrificial, and rooted in God's own.

Love that conquers hatred

Loving enemies is not sentimentalism. It is the most powerful force for transformation in the world. Hatred perpetuates cycles of violence and retribution. Love breaks those cycles. It confronts evil not with equal force but with something greater. Paul echoes this in Romans 12:20–21: *"If your enemy is hungry, feed him; if he is thirsty, give him something to drink… Do not be overcome by evil, but overcome evil with good."* Loving enemies is not passive; it is aggressive goodness. It disarms hostility, exposes injustice, and opens the door for reconciliation.

The difficulty and the possibility

This command is humanly impossible apart from divine grace. On our own, we cannot love those who wound us. But through the Holy Spirit, God pours His love into our hearts (Romans 5:5), enabling us to extend what we have received.

The key is remembering that we were once God's enemies. Romans 5:10 says, *"While we were God's enemies, we were reconciled to him through the death of his Son."* Our love for enemies flows from the recognition that God loved us when we were hostile to Him. As recipients of such mercy, how can we withhold it from others?

Practical ways to love our enemies

Jesus' command is radical, but it is not abstract. Loving enemies is a concrete, Spirit-enabled choice expressed through specific actions. Here are ways we can live this out in daily life:

1. Pray for them consistently

Prayer is the starting point because it aligns our hearts with God's. It's difficult to hate someone while interceding for them. Pray for their well-being, for God's mercy in their lives, and for their hearts to be transformed.

As Jesus commands in Luke 6:28: *"Bless those who curse you, pray for those who mistreat you."* Prayer reshapes not only our view of our enemies but also our whole posture toward them. It softens bitterness and replaces it with compassion.

2. Refuse to retaliate

Loving enemies includes withholding vengeance, even when it feels justified. This does not mean condoning evil or ignoring wrongdoing but relinquishing the desire to *"get even."*

Romans 12:19 reminds us: *"Do not take revenge... but leave room for God's wrath."* Instead of retaliation, we entrust justice to God. This act of surrender frees us from being controlled by anger and demonstrates faith in God's righteous judgment.

3. Do good to them

Love is active, not passive. Jesus calls for tangible acts of kindness toward enemies. This echoes His teaching in Luke 6:27: *"Do good to those who hate you."* This might mean offering help when they are in need, speaking respectfully even when insulted, or showing generosity where hostility exists.

Such actions can be disarming. They expose the futility of enmity and reflect the unexpected nature of grace. They communicate that our love is not transactional but rooted in God's character.

4. Speak well of them

Our words always reveal our hearts (Matthew 12:34). Instead of slandering or belittling those who oppose us, we can choose to speak truthfully but charitably. This doesn't mean ignoring wrongdoing, but it does mean refusing to demonize others or perpetuate hatred in how we talk about them.

Paul exhorts in Ephesians 4:29: *"Do not let any unwholesome talk come out of your mouths, but only what is helpful for building others up."* Loving our enemies includes restraining speech that fuels division.

5. Seek opportunities for reconciliation

Wherever it is possible, take some steps toward restoring broken relationships. This may not always be feasible or safe, but when it seems appropriate, initiating dialogue or offering forgiveness demonstrates Christlike love. As Paul writes in Romans 12:18: *"If it is possible, as far as it depends on you, live at peace with everyone."* Love sometimes means making the first move, even when the other party shows no interest in reconciliation.

Historical examples of loving enemies

Throughout history, countless believers have embodied the teaching of Jesus in transformative ways, offering living proof of its power.

1. Jesus on the cross

The ultimate example is Jesus Himself. As He hung on the cross, unjustly condemned and surrounded by mockers, He prayed: *"Father, forgive them, for they do not know what they are doing."* (Luke 23:34). His prayer for His executioners epitomizes enemy-love, demonstrating mercy even in the face of unimaginable cruelty.

2. Stephen the martyr

In Acts 7:59–60, as Stephen was stoned to death for his testimony, he echoed Jesus' words: *"Lord, do not hold this sin against them."* His plea for his killers revealed a heart free from hatred, shining the light of Christ in his final moments. This act profoundly impacted Saul of Tarsus (later Paul), who witnessed it and later became the greatest apostle to the Gentiles.

3. Corrie ten Boom and forgiveness

As mentioned last chapter, Corrie ten Boom, after surviving the Nazi concentration camp, encountered one of her former guards at a postwar meeting. When he asked for her forgiveness, she struggled internally but ultimately extended her hand and forgave him. She later wrote:

"Forgiveness is an act of the will, and the will can function regardless of the temperature of the heart." Corrie ten Boom's story powerfully illustrates how enemy-love is always a deliberate choice which is rooted in obedience, even when emotions lag behind.

4. Martin Luther King Jr. and civil rights

Dr. King's famous philosophy of nonviolence was grounded in Jesus' command to love enemies. He insisted: *"Love is the only force which is capable of transforming an enemy into a friend."* His movement's refusal to retaliate in the face of violence exposed the moral bankruptcy of segregation and pointed powerfully to the kingdom ethic of enemy-love.

Why enemy-love is central to the Gospel

Loving enemies is not just an ethical ideal; it lies at the very heart of the gospel. Paul explains in Romans 5:10: *"While we were God's enemies, we were reconciled to him through the death of his Son."* We once stood opposed to God, yet He loved us and gave His Son to restore us.

Thus, our love for enemies flows directly from God's prior love for us. We are not merely following a command; we are imitating what has already been done for us. This makes enemy-love both possible and necessary. We forgive because we have been forgiven (Ephesians 4:32). We love because He first loved us (1 John 4:19).

Enemy-love as kingdom witness

When Christians love enemies, they display the reality of the kingdom in ways words alone cannot. Such love is inexplicable apart from divine transformation. It draws attention to the God who makes it possible and invites others to encounter Him.

Jesus Himself said: *"By this everyone will know that you are my disciples, if you love one another."* (John 13:35). Extending love beyond even our community - to our enemies - magnifies this witness exponentially. It is a living apologetic for the gospel, showcasing grace that defies human logic.

The challenge and the power

I must acknowledge that loving enemies is profoundly difficult. It confronts our pride, our pain, and our sense of justice. But it is precisely because it is so hard that it is so powerful. It forces us to rely on the Spirit's strength rather than our own. Paul reminds us in Galatians 5:22–23 that love is the fruit of the Spirit, not human effort. Through prayer, surrender, and meditation on God's love, He produces in us what we could never manufacture ourselves.

From enemy-love to perfection in love

Jesus concludes with the call to *"be perfect... as your heavenly Father is perfect."* (Matthew 5:48). This *"perfection"* is not flawless performance but fullness of love. To love enemies is to reach maturity in reflecting the Father's character. It is to live as true children of God, embodying His generous, indiscriminate love.

As we move into Matthew 6, Jesus will shift from interpersonal commands to personal piety - examining how our relationship with God shapes prayer, giving, and devotion. Yet the command to love enemies remains the pinnacle of His teaching in chapter 5, summoning us to nothing less than the heart of God Himself.

Cultivating the capacity to love enemies

Loving enemies does not happen automatically; it is a fruit of discipleship. Jesus calls His followers to a love so radical that it requires daily formation by the Spirit. Here are practical habits to cultivate this capacity.

1. Daily reflection on God's love for us

We love our enemies because God first loved us - even when we were His enemies (Romans 5:10). Regular meditation on this truth deepens our gratitude and our humility. Passages such as Ephesians 2:1–7 remind us of our former alienation and God's mercy, fuelling compassion for others who oppose us. When we see ourselves as recipients of unearned grace, it becomes harder to withhold grace from those who wrong us.

2. Praying for our enemies by name

Jesus' command in Matthew 5:44 to *"pray for those who persecute you,"* is an act of obedience and a pathway to transformation. Naming those who have hurt us in prayer personalizes the command. It shifts them from abstract *"enemies"* to individuals seen through God's eyes.

Start with simple petitions: asking God to bless them, soften their hearts, or bring them to repentance. Over time, such prayer reshapes our emotions, aligning our hearts with God's mercy rather than resentment.

3. Practicing acts of kindness

Enemy-love is demonstrated through action. Romans 12:20 exhorts, *"If your enemy is hungry, feed him; if he is thirsty, give him something to drink."* Deliberate acts of kindness disrupt hostility. These can be small gestures: sending an encouraging note, offering help in need, or choosing words of kindness rather than retaliation. Even modest actions can dismantle barriers and open doors for reconciliation.

4. Surrendering vengeance to God

Bitterness often lingers because we cling to the need for justice. Yet Scripture calls us to release vengeance into God's hands: *"It is mine to avenge; I will repay."* (Romans 12:19). Entrusting wrongs to God frees us from carrying burdens we were never meant to bear. This surrender is not denial; it is faith. We trust that God's justice is perfect and His timing sure, allowing us to respond with grace rather than retaliation.

5. Immersing ourselves in the Gospels

Enemy-love flows from union with Christ. Immersing ourselves in the Gospels keeps His example before us: His patience with His accusers, His forgiveness of those who mocked Him, and His sacrificial death for sinners. Regularly revisiting these scenes strengthens our resolve to imitate Him. When faced with hostility, we can ask: *How did Jesus respond?* The answer always points us toward mercy, restraint, and love that costs something.

The transformative power of enemy-love in communities

When Christians live out Jesus' command to love enemies, it does so much more than transform individuals - it reshapes entire communities.

1. Breaking cycles of retaliation

In societies dominated by vengeance and rivalry, enemy-love halts escalating hostility. Instead of perpetuating harm, it introduces forgiveness and grace. Over time, this disrupts entrenched divisions, paving the way for true peace.

Examples abound in conflict zones around the world where believers have chosen forgiveness over revenge. Their witness often sparks reconciliation that political solutions fail to achieve.

2. Creating a countercultural witness

Enemy-love distinguishes the church from the world. When outsiders see Christians responding to hatred with kindness, they encounter a reality they cannot explain apart from God. This draws attention to the gospel and invites curiosity: *What kind of love is this?*

Tertullian observed this dynamic in the early church: *"See how they love one another, and how they are ready to die for one another!"* Such love - including love for enemies - was the church's most persuasive apologetic.

3. Restoring divided relationships

On a personal level, enemy-love has the power to restore relationships fractured by resentment. Families estranged for years have been reconciled when one party chose to forgive rather than retaliate. Friendships broken by betrayal have been rebuilt through persistent acts of grace.

While reconciliation is not always possible - particularly in cases where there is ongoing harm - enemy-love still breaks the chains of bitterness, even if only in our own hearts.

Enemy-love as spiritual formation

Jesus' command to love enemies is not merely ethical; it is deeply formative. It trains us in Christlikeness, stripping away self-centeredness and pride. Each act of enemy-love is a step toward maturity in holiness.

This is why Jesus concludes this section with the words, *"Be perfect, therefore, as your heavenly Father is perfect."* (Matthew 5:48). The perfection He calls for is completeness in love - a love that mirrors God's indiscriminate goodness. As we learn to love enemies, we become more like Him.

Enemy-love thus functions as a litmus test of discipleship. Anyone can love friends or family; only Spirit-filled followers of Jesus can extend love to adversaries. This is what sets kingdom citizens apart: they love beyond natural limits because they draw from a supernatural source.

The cost of enemy-love

We must also be honest with ourselves here: loving enemies can be costly. It may mean relinquishing our right to vindication, enduring misunderstanding, or absorbing further hurt without retaliation. Jesus never hid this cost. He warned that following Him would involve bearing a cross (Luke 9:23).

Yet this cost pales beside the reward: intimacy with Christ, freedom from bitterness, and participation in God's redemptive work. By loving enemies, we enter deeply into the pattern of Jesus' own life and reflect His kingdom in tangible ways.

Preparing for Matthew 6: Practicing righteousness before God

As Jesus now concludes Matthew 5 with the command to love enemies and reflect the Father's perfect love, He then pivots in Matthew 6 toward personal devotion: giving, prayer, and fasting. These two sections of the Sermon are deeply connected. Loving enemies requires a heart transformed by God's love; such transformation is nurtured through communion with Him.

The practices of Matthew 6 - done in secret, before the Father - fuel the inner life that makes enemy-love possible. Without intimacy with God, loving enemies will remain an impossible burden. With it, it becomes the natural overflow of His presence within us.

Conclusion: The pinnacle of kingdom ethics

Loving our enemies is the climax of Jesus' ethical teaching in Matthew 5. It brings His vision of kingdom righteousness to its highest point: a love that mirrors God's own. It invites us into the divine life, where grace triumphs over hostility and mercy triumphs over judgment.

This command is not peripheral; it is central. It encapsulates the heart of the gospel: God loved His enemies - you and me - and reconciled us through Christ. As His children, we now go and do likewise.

As we move now into chapter 6, Jesus will shift from outward relationships to inward devotion, teaching us how to cultivate a hidden life with God. Yet the call to love enemies lingers, shaping everything that follows. For only those rooted in God's perfect love can live out the radical righteousness of His kingdom.

18

PRACTICING RIGHTEOUSNESS IN SECRET: GIVING, PRAYER, AND FASTING

Matthew 6:1–18

"Be careful not to practice your righteousness in front of others to be seen by them. If you do, you will have no reward from your Father in heaven. So when you give to the needy, do not announce it with trumpets, as the hypocrites do in the synagogues and on the streets, to be honoured by others. Truly I tell you, they have received their reward in full. But when you give to the needy, do not let your left hand know what your right hand is doing, so that your giving may be in secret. Then your Father, who sees what is done in secret, will reward you.

And when you pray, do not be like the hypocrites, for they love to pray standing in the synagogues and on the street corners to be seen by others. Truly I tell you, they have received their reward in full. But when you pray, go into your room, close the door and pray to your Father, who is unseen. Then your Father, who sees what is done in secret, will reward you.

And when you fast, do not look sombre as the hypocrites do, for they disfigure their faces to show others they are fasting. Truly I tell you, they have received their reward in full. But when you fast, put oil on your head and wash your face, so that it will not be obvious to others that you are fasting, but only to your Father, who is unseen; and your Father, who sees what is done in secret, will reward you."

The shift from public ethics to private devotion

In Matthew 5, Jesus addressed the outward relationships and ethical demands of kingdom life: anger, lust, marriage, integrity, generosity, and enemy-love. Now, in this chapter, Jesus turns inward, focusing on the hidden life of devotion to God.

Here, Jesus warns against a new danger: performing acts of righteousness to gain human approval rather than to please the Father.

He begins with a broad principle: *"Be careful not to practice your righteousness in front of others to be seen by them."* (v. 1). This is not a prohibition against public good works (cf. Matthew 5:16, where He tells us to *"let your light shine before others"*). Instead, Jesus addresses motive. The issue is whether our acts of righteousness flow from our genuine devotion to God or from our desire for recognition and praise.

Hypocrisy: The quest for human approval

Jesus repeatedly uses the word *"hypocrites"* (vv. 2, 5, 16) as He describes those who give, pray, or fast for show. The term *"hypocrite"* originally referred to an actor wearing a mask in the Greek theatre - someone pretending to be someone else. In the same way, religious hypocrisy masks self-centred motives under the appearance of piety.

When righteousness is performed to impress others, it ceases to be righteousness. Such acts become self-serving, seeking human applause rather than divine approval. Jesus' verdict is sobering: *"They have received their reward in full."* (v. 2). Public recognition is all they will get. God owes them nothing because their devotion was never truly for Him.

This warning speaks to every generation. The temptation to parade spirituality is universal, whether through ostentatious charity, verbose prayers designed to impress, or conspicuous fasting meant to signal devotion. Jesus exposes the heart beneath such behaviour: it craves approval from people rather than intimacy with God.

Practicing righteousness "in secret"

Jesus contrasts public religiosity with hidden devotion. He commands His disciples to give, pray, and fast in ways seen only by "your Father, who is unseen" (vv. 4, 6, 18). This does not mean literal secrecy in all circumstances but cultivating a posture where the audience for our devotion is God alone. The repeated refrain - *"your Father, who sees what is done in secret, will reward you"* – assures us that nothing done for God escapes His notice.

True righteousness seeks God's pleasure, never the applause of others. It delights in intimacy with the Father rather than public image.

Giving to the needy: Quiet generosity

Jesus begins with almsgiving: *"When you give to the needy, do not announce it with trumpets... But when you give... do not let your left hand know what your right hand is doing."* (vv. 2–3). In Jewish culture, giving to the poor was an established duty rooted in God's law (Deuteronomy 15:7–11). Yet some gave publicly in ways designed to enhance their reputation. Whether literal trumpets were used or Jesus is speaking figuratively, His point is clear: generosity distorted by self-promotion is not generosity at all.

Instead, He calls for such quiet, almost unconscious giving that *"your left hand does not know what your right hand is doing."* This hyperbolic image underscores the purity of motive required: giving should be so natural and unselfconscious that it seeks no recognition, not even from oneself.

Paul reflects this same ethic in 2 Corinthians 9:7: *"Each of you should give what you have decided in your heart to give, not reluctantly or under compulsion, for God loves a cheerful giver."* True generosity is joyful, humble, and God-directed, not image-driven.

Prayer: Intimacy, not performance

Jesus next addresses prayer. He warns against *"hypocrites"* who *"love to pray standing in the synagogues and on the street corners to be seen by others."* (v. 5). Public prayer in itself was not wrong; Jewish custom included public blessings and prayers. The issue, once again, is motive: prayer that becomes a platform for display loses its essence. Jesus calls His followers instead to private prayer: *"Go into your room, close the door and pray to your Father."* (v.6). This image evokes intimacy rather than performance. Prayer is not about impressing others with eloquence or piety but communing with God in the quiet place where no audience exists but Him.

This instruction echoes Psalm 91:1: *"Whoever dwells in the shelter of the Most High will rest in the shadow of the Almighty."* Prayer is dwelling in that hidden shelter, seeking the Father's face away from the gaze of the crowd.

Fasting: Joyful secrecy

Finally, Jesus addresses fasting. In Jewish tradition, fasting expressed repentance, mourning, or intense devotion (Joel 2:12; Ezra 8:23). By Jesus' day, it was common for devout Jews to fast twice a week (Luke 18:12). Yet some made a show of their fasting, *"disfiguring their faces"* (v. 16) to elicit admiration for their self-denial.

Jesus instructs: *"When you fast, put oil on your head and wash your face."* (v. 17) - in other words, look normal. Fasting should be a private matter of devotion between the believer and God, not an exercise in public image. Like giving and prayer, fasting must be Godward in motive and hidden from human view.

The common thread: An audience of one

Across giving, prayer, and fasting, Jesus underscores a single principle: live before the Father's eyes alone. His repeated phrase - *"your Father, who sees what is done in secret, will reward you"* - draws our attention upward. Our reward is not fleeting human praise but eternal fellowship with God Himself.

This hiddenness also protects against pride. When we cultivate a secret devotional life - generosity unknown to others, prayers uttered in solitude, fasting invisible to all but God - we train our hearts to seek Him alone. This is the antidote to spiritual hypocrisy.

Kingdom righteousness: Inside out

Matthew 6 marks a shift from outward righteousness (how we treat others) to inward righteousness (our relationship with God). Both are essential. Kingdom living is not merely about ethical behaviour toward others but also about cultivating a heart fixed on the Father.

Jesus warns us: it is possible to *"do the right things"* for the wrong reasons. The Pharisees exemplified this - scrupulously religious but inwardly far from God (Matthew 23:27). True discipleship demands a righteousness deeper than external compliance; it flows from a heart whose reward is found in God alone.

"Give us today our daily bread" – Daily dependence

Here Jesus teaches simplicity in petition. We ask not for luxury or excess but for "daily bread" — enough for today. This reflects trust in God's ongoing provision, echoing Israel's manna in the wilderness (Exodus 16). It reminds us to live in present dependence rather than anxious stockpiling for the future.

Forgiveness and spiritual protection

Jesus' prayer also prioritizes relational and spiritual needs:

➢ *"Forgive us our debts, as we also have forgiven our debtors" (v. 12):* Prayer involves confession and grace. As recipients of forgiveness, we extend it to others.
➢ *"Deliver us from the evil one" (v. 13):* Prayer acknowledges our vulnerability and asks God for His spiritual protection, recognizing that we live amid ongoing temptation and opposition.

These petitions ground us in humility and dependence, reinforcing that hidden righteousness is not self-sufficiency but continual reliance on God.

Prayer as the heart of secret righteousness

In teaching the Lord's Prayer, Jesus shows that prayer is the engine of hidden devotion. It sustains giving and fasting, nurtures intimacy with the Father, and shapes the inner life from which all outward righteousness flows.

The Lord's Prayer trains us to seek first God's name, His kingdom, and His will. It aligns us with His priorities and forms us into people whose hidden life with Him is rich and vibrant.

Note: For an in-depth examination of The Lord's Prayer, please see my book, *"Lord, Teach us to Pray."*

Forgiveness and prayer: A critical connection

Immediately following The Lord's Prayer, Jesus underscores one petition in particular: forgiveness. He says, *"For if you forgive other people when they sin against you, your heavenly Father will also forgive you. But if you do not forgive others their sins, your Father will not forgive your sins."* (Matthew 6:14–15).

This direct statement highlights the inseparable link between our experience of God's forgiveness and our willingness to forgive others. As you will know from your broader reading of the New Testament, forgiveness is never earned by forgiving others, but it is evidence that we truly grasp the mercy we've received. A heart that clings to resentment reveals it has not fully understood grace, and therefore, it will not fully experience the power of God's forgiveness.

In kingdom living, forgiveness is paramount because it mirrors God's own heart. When we refuse to forgive, we erect barriers to intimacy with Him. Jesus emphasizes this connection because forgiveness is foundational to prayer: we cannot stand in God's presence, revelling in His mercy, while withholding mercy from others.

Forgiveness as an act of obedience

Forgiving those who have wronged us is rarely easy, but it is an act of obedience grounded in trust. We release our claim to vengeance not because the offense is too trivial but because we choose to entrust justice to God (Romans 12:19). As we forgive, we experience a deeper freedom and a clearer channel of communion with the Father.

Fasting: Dependence, Not display

Jesus concludes this section with fasting, warning: *"When you fast, do not look sombre as the hypocrites do... But when you fast, put oil on your head and wash your face."* (Matthew 6:16–17).

Fasting, like giving and prayer, was a respected practice in Jewish piety. Yet many turned it into a stage for self-promotion, drawing attention to their sacrifice. By contrast, Jesus reframes fasting as a private expression of our dependence on God. Its purpose is not deprivation just for deprivation's sake but the reorientation of our appetites toward Him. In fasting, we declare that God is our true sustenance: *"Man shall not live on bread alone, but on every word that comes from the mouth of God."* (Matthew 4:4).

Fasting as spiritual hunger

Fasting creates space to seek God with undivided focus. As we abstain from food or other comforts, we allow physical hunger to remind us of our deeper hunger for God. This is why Joel 2:12 links fasting with returning to God *"with all your heart."*

Hidden fasting intensifies prayer and dependence. It strips away self-reliance and trains us to find satisfaction not in earthly provisions but in the Father's presence. It shifts our question from, *"What am I giving up?"* to *"What am I seeking?"*

The reward of hidden devotion

Jesus repeats the refrain three times: *"Your Father, who sees what is done in secret, will reward you."* (vv. 4, 6, 18). This promise frames this entire passage. The reward is not the applause of others, admiration, or earthly gain. It is deeper communion with God Himself - seeing His face, knowing His presence, and being shaped into His likeness.

Hidden righteousness reorients our lives around this reward. We learn to live for an audience of One, confident that His gaze is enough. This is the heart of kingdom living: trading fleeting approval from people for eternal delight in God.

Contrast with Performative Religion

Jesus' critique of hypocrisy exposes the complete emptiness of performative religion. Religion performed for human eyes is hollow, seeking honour now but forfeiting eternal reward.

True righteousness is unseen not because it is hiding from accountability but because it rests securely in God's sight alone. This principle runs throughout Scripture.

In 1 Samuel 16:7, God reminds Samuel: *"The Lord does not look at the things people look at. People look at the outward appearance, but the Lord looks at the heart."* Kingdom righteousness is heart-deep. It is invisible to many but fully visible to God.

Living before the Father's eyes

The phrase *"your Father who sees"* is one of the most comforting truths in this whole passage. We are never unnoticed. Our quiet prayers, hidden sacrifices, and unseen obedience are fully known and cherished by Him.

Psalm 56:8 beautifully captures this reality: *"You keep track of all my sorrows. You have collected all my tears in your bottle. You have recorded each one in your book."* Nothing escapes His gaze. This frees us from the exhausting cycle of seeking human recognition. Our lives are lived under His tender and attentive eye.

The inner life as the root of the outer life

Matthew 6 teaches that public righteousness flows from private devotion. Jesus is not dismissing public acts of faith – back in Matthew 5:14 He has already called His disciples to be, *"the light of the world"* - but He insists that the light we shine must be fuelled by the oil of a hidden life with God.

Without this hidden root system, public righteousness becomes brittle, performative, and unsustainable. Just as a tree cannot bear fruit without deep roots, our outward witness cannot endure without secret communion with the Father.

Practicing hiddenness in a public world

In our modern culture, where social media and constant visibility tempt us to display every good deed, Jesus' words are more urgent than ever. We must intentionally cultivate these hidden practices:

- Give anonymously where possible.
- Pray without broadcasting our piety.
- Fast quietly, resisting the urge to signal our devotion.

These habits silence the craving for recognition and train us to find sufficiency in God alone.

Transitioning to the next section: Treasures in heaven

This teaching on hidden righteousness seamlessly leads into Jesus' next warning against storing up *"treasures on earth"* (Matthew 6:19). Both address the heart's orientation: do we live for human praise or for God's reward? Do we seek security in what is visible or in what is unseen?

By grounding righteousness in secret devotion, Jesus prepares His disciples to renounce earthly treasure and set their hearts wholly on heaven. The unseen life before God fuels the visible life of kingdom obedience.

The Father Who sees in secret

Jesus' call to practice righteousness in secret is not about withdrawing from the world but about anchoring our lives in the Father's gaze. True righteousness is not validated by applause but by intimacy with Him. Giving, prayer, and fasting are not performances to be displayed but lifelines drawing us deeper into His heart.

When we live this way, our outward witness becomes authentic and compelling - not because we seek to impress, but because we have been transformed in the secret place. The world sees the fruit, but only the Father knows the root.

As Jesus now turns in Matthew 6:19-34 to treasures, worry, and trust, He continues this theme: living for the unseen, eternal realities of His kingdom rather than the fleeting approval or security of this world. Hidden devotion is the foundation for this freedom.

- 19 -

TREASURES IN HEAVEN: WHERE YOUR HEART IS

Matthew 6:19–24

"Do not store up for yourselves treasures on earth, where moths and vermin destroy, and where thieves break in and steal. But store up for yourselves treasures in heaven, where moths and vermin do not destroy, and where thieves do not break in and steal. For where your treasure is, there your heart will be also.

The eye is the lamp of the body. If your eyes are healthy, your whole body will be full of light. But if your eyes are unhealthy, your whole body will be full of darkness. If then the light within you is darkness, how great is that darkness!

No one can serve two masters. Either you will hate the one and love the other, or you will be devoted to the one and despise the other. You cannot serve both God and money."

The call to redirect our treasure

In this section of the Sermon on the Mount, Jesus addresses the fundamental question of what we value most. His opening command is stark: *"Do not store up for yourselves treasures on earth."* (v. 19). Earthly treasures are so vulnerable - moths eat clothing, vermin ruin stored grain, and thieves steal wealth. In other words, everything in this world is subject to decay and loss.

Instead, Jesus calls His disciples to invest in *"treasures in heaven."* (v.20) - lasting riches that can never be corroded, or stolen, or diminished. These heavenly treasures are not material but spiritual: they include righteousness, acts of mercy, sacrificial generosity, obedience, faithfulness, and the reward of intimacy with God. This teaching echoes His earlier command: "Your Father, who sees what is done in secret, will reward you" (Matthew 6:4, 6, 18). Jesus shifts our focus from temporary wealth and acclaim to eternal realities. His logic is simple: if earthly treasures perish and heavenly treasures endure, why would we stake our lives on what we cannot keep?

Treasures reveal the heart

Jesus' statement, *"For where your treasure is, there your heart will be also."* (v. 21), is pivotal. Our treasures are not merely indicators of our priorities; they actively shape our hearts. Whatever we prize most will command our affection, direct our decisions, and capture our loyalty.

If we store up earthly wealth, our hearts become tethered to this world, consumed by anxiety over protecting and increasing what we have. If we invest in heavenly treasure, our hearts become oriented toward God's kingdom, seeking first His righteousness (Matthew 6:33).

This truth forces us to ask probing questions:

➢ What do I value most?
➢ Where do my time, energy, and resources go?
➢ What does my spending, giving, and dreaming reveal about where my heart truly is?

Our treasure and our heart are inseparable. One always follows the other.

Earthly treasures: The illusion of security

We often pursue earthly treasure because it promises security, identity, and satisfaction. Wealth appears to offer control over our lives and insulation from uncertainty. Yet Jesus dismantles this illusion. Material wealth is inherently temporary and fragile. A single economic downturn, natural disaster, or personal crisis can strip it away.

Proverbs 23:4–5 warns: *"Do not wear yourself out to get rich... Cast but a glance at riches, and they are gone, for they will surely sprout wings and fly off to the sky like an eagle."* Wealth is fleeting by nature; tying our hearts to it is like anchoring ourselves to smoke. Moreover, earthly treasures compete for our devotion. They subtly enslave us, demanding attention and affection that rightly belong to God. As Jesus will conclude in verse 24: *"You cannot serve both God and money."*

Heavenly treasures: A lasting investment

In contrast, heavenly treasures are incorruptible. They are not susceptible to moth, rust, or theft because they exist in the eternal realm where God reigns. These treasures include:

> *Character shaped by righteousness:* Every step of obedience stores eternal value (Galatians 6:8–9).

> *Acts of love and mercy:* Jesus said that even giving *"a cup of cold water"* in His name will not go unrewarded (Matthew 10:42).

> *Generosity toward the poor:* Proverbs 19:17 declares, *"Whoever is kind to the poor lends to the Lord, and he will reward them for what they have done."*

> *Faithfulness in suffering:* Enduring trials for Christ builds treasure in heaven (2 Corinthians 4:17–18).

Heavenly treasure is not earned salvation but the fruit of kingdom living. These are the riches that follow us into eternity, reflecting lives aligned with God's purposes.

The eye as the lamp of the body

Jesus then shifts to a metaphor in verse 22: *"The eye is the lamp of the body."* In Jewish thought, the eye symbolized focus and intention. A *"healthy"* (literally *"single"* or *"clear"*) eye represents undivided vision fixed on God. When our focus is pure, our whole life is *"full of light"* - illuminated by His truth and oriented toward His kingdom.

By contrast, an *"unhealthy"* (literally *"evil"*) eye is clouded by greed, envy, or divided loyalties. Such vision fills the body with "darkness," distorting our perception and leading us astray. Jesus warns: *"If then the light within you is darkness, how great is that darkness!"* (v. 23). Spiritual blindness is devastating because it mistakes darkness for light. This imagery connects directly to treasure: what we fix our gaze upon shapes our entire being. If our eyes are set on earthly wealth, our lives will be darkened by its deceit. If our eyes are fixed on God and His kingdom, His light floods every area of our lives.

Singleness of vision and devotion

The *"healthy eye"* calls for single-minded devotion. James 1:8 warns that *"the double-minded person is unstable in all they do."* Divided focus produces divided loyalties, leaving us torn between competing masters. Jesus presses this point to its climax in verse 24.

Two masters: God or money

"No one can serve two masters," Jesus declares (v. 24). This is not merely some advice about priorities but a statement of fact. Servanthood in Jesus' time implied exclusive ownership; a slave could not belong to two masters simultaneously. In the same way, we cannot live under the lordship of both God and money.

Jesus personifies money (the Greek term is *mammon*) as a rival deity vying for our worship. To serve mammon is to place ultimate trust in wealth for security, identity, and meaning. But devotion to money inevitably displaces devotion to God. As Jesus says, *"You will hate the one and love the other… You cannot serve both."*

This forces a clear choice: Who will be our master? Will we anchor our hearts in God's eternal kingdom or in the fragile economy of this world?

The heart of the matter: Allegiance

At its core, this teaching is not just about money; it is about allegiance. Jesus is calling His disciples to undivided loyalty to God. Treasure, vision, and master are all interconnected:

> What we **treasure** determines where our hearts dwell.
> What our **eyes** focus on determines how we see reality.
> What **master** we serve determines whom we ultimately obey.

Kingdom living requires a reorientation of all three - fixing our hearts on heaven, our gaze upon God, and our service to Him alone.

Investing in heavenly treasure

Jesus' command to *"store up for yourselves treasures in heaven."* (v. 20) is not merely negative (avoiding earthly hoarding) but profoundly positive. He invites us to redirect our resources, time, and energy into what has eternal value. How do we do this in practical terms?

1. Generosity toward the poor and needy

One direct way we can lay up heavenly treasure now is through generosity. Scripture consistently links giving to eternal reward. In Matthew 19:21 Jesus told the rich young ruler , *"Sell your possessions and give to the poor, and you will have treasure in heaven."*

Generosity loosens our grip on material wealth and reflects God's own character as a giver. Proverbs 19:17 assures us: *"Whoever is kind to the poor lends to the Lord, and he will reward them for what they have done."* When we bless others, we are investing in what cannot be taken from us.

2. Serving others in Christ's name

Acts of service, whether public or unseen, build eternal treasure as they mirror Christ's own servant heart. Matthew 25:34–36 depicts the final judgment where Jesus rewards those who fed the hungry, welcomed strangers, and clothed the naked, saying, *"Whatever you did for one of the least of these brothers and sisters of mine, you did for me."* Every simple act of kindness done in His name has eternal weight. Serving others shifts our focus from self-centred accumulation to kingdom-centred generosity.

3. Pursuing kingdom priorities

We store up heavenly treasure by orienting our lives around God's mission. This includes proclaiming the gospel, discipling others, supporting missions, and using our gifts to advance His kingdom. Paul describes this investment in Philippians 4:17, where he commends the Philippians' financial support of his ministry: *"Not that I desire your gifts; what I desire is that more be credited to your account."* Kingdom work produces fruit that carries eternal reward.

4. Cultivating Godly character

Treasure is not only about what we do but who we become. The fruit of the Spirit (Galatians 5:22–23) - love, joy, peace, patience, kindness, goodness, faithfulness, gentleness, and self-control - forms part of our eternal inheritance. As our hearts become conformed to Christ, we reflect His glory and invest in the one treasure that cannot be lost: likeness to Him.

The dangers of materialism

Jesus' warning here about earthly treasure is especially relevant for today, where consumerism dominates culture. Materialism promises happiness but delivers bondage. It enslaves us to the endless pursuit of more, while fuelling anxiety about what we already have.

1. The illusion of control

We often think wealth can shield us from life's uncertainties. But Jesus calls this foolishness. In Luke 12:16–21, He tells the parable of the rich fool who built bigger barns to store his grain, only to die that very night. *"This is how it will be with whoever stores up things for themselves but is not rich toward God."* (v. 21). Wealth can create the illusion of control, but it cannot secure our lives.

2. The subtle tyranny of "mammon"

Jesus personifies money (*mammon*) as a rival master because it demands worship-like devotion. We check our investments obsessively, fear losing our possessions, and evaluate worth by net worth. Before long, money dictates our choices, relationships, and priorities. Paul warns of this in 1 Timothy 6:9–10: *"Those who want to get rich fall into temptation and a trap... For the love of money is a root of all kinds of evil."* The danger is not in wealth itself but in its capacity to dominate our hearts.

3. Anxiety and attachment

Materialism breeds anxiety. The more we own today, the more we worry about protecting it. This is why Jesus later says, *"Do not worry about your life."* (Matthew 6:25).

Hoarded treasure ties our hearts to this world, making us fearful of loss and reluctant to give. In contrast, detachment from material wealth brings peace. When our treasure is in heaven, we are free from the tyranny of *"what if."* We can hold possessions loosely because our security is anchored elsewhere.

The freedom of singleness of devotion

Jesus' statement, *"No one can serve two masters."* (v. 24), confronts us with a stark choice: Who or what will rule our lives? We cannot serve both God and money because each demands exclusive loyalty. Divided allegiance drains us spiritually, leaving us torn between incompatible loves.

1. The clarity of single focus

A *"healthy eye"* (v. 22) is one fixed singularly on God. When our vision is clear, our lives are flooded with His light. We see possessions not as ultimate but as tools for kingdom purposes. We see success not as wealth accumulation but as faithfulness to Him. Single-hearted devotion simplifies life. It frees us from chasing competing gods and allows us to pour ourselves fully into the service of one: the living God.

2. Joyful release of earthly claims

When God is our master, we hold possessions lightly. We become stewards rather than owners, seeing our resources as entrusted by Him for His glory. This perspective enables joyful giving rather than reluctant obligation, because we know our true treasure lies elsewhere.

Hebrews 10:34 describes early Christians who *"joyfully accepted the confiscation of your property, because you knew that you yourselves had better and lasting possessions."* Their grip on earthly treasure was loosened by their confidence in heavenly reward.

3. Rest from the burden of rival masters

Serving money is exhausting because it is never satisfied. No matter how much we earn or save, it whispers, *"Just a little more."*

By contrast, serving God brings rest: *"Come to me, all you who are weary and burdened, and I will give you rest."* (Matthew 11:28). Single devotion will lift that crushing burden of striving for approval, status, or financial security. We discover the joy of living under the care of a generous Father.

Practical steps toward kingdom treasuring

To realign our hearts and treasures, we can take intentional steps:

- ➢ *Audit our spending:* Where our money goes reveals where our heart is. Redirecting even small amounts toward generosity trains us to value eternal priorities.
- ➢ *Practice gratitude:* Regularly thank God for what you have, loosening envy and discontent.
- ➢ *Simplify:* Deliberately resist consumer pressures by choosing contentment and freeing resources for kingdom purposes.
- ➢ *Give sacrificially:* Stretching generosity breaks materialism's grip and lays up heavenly treasure.
- ➢ *Refocus vision daily:* Begin each day praying, *"Lord, fix my eyes on You, not on earthly things."*

Living with an eternal perspective

Paul captures Jesus' teaching in Colossians 3:1–2: *"Since, then, you have been raised with Christ, set your hearts on things above... Set your minds on things above, not on earthly things."* This eternal perspective reshapes how we view money, time, and ambition. When our hearts are anchored in heaven, earthly wealth loses its power. We see ourselves as pilgrims passing through, investing in what will matter forever.

The treasure test

Ultimately, Jesus' teaching on treasure is a test of allegiance. It asks: Where is your heart? What do you love most? What are you building your life upon? Treasures on earth are fragile, fleeting, and vulnerable.

Treasures in heaven are secure, eternal, and anchored in God Himself. Choosing between them is not merely about financial priorities but about ultimate loyalty. As Jesus concludes this section with *"You cannot serve both God and money."* (v. 24), He draws a clear line. True disciples must choose their master. The freedom, joy, and security of kingdom living belong to those who serve God alone, investing in the treasure that cannot be lost.

Diagnosing divided loyalties

Jesus' teaching exposes a tension many of us feel: the pull between God and money, between eternal priorities and temporal concerns. Diagnosing this tension is crucial because divided loyalties weaken discipleship and dim our spiritual vision.

1. Signs of serving money over God

We may not consciously *"serve"* money, but subtle patterns will reveal its influence:

> *Anxiety over finances:* Persistent worry about provision may indicate misplaced trust.
> *Stinginess or reluctance to give:* When generosity feels threatening rather than joyful, our hearts may be clinging to possessions.
> *Identity tied to wealth or status:* If success, value, or self-worth depend on financial standing, money has become a master.
> *Decisions driven by profit over principle:* Prioritizing gain over obedience reveals compromised allegiance.

Jesus' words in Matthew 6:21 - *"Where your treasure is, there your heart will be also"* - invite honest self-examination. What we prize most reveals who we truly serve.

2. The subtle drift of compromise

Divided loyalty often develops gradually. We begin by desiring financial security or comfort, but over time those desires can displace kingdom priorities.

Like the seed *"choked by the worries of this life and the deceitfulness of wealth."* (Matthew 13:22), spiritual fruit withers when our hearts are entangled in earthly pursuits. This is why Jesus insists on an either/or: *"You cannot serve both God and money."* (v. 24). Half-measures are impossible because each master demands exclusive devotion. One will inevitably dominate.

Examples of radical generosity

Throughout Scripture and church history, we see vivid examples of believers who broke free from divided loyalties through radical generosity. Their lives illustrate Jesus' teaching in action.

1. The transformation of Zacchaeus (Luke 19:1–10)

When Zacchaeus encountered Jesus, his grip on wealth was instantly loosened: *"Look, Lord! Here and now I give half of my possessions to the poor, and if I have cheated anybody… I will pay back four times the amount."* (v. 8). His generosity was not coerced; it was the spontaneous overflow of a heart which had been newly captured by Christ. Jesus' response - *"Today salvation has come to this house."* (v. 9) - shows that Zacchaeus' open-handedness was evidence of genuine conversion. His treasure shifted from riches to relationship with Jesus.

2. The widow's offering (Mark 12:41–44)

Jesus praised the widow who gave *"two very small copper coins"* because she gave *"all she had to live on."* Her offering was tiny by worldly standards but immense in devotion. Unlike the rich who gave surplus, she entrusted herself wholly to God's care. Her treasure was not her last coins but her faith in Him.

3. The early Church (Acts 2:44–45)

In Jerusalem, the first believers *"sold property and possessions to give to anyone who had need."* Their radical generosity flowed from their newfound identity in Christ and anticipation of His kingdom. By loosening their hold on their possessions, they demonstrated that their true treasure was eternal and communal rather than individual. This spirit of open-handedness fuelled the church's explosive growth. Outsiders were drawn not only to their preaching but to their countercultural generosity, which testified to a new way of life.

4. Modern examples

Even today, countless believers are practicing this kingdom ethic. Stories abound of families downsizing to free resources for missions, professionals refusing very lucrative and yet unethical opportunities, or churches pooling resources to eliminate debt burdens within their communities. These examples remind us: treasure-shifting is not abstract theology; it is lived daily in choices that reflect trust in God's reward over earthly gain.

Freedom found in surrender

Paradoxically, releasing our grip on earthly treasure liberates us. When our hearts are anchored in heaven, we are no longer enslaved by fear of loss, competition, or comparison. We can live with open hands, knowing that our inheritance *"can never perish, spoil or fade."* (1 Peter 1:4).

This freedom also dismantles anxiety. As Jesus will soon teach in Matthew 6:25–34, our worry over provision dissipates when we remember that our Father feeds the birds and clothes the lilies. If our treasure is with Him, our hearts can rest secure.

Training the heart for heaven

Because *"where your treasure is, there your heart will be also,"* shifting treasure also trains the heart. As we deliberately invest in heavenly pursuits - through generosity, service, worship, and obedience - our affections follow. Giving aligns our hearts with God's priorities, deepening our love for Him and loosening worldly attachments.

This principle works both ways:

➤ Hoarding earthly treasure strengthens love for the world.
➤ Investing in heavenly treasure strengthens love for God.

Spiritual practices like regular giving and intentional simplicity are not merely duties; they are tools for reorienting desire. They teach our hearts to treasure what is truly valuable.

The link to trust and anxiety

Jesus' teaching here on treasure naturally flows into His next command: *"Do not worry about your life"* (Matthew 6:25). Anxiety about provision often springs from misplaced treasure. When we store up earthly wealth, we feel vulnerable because it can be lost. But when our treasure is in heaven, we are freed from fear because nothing can touch what matters most.

In other words, our treasure will dictate our trust. If our security rests in our bank accounts, possessions, or career, we will be consumed by worry. But if our confidence is in God, we can live lightly in this world, trusting our Father's care. This is why Jesus moves seamlessly from treasure to trust. He is inviting His disciples into a worry-free life grounded in the assurance of God's provision.

The exclusive claim of God's kingdom

Ultimately, Jesus' call is to undivided allegiance. His language - *"You will hate the one and love the other… You cannot serve both"* - reveals that the kingdom tolerates no rivals. We must choose: either God is our supreme treasure or something else is.

This exclusivity is not harsh but liberating. Serving two masters is exhausting; it divides our loyalties and burdens our hearts. Serving God alone brings clarity, rest, and freedom because our lives are simplified under His reign.

The heart examined by treasure

Jesus' teaching compels us to examine ourselves:

> ➢ What dominates my thoughts - God's kingdom or my financial goals?
> ➢ Do I give generously, or do I hold back out of fear?
> ➢ Do I make decisions based on eternal values or short-term gain?
> ➢ When I feel insecure, do I run to my bank account or to my Father?

These questions help us discern whether our treasure truly lies in heaven or whether earthly wealth has subtly captured our hearts.

Preparing for the call to trust (Matthew 6:25–34)

This section sets the stage for one of Jesus' most comforting teachings: freedom from worry. The link is clear: once we shift our treasure to heaven and submit wholly to God as Master, we can rest in His provision. Anxiety fades because our hearts are anchored in Him, not in fragile earthly security.

This transition is crucial: Jesus moves from what we treasure to how we trust. The heart released from materialism is now ready to hear, *"Seek first his kingdom and his righteousness, and all these things will be given to you as well."* (Matthew 6:33).

Choosing our treasure, fixing our eyes

Matthew 6:19–24 calls us to a decisive reordering of our lives. Jesus confronts us with two treasures (earthly vs. heavenly), two visions (light vs. darkness), and two masters (God vs. money). Neutrality is impossible; our hearts will serve one or the other.

Choosing heavenly treasure frees us from anxiety, reshapes our desires, and aligns us with the kingdom. It opens the door to the trust-filled life Jesus describes next - a life liberated from fear because it rests securely in the Father's care.

- 20 -

TRUSTING THE FATHER'S PROVISION

Matthew 6:25–34

"Therefore I tell you, do not worry about your life, what you will eat or drink; or about your body, what you will wear. Is not life more than food, and the body more than clothes? Look at the birds of the air; they do not sow or reap or store away in barns, and yet your heavenly Father feeds them. Are you not much more valuable than they? Can any one of you by worrying add a single hour to your life?

And why do you worry about clothes? See how the flowers of the field grow. They do not labour or spin. Yet I tell you that not even Solomon in all his splendour was dressed like one of these. If that is how God clothes the grass of the field, which is here today and tomorrow is thrown into the fire, will he not much more clothe you — you of little faith?

So do not worry, saying, 'What shall we eat?' or 'What shall we drink?' or 'What shall we wear?' For the pagans run after all these things, and your heavenly Father knows that you need them. But seek first his kingdom and his righteousness, and all these things will be given to you as well. Therefore, do not worry about tomorrow, for tomorrow will worry about itself. Each day has enough trouble of its own."

The connection to treasure and trust

Jesus begins with *"Therefore,"* clearly linking this teaching to His previous words about treasure and masters (Matthew 6:19–24). Once we choose God over money as our ultimate master and shift our treasure to heaven, we are free to live without anxiety. Worry is rooted in misplaced trust - when our hearts are tied to earthly security, fear inevitably follows.

If our treasure is fragile and our master is uncertain, anxiety dominates. But if God is our treasure and our Father, we can rest in His care. This passage builds upon that truth, inviting us into a life of deep trust in His provision.

The nature of worry

Jesus addresses three fundamental human concerns: food, drink, and clothing - the basic necessities of life. He is not dismissing their importance but challenging our tendency to obsess over them. Worry magnifies needs until they dominate our minds, crowding out trust in God.

In the Greek, the word for *"worry"* (*merimnao*) literally means *"to be divided"* or *"pulled apart."* Worry fractures our focus, splitting our hearts between fear and faith. It drains energy from the present and projects us into imagined futures we cannot control.

Jesus gently but firmly asks: *"Can any one of you by worrying add a single hour to your life?"* (v. 27). Worry is futile. It changes nothing about tomorrow and only robs today of peace.

The birds of the air: Lessons in provision

Jesus directs His disciples to creation: *"Look at the birds of the air."* (v. 26). Birds neither sow nor reap nor store in barns, yet God feeds them. They live in daily dependence on His provision without anxious toil. The point is not that we should be idle. Birds still work - they gather food diligently - but they do so without worry because they live within the natural rhythms God has designed. Their provision comes ultimately from His hand.

Jesus then makes the key comparison: *"Are you not much more valuable than they?"* If God cares for birds - creatures of small worth - how much more will He care for His children, who bear His image and are redeemed by His Son? This is an argument from lesser to greater: if God provides for the least, He will certainly provide for the greatest.

The flowers of the field: Lessons in beauty

Jesus next turns to the lilies: *"See how the flowers of the field grow. They do not labour or spin. Yet I tell you that not even Solomon in all his splendour was dressed like one of these."* (vv. 28–29). The beauty of wildflowers, fleeting and unlaboured, surpasses even the wealth of Israel's greatest king.

If God lavishes such splendour on grass that *"is here today and tomorrow is thrown into the fire."* (v. 30), how much more will He clothe His children? Jesus uses this vivid image to rebuke *"little faith."* Worry reveals that we doubt either God's care or His power. Trusting His provision frees us from anxious striving over appearances or status.

The pagan pursuit

Jesus contrasts His disciples with *"the pagans"* who *"run after all these things."* (v. 32). The word *"run after"* (*epizēteō*) suggests a frantic pursuit. Those who do not know God scramble to secure their needs because they believe their lives depend solely on their own efforts.

In a world without a heavenly Father, anxiety will be inevitable. Survival depends entirely on what you can acquire and protect. But Jesus' followers live in a different reality: *"Your heavenly Father knows that you need them."* We are not abandoned to self-sufficiency; we are cared for by One who knows us intimately and provides for us lovingly.

Seek first His kingdom and His righteousness

At the heart of this passage is Jesus' positive command: *"Seek first his kingdom and his righteousness, and all these things will be given to you as well."* (v. 33). This is the best possible antidote to worry. Instead of chasing provision, we pursue the reign of God in our lives and trust Him to supply our needs.

Seeking God's kingdom means aligning our lives with His rule - prioritizing His purposes, submitting to His will, and living out His righteousness. It means our chief concern is not what we eat, drink, or wear but how we honour Him and advance His kingdom.

When we reorder all our priorities around God's kingdom, provision falls into its rightful place. The Father knows what we need, and He promises to meet those needs as we put Him first. This does not guarantee luxury, but sufficiency rooted in His faithfulness.

Freedom from tomorrow's anxiety

Jesus concludes with a final exhortation: *"Do not worry about tomorrow, for tomorrow will worry about itself. Each day has enough trouble of its own."* (v. 34). This is not a call to recklessness or irresponsibility but to trust-filled living one day at a time. Worry projects us into future problems we cannot control. Jesus invites us to stay in today's grace. God gives strength for the present moment, not for hypothetical futures. By focusing on today's faithfulness rather than tomorrow's fears, we experience His peace.

This echoes Lamentations 3:22–23: *"Because of the Lord's great love we are not consumed... They are new every morning; great is your faithfulness."* God's provision and mercies are daily, not stored in advance. Like Israel (in Exodus 16), gathering manna whilst in the wilderness, we learn to depend on Him afresh each day.

The root of worry: Little faith

Jesus identifies worry as a faith issue: *"You of little faith"* (v. 30). Anxiety reveals where our trust is thin. It exposes doubts about God's goodness, His attentiveness, or His ability to provide. This diagnosis is not condemnation but invitation. Jesus calls His disciples into deeper trust, reminding them of the Father's care. Faith grows as we recall His past provision, meditate on His promises, and choose to surrender our fears to Him.

The Fatherhood of God: The basis of trust

The foundation of this passage is the fatherhood of God. Over and over, Jesus anchors His commands in this powerful truth: *"Your heavenly Father knows."* Unlike pagan deities who are indifferent or capricious, our God is relational, attentive, and loving. Romans 8:32 reinforces this confidence: *"He who did not spare his own Son, but gave him up for us all – how will he not also, along with him, graciously give us all things?"* If God has already given us His greatest gift - His Son - how can we doubt His willingness to provide for our lesser needs? Knowing God as our Father transforms how we approach life. Anxiety diminishes when we rest in His care, like children secure in a parent's arms.

Practical steps to overcome worry

Jesus' command *"do not worry"* is both simple and profoundly challenging. He does not merely tell us to stop worrying but redirects our hearts toward active trust in the Father. Overcoming worry involves intentional practices that shift our focus from fear to faith.

1. Replace worry with prayer

Paul echoes Jesus' teaching here in Philippians 4:6–7: *"Do not be anxious about anything, but in every situation, by prayer and petition, with thanksgiving, present your requests to God. And the peace of God… will guard your hearts and your minds in Christ Jesus."*

Prayer is the antidote to anxiety because it transfers the burden from our shoulders to God's. Each time worry arises, we can turn it into prayer:

➢ **Worry says:** *"What if I don't have enough?"*
➢ **Prayer says:** *"Father, You know my needs. I trust You to provide."*

This habit retrains our reflexes, teaching us to cast *"all your anxiety on him because he cares for you."* (1 Peter 5:7).

2. Focus on today's grace

Jesus calls us to live one day at a time: *"Do not worry about tomorrow… Each day has enough trouble of its own."* (Matthew 6:34). Much of our anxiety is future-oriented, rooted in "what ifs" that may never come to pass. To combat this, we practice staying present. We remind ourselves: God has given grace for today, and tomorrow's grace will meet tomorrow's needs. Like Israel gathering manna daily, we rely on fresh provision each morning (Exodus 16:4).

A practical exercise is to begin each day with this *"Lord, thank You for today's mercies. Help me to trust You for what I need now and leave tomorrow in Your hands."*

3. Meditate on God's creation

Jesus points us to the birds and flowers as living parables of God's care. Nature preaches to us daily if we have eyes to see. Watching birds fed without barns or flowers clothed in beauty they did not labour for is reminding us of our Father's faithful provision. Spending time outdoors, pausing to observe creation, or even keeping a nature journal can cultivate this perspective. Every sparrow and lily whispers: *If God cares for these, how much more for you?*

4. Memorize God's promises

Fighting worry requires filling our minds with Scripture. Verses such as these anchor our hearts in truth:

➢ *"My God will meet all your needs according to the riches of his glory in Christ Jesus."* (Philippians 4:19).
➢ *"The Lord is my shepherd; I lack nothing."* (Psalm 23:1).
➢ *"Those who seek the Lord lack no good thing."* (Psalm 34:10).

When worry strikes, speaking these promises aloud counters fear with faith. Scripture fortifies our minds, reminding us that our Father's provision is sure.

5. Practice gratitude daily

Thanksgiving redirects our focus from what we lack to what we have. By listing daily blessings, we train our hearts to see evidence of God's care. Gratitude combats the scarcity mindset that fuels our worry. Keeping a gratitude journal can often be transformative: writing down even the smallest provisions - an encouraging word, an answered prayer, a meal provided - builds a cumulative record of God's faithfulness.

Seeking the kingdom first

The hinge of Jesus' teaching is His command: *"Seek first his kingdom and his righteousness."* (v. 33). Worry fades when we realign our priorities. Instead of chasing material needs as our highest goal, we fix our hearts on God's reign.

What does it mean to seek the kingdom?

Seeking God's kingdom means:

> *Submitting to His rule in our lives:* Allowing His Word to shape our values, choices, and desires.

> *Prioritizing His mission:* Sharing the gospel, making disciples, and serving others as expressions of His reign.

> *Pursuing righteousness:* Living in obedience, integrity, and holiness, reflecting His character to the world.

When we make His kingdom our first pursuit, material concerns fall into proper perspective. Provision becomes a byproduct, not the focus.

God knows what you need

Jesus reassures us: *"Your heavenly Father knows that you need them."* (v. 32). This statement is profoundly comforting. We do not have to convince God of our needs; He already knows and cares. This is not permission for idleness but liberation from anxiety-driven striving. Our Father's awareness is intimate and personal.

Psalm 139:1–3 declares: *"You have searched me, Lord, and you know me… You are familiar with all my ways."* The One who numbers our hairs (Luke 12:7) will not overlook our daily bread.

The difference between needs and wants

Part of trusting God's provision involves distinguishing between needs and wants. Jesus promises to meet our <u>needs</u> - food, drink, clothing - not every desire we label as essential. Modern culture often blurs this line, feeding discontentment and worry.

Learning contentment, as Paul describes in Philippians 4:11–12, is key: *"I have learned to be content whatever the circumstances… I have learned the secret of being content in any and every situation."* Contentment does not mean apathy; it means resting in God's provision without craving more than He gives. It frees us from worry rooted in comparison or consumerism.

Trust and the character of God

At the core of this passage is the question: *What kind of God do we believe in?* If we see Him as distant or indifferent, worry will dominate our life. But if we see Him as loving Father, intimately involved and perfectly wise, we can release anxiety. Romans 8:28 reinforces this trust: *"We know that in all things God works for the good of those who love him."* Even when provision comes to us differently than we expect, we believe He is working for our ultimate good.

Overcoming the root of "little faith"

Jesus identifies worry as rooted in *"little faith"* (v. 30). This is not a harsh rebuke but an invitation to grow. Faith matures through exercise. Each time we choose trust over fear, our confidence deepens. One practical way to build faith is to record answered prayers and past provisions. Reviewing these testimonies reminds us of God's track record. If He has been faithful before, He will be faithful again.

Daily trust: Living in the present

Jesus' final command - *"Do not worry about tomorrow"* - calls us to live fully in the present. Tomorrow's problems will come with tomorrow's grace. Anxiety collapses when we stay rooted in today. This is not passivity. We plan wisely for the future, but we refuse to live there mentally. We refuse to be consumed by all the imagined "what ifs" that rob us of present peace.

Psalm 118:24 captures this mindset: *"This is the day the Lord has made; let us rejoice and be glad in it."* Trust thrives when we embrace one day at a time, knowing our Father holds both today and tomorrow.

Trust as witness to the world

Finally, living free from worry is itself a powerful witness. In a world riddled with anxiety, peace rooted in God's care is countercultural. When we remain calm amid uncertainty, we display a confidence that draws others to ask: *Where does this peace come from?*

Isaiah 26:3 promises: *"You will keep in perfect peace those whose minds are steadfast, because they trust in you."* Our worry-free trust showcases the reality of our Father's kingdom and invites others into it.

Real-life examples of God's provision

Throughout Scripture and history, we see vivid demonstrations of God's faithful provision. These accounts strengthen our faith, reminding us that the Father who cared for His people then continues to care for us today.

1. Israel's daily manna (Exodus 16:4–30)

When Israel journeyed through the wilderness, they had no means of sustenance. Yet God provided manna each morning, enough for that day only. Attempts to hoard it resulted in spoilage. Through this pattern, God taught His people daily dependence: *"The one who gathered much did not have too much, and the one who gathered little did not have too little."* (Exodus 16:18).

This story parallels Jesus' teaching in Matthew 6: we are to rely on God's provision day by day, trusting Him for each new morning rather than stockpiling anxiously for the future.

2. Elijah and the widow at Zarephath (1 Kings 17:8–16)

In a time of famine, God sent Elijah to a destitute widow with only a handful of flour and a little oil. Yet when she obeyed God's word and shared her last meal, *"the jar of flour was not used up and the jug of oil did not run dry."* God's provision was not lavish but sufficient - enough for each day until the drought ended. This narrative illustrates that God's supply often comes in ordinary, steady ways. He meets needs faithfully, one day at a time.

3. Jesus feeding the multitudes (Matthew 14:13–21)

When faced with thousands of hungry people, Jesus multiplied five loaves and two fish into an abundant feast. The disciples' worry - *"We have here only five loaves"* - was met with Jesus' sufficiency: *"Bring them here to me."*

Jesus then blessed the meagre offering, and it became more than enough. This miracle reminds us that our insufficiency is no obstacle for God. He delights in providing abundantly when we bring Him what little we have.

4. Modern testimonies of provision

Even today, countless believers can attest to God's care:

> ➤ Bills paid unexpectedly at the last moment.
> ➤ Groceries appearing when cupboards were bare.
> ➤ Jobs opening after fervent prayer.

These stories, large and small, testify that Jesus' words are not mere idealism but a lived reality for those who seek first His kingdom.

Habits that strengthen trust

Faith in God's provision is not passive; it grows through deliberate habits that anchor our hearts in His care.

1. Daily surrender in prayer

Begin each day by placing your needs and concerns before God. A simple prayer such as, *"Father, I trust You for today. Provide what I need, guide my steps, and help me rest in Your care,"* frames the day in dependence rather than worry. This daily surrender mirrors Jesus' prayer: *"Give us today our daily bread."* (Matthew 6:11), reminding us to look to Him moment by moment.

2. Keeping a provision journal

Recording instances of God's provision - answers to prayer, financial help, encouragement received - builds a personal history of His faithfulness. In moments of worry, reviewing these entries reassures us: *He provided then; He will provide again.*

3. Intentional simplicity

Practicing simplicity helps us to break anxiety's grip. This might involve decluttering our possessions, reducing our unnecessary spending, or resisting consumer-driven pressure to *"keep up."*

Simplicity quiets our hearts, allowing us to focus on what matters: God's kingdom and His righteousness. Paul models this mindset in 1 Timothy 6:6–8: *"Godliness with contentment is great gain... If we have food and clothing, we will be content with that."*

4. Sharing testimonies in community

Hearing and sharing stories of God's provision strengthens not only personal trust but the faith of the whole church. Testimonies remind us that God is active and faithful. They reframe anxiety as opportunities for God to display His care.

5. Practicing generosity even in lack

Counterintuitively, generosity deepens trust. When we give - even when resources feel tight - we declare that God is our provider, not our bank account.

Malachi 3:10 captures this principle: *"Bring the whole tithe into the storehouse... Test me in this... and see if I will not throw open the floodgates of heaven."* Generosity is not about testing God selfishly but about stepping into His promises and loosening fear's grip.

Trust as kingdom living

When Jesus says we should, *"Seek first his kingdom,"* He ties provision directly to kingdom priorities. Trust in God's care is not separate from discipleship; it is central to it.

A worried heart cannot fully serve God's kingdom because it is preoccupied with self-preservation. But when we rest in the Father's care, we are liberated to pour ourselves into His purposes. We can focus on loving, serving, and proclaiming Christ without being consumed by survival.

Kingdom living means:

➢ Confidence that God's provision frees us from distraction.
➢ Contentment rooted in His sufficiency, not our surplus.
➢ Courage to live generously because we know we are secure in Him.

How this teaching leads into Matthew 7

This passage naturally flows into Matthew 7, where Jesus addresses judgment, prayer, and trust. After calling His disciples to rest in the Father's provision, He will soon invite them to approach that same Father boldly in prayer (Matthew 7:7–11).

This progression is significant:

➤ *Choose your treasure (6:19–24):* Orient your heart toward God.
➤ *Trust the Father's provision (6:25–34):* Release anxiety by resting in His care.
➤ *Approach Him in prayer (7:7–11):* Boldly ask, seek, and knock, confident in His fatherly goodness.

By grounding His disciples in trust, Jesus prepares them for the relational confidence needed to pray persistently and to live without fear of scarcity.

The peace of trusting the Father

Isaiah 26:3 encapsulates this teaching: *"You will keep in perfect peace those whose minds are steadfast, because they trust in you."* Trust and peace are inseparable. As we anchor our minds in God's faithfulness, peace replaces worry.

This is not a naive denial of life's difficulties. Jesus acknowledges that *"each day has enough trouble of its own,"* (Matthew 6:34). But He invites us to face those troubles without fear because the Father's provision is certain.

Trusting God does not remove challenges, but it transforms how we navigate them - with calm assurance rather than restless anxiety.

Conclusion: living free from worry

Jesus' words in Matthew 6:25–34 are both deeply practical and profoundly theological.

They remind us:

> ➤ Life is more than food and clothing.
> ➤ Our value to God surpasses that of birds and flowers.
> ➤ Worry is futile, but trust is fruitful.
> ➤ Seeking God's kingdom first unlocks freedom from anxiety.

To live this way is to embrace our identity as children of a loving Father. It is to wake each morning confident that His mercies are new, His provision is sure, and His kingdom is worth our undivided pursuit.

As we step into Matthew 7, we do so grounded in this assurance: the God Who commands us not to worry is the same God who opens His hands to provide, invites us to pray boldly, and promises to answer as a Father delights in giving good gifts to His children.

21

LIVING IN GRACE AND PRAYER

Matthew 7:1–12

"Do not judge, or you too will be judged. For in the same way you judge others, you will be judged, and with the measure you use, it will be measured to you. Why do you look at the speck of sawdust in your brother's eye and pay no attention to the plank in your own eye? How can you say to your brother, 'Let me take the speck out of your eye,' when all the time there is a plank in your own eye? You hypocrite, first take the plank out of your own eye, and then you will see clearly to remove the speck from your brother's eye.

Do not give dogs what is sacred; do not throw your pearls to pigs. If you do, they may trample them under their feet, and turn and tear you to pieces. Ask and it will be given to you; seek and you will find; knock and the door will be opened to you. For everyone who asks receives; the one who seeks finds; and to the one who knocks, the door will be opened.

Which of you, if your son asks for bread, will give him a stone? Or if he asks for a fish, will give him a snake? If you, then, though you are evil, know how to give good gifts to your children, how much more will your Father in heaven give good gifts to those who ask him! So in everything, do to others what you would have them do to you, for this sums up the Law and the Prophets."

The call to resist judgmentalism

Jesus begins this section with a blunt command: *"Do not judge."* This verse is among the most quoted and misunderstood in Scripture. He is not prohibiting discernment or moral evaluation Later in this passage He calls for wise judgment regarding *"dogs"* and *"pigs"* (v.6). Instead, Jesus condemns this harsh, hypocritical, and self-righteous spirit that sets us up as ultimate arbiters of others. Judging in this sense involves condemning others from a posture of superiority, delighting in their faults while ignoring our own. Jesus warns: *"In the same way you judge others, you will be judged."* (v. 2).

The standard we apply to others will be applied to us - whether by human reciprocity or divine accountability. This principle reflects James 2:13: *"Judgment without mercy will be shown to anyone who has not been merciful. Mercy triumphs over judgment."* Kingdom living calls for mercy and humility, not the harshness that often masquerades as righteousness.

The speck and the plank: Self-examination first

Jesus illustrates His point with humour and hyperbole: we fixate on a *"speck of sawdust"* in another's eye while ignoring the *"plank"* in our own (vv. 3-4). The image is absurd - trying to perform delicate eye surgery while a beam protrudes from our own face. This metaphor exposes the hypocrisy of judgmentalism. We are often blind to our own faults while magnifying the minor failings of others. Jesus' solution is clear: *"First take the plank out of your own eye, and then you will see clearly."* (v. 5). Self-examination must precede correction.

This is not a call to ignore sin in others but to approach it with humility and self-awareness. Galatians 6:1 captures this posture: *"If someone is caught in a sin, you who live by the Spirit should restore that person gently. But watch yourselves, or you also may be tempted."*

Judging with discernment, not condemnation

After warning against judgmentalism, Jesus adds: *"Do not give dogs what is sacred; do not throw your pearls to pigs."* (v. 6). Here He calls for discernment in sharing the truths of the kingdom of God. The *"dogs"* and *"pigs"* symbolized those who are hostile to God's ways - people who would trample His wisdom and lash out in response.

This verse balances the earlier command of Jesus. We must avoid hypocritical judgment, but we must also have wise discernment. Kingdom love is neither naive nor indiscriminate. It requires Spirit-led wisdom for us to know when correction or counsel will be fruitful and when it may be futile or even dangerous. This reflects Proverbs 9:8: *"Do not rebuke mockers or they will hate you; rebuke the wise and they will love you."* Wisdom discerns when to speak and when to remain silent.

From judgment to prayer

After addressing relationships with others, Jesus shifts to our relationship with God: *"Ask and it will be given to you; seek and you will find; knock and the door will be opened."* (v. 7).

These three verbs - ask, seek, knock - suggest persistence and growing intensity in prayer.

The progression is striking:

➤ *Ask:* Express dependence on God by bringing needs before Him.

➤ *Seek:* Pursue His will actively, aligning our hearts with His purposes.

➤ *Knock:* Persistently approach Him, trusting His readiness to receive us.

Prayer, in this sense, is not passive but active engagement with the Father. It flows naturally from the trust Jesus cultivated in Matthew 6: if we believe God cares for us and knows our needs, we will confidently ask.

The Father's generosity in prayer

Jesus strengthens our confidence in prayer with a vivid analogy: *"Which of you, if your son asks for bread, will give him a stone? Or... asks for a fish, will give him a snake?"* (vv. 9–10). No loving parent would mock a child's need with cruelty.

He then argues from lesser to greater: *"If you... know how to give good gifts to your children, how much more will your Father in heaven give good gifts to those who ask him!"* (v. 11). Earthly parents, flawed though they may be, still provide for their children. How much more will our perfect heavenly Father delight to answer prayer?

This teaching echoes James 1:17: *"Every good and perfect gift is from above, coming down from the Father of the heavenly lights."* Prayer is grounded not in our eloquence but in His goodness.

The interplay of relationships and prayer

Notice how Jesus intertwines relationships with others and communion with God. He calls us to humility and mercy toward others, then to bold dependence on the Father. These are inseparable: our posture toward God shapes our posture toward people, and vice versa.

A judgmental heart cannot pray with confidence; a prayerful heart marked by grace will treat others with mercy. Kingdom living flows from this integration: receiving grace vertically from the Father and extending it horizontally to those around us.

Persistent prayer: ask, seek, knock

Jesus' call to *"ask, seek, knock"* (v. 7) is not a one-time invitation but an ongoing posture of dependence. The Greek verbs are in the present continuous tense, suggesting ongoing action: *"keep on asking," "keep on seeking," "keep on knocking."*

1. Prayer as ongoing dependence

Prayer is not a single event but a sustained relationship with the Father. Just as children repeatedly ask their parents for help or provision, so too do we come to God continually.

This persistence reflects both our need and our confidence in His readiness to respond. Luke's parallel teaching (Luke 11:5–10) includes a parable of a man knocking at his neighbour's door at midnight, persistently requesting bread. Jesus' point is not that God is reluctant and must be pressured but that persistence demonstrates faith and desire for His help.

2. Seeking beyond asking

Seeking goes deeper than asking. It involves active pursuit of God's will and presence, not merely presenting requests. Psalm 105:4 exhorts: *"Look to the Lord and his strength; seek his face always."* To seek God in prayer is to desire Him above His gifts, aligning our hearts with His purposes. This means searching Scripture, listening for His voice, and orienting our lives toward His kingdom.

3. Knocking with expectation

Knocking conveys persistence and expectation. When we knock, we anticipate an answer. This image reassures us that God is not distant or inaccessible. His door is open to His children.

Hebrews 4:16 invites us to *"approach God's throne of grace with confidence, so that we may receive mercy and find grace to help us in our time of need."* Prayer thus moves from petition (asking), to pursuit (seeking), to persistence (knocking), culminating in confident reception.

The Father's delight in giving

Jesus grounds our confidence in prayer in the character of God: *"If you... know how to give good gifts to your children, how much more will your Father in heaven give good gifts."* (v. 11).

1. The parent-child analogy

Earthly parents, though flawed ("though you are evil"), still respond to their children's needs with generosity. They do not give stones when asked for bread or snakes when asked for fish.

Their instinct is to provide what is good and appropriate.
If this is true of human parents, how much more of our perfect, loving Father? This argument from lesser to greater magnifies God's goodness. He not only meets needs but delights to bless His children.

2. What are "good gifts"?

The phrase *"good gifts"* does not mean God grants every request exactly as we ask. Instead, He gives what is truly good for us in light of His wisdom and purposes. Like a wise parent, He knows when to say *"yes," "no,"* or *"not yet."* James 4:3 cautions: *"When you ask, you do not receive, because you ask with wrong motives."*

Prayer is not a blank check but a means of aligning our desires with God's. As we grow in faith, we learn to trust that His definition of *"good"* is better than ours - even when it involves delays or denials.

3. The greatest gift: Himself

Ultimately, the best gift God gives is Himself. Luke's version of this teaching (Luke 11:13) says, *"How much more will your Father in heaven give the Holy Spirit to those who ask him!"* God's greatest provision is His presence through the Spirit, who comforts, guides, and empowers us. This transforms how we pray. We don't simply seek things from God but God Himself. In doing so, we receive the deepest answer to every prayer: His sustaining, transforming presence.

The Golden Rule: Grace in action

Jesus concludes this section with the famous Golden Rule: *"So in everything, do to others what you would have them do to you."* (v. 12). This principle flows naturally from the preceding verses: those who experience the Father's generosity extend that generosity outward.

1. Positive and proactive

Many ancient cultures expressed similar ethical maxims in negative form *("Do not do to others what you would not want done to you")*. Jesus goes further, making it active: *"Do to others..."* His ethic is not mere restraint from harm but proactive goodness.

This requires initiative. Instead of waiting to be treated kindly, we treat others kindly first. Instead of passively avoiding injustice, we actively pursue justice and mercy. It is a call to creativity in love: imagining how we wish to be treated and doing likewise.

2. The fulfilment of the Law and Prophets

Jesus declares that this rule "sums up the Law and the Prophets" (v. 12). This is parallel to His later teaching in Matthew 22:37-40, where He says that loving God and loving neighbour fulfils the law. The Golden Rule distils neighbour-love into practical, everyday action. To live this way is to embody kingdom righteousness. It is not enough to avoid condemning others; we must also actively bless, serve, forgive, and encourage them - reflecting the generosity we have received from God.

Practical applications of the Golden Rule

What does it look like to live out "do to others what you would have them do to you" in daily life?

1. In speech

We consider how our words affect others. If we desire encouragement rather than criticism, we speak encouragement. If we value honesty, we communicate truthfully but with grace (Ephesians 4:29).

2. In relationships

We treat others with empathy, putting ourselves in their position. This means listening well, forgiving quickly, and bearing with weaknesses. We offer patience because we hope to receive patience ourselves.

3. In conflict

The Golden Rule reframes disputes: if we desire understanding rather than hostility, we extend understanding first. Instead of retaliating, we choose reconciliation (Romans 12:18).

4. In generosity

We give as we would always hope to receive - freely and without resentment. This could mean sharing our resources, offering hospitality, or meeting practical needs, imitating the Father's open-handedness.

Integrating prayer and grace

The structure of this passage is deliberate. Jesus places prayer (ask, seek, knock) between His commands about judgment and the Golden Rule. Why? Because prayer fuels the humility and love needed to live graciously. We cannot resist judgmentalism or live out the Golden Rule apart from the transforming grace we receive in prayer. Our interactions with others flow from our interaction with God. As we experience His generosity in prayer, we become generous toward others.

Grace begets grace

This interplay reflects Jesus' broader kingdom ethic: recipients of grace become agents of grace. Just as forgiven people forgive (Matthew 6:14–15), so provided-for people provide, and loved people love. This dynamic will transform communities. When judgment is replaced with mercy and selfishness replaced with prayer-fuelled generosity, the church becomes a living picture of the Father's kingdom.

Wisdom in discernment: *"dogs"* and *"pigs"*

After warning against judgmentalism, Jesus includes an unusual but important instruction: *"Do not give dogs what is sacred; do not throw your pearls to pigs."* (v. 6). At first glance, this might seem very harsh, but it actually reinforces His call to balance mercy with discernment.

1. Understanding the imagery

In Jewish culture, dogs were not pampered pets but often scavengers roaming around the streets, viewed as unclean and aggressive. Pigs were forbidden under the Law (Leviticus 11:7), symbolized impurity. Both images convey rejection of what is holy. *"Sacred"* things and *"pearls"* refer to precious truths of God's kingdom - wisdom, correction, and the gospel itself. Jesus warns against offering these treasures to those who are openly hostile or contemptuous, lest they *"trample them under their feet"* and *"turn and tear you to pieces."*

2. Balancing grace and wisdom

This is not a license for elitism or withholding truth from those who are merely ignorant or struggling. Rather, it cautions against wasting energy or risking harm by pressing sacred truths on those who persistently and aggressively reject them.

Proverbs 23:9 echoes this: *"Do not speak to fools, for they will scorn your prudent words."* Kingdom discernment requires knowing when to share, when to pause, and when to entrust resistant hearts to God's timing.

3. Practical Discernment

This principle applies in various contexts:

> ➢ *Personal correction:* Gently confronting sin is appropriate (Galatians 6:1), but if met with hostility, further confrontation may be unwise.

> ➢ *Evangelism:* Persistent rejection of the gospel may call for withdrawing and focusing efforts elsewhere, as Paul and Barnabas did in Acts 13:46.

> ➢ *Boundaries in relationships:* Extending grace does not mean enabling abuse. Sometimes wisdom involves stepping back while continuing to pray.

Discernment ensures that grace is not naïve but always Spirit-led, preserving the dignity of both giver and receiver.

Prayer as the engine of relational grace

Jesus' sequence - judging others (vv. 1–5), discernment (v. 6), persistent prayer (vv. 7–11), and the Golden Rule (v. 12) - reveals a profound connection: prayer fuels grace toward others.

1. Prayer humility softens judgment

We cannot persist in prayer without being reminded of our own dependence on God's mercy. Standing before a holy Father exposes our need for forgiveness and humbles our hearts. This self-awareness disarms judgmentalism.

As we pray, *"forgive us our sins."* (Matthew 6:12), we recall our own failures and God's patience with us. This posture softens our approach to others: we always correct gently, forgive readily, and refrain from harsh condemnation.

2. Prayer shapes our vision of others

Persistent prayer for others transforms how we see them. When we intercede for those who frustrate or wound us, resentment diminishes. We begin to see them through the Father's eyes — beloved yet broken, in need of grace just as we are.

Jesus modelled this even on the cross: *"Father, forgive them, for they do not know what they are doing."* (Luke 23:34). His prayer redefined His enemies not as irredeemable adversaries but as blind souls in need of mercy.

3. Prayer strengthens discernment

Prayer also sharpens wisdom. Before confronting someone or sharing difficult truth, prayer aligns our motives with God's and tunes our hearts to His Spirit. James 1:5 promises: *"If any of you lacks wisdom, you should ask God... and it will be given to you."* Discernment about when to speak or remain silent is not innate; it flows from time spent in communion with the Father.

The Golden Rule as the crown of this section

Notice again the first word in the Golden Rule verse: *"So in everything, do to others what you would have them do to you."* (v. 12). The *"so"* links this directly to what precedes it. Because God is generous in answering prayer, we are to imitate His generosity toward others.

1. Grace received becomes grace given

Those who keep on asking, seeking, and knocking, experience the Father's open-handed goodness. Having received mercy, we naturally extend it outward. The Golden Rule thus encapsulates a life transformed by prayer: vertical grace (from God) flows horizontally (to people). This fulfils Jesus' summary: *"for this sums up the Law and the Prophets."* The entire Old Testament's moral teaching is distilled into this principle of proactive, self-giving love grounded in God's own character.

2. Practical Outworking of the Golden Rule

Living the Golden Rule reshapes every sphere:

➢ *Workplace:* Treat colleagues with respect, support, and honesty as you would wish to be treated.
➢ *Family:* Offer forgiveness and patience, especially where tension arises, reflecting the Father's patience with you.

> *Church:* Extend hospitality, care for those in need, and bear others' burdens (Galatians 6:2) as you would desire support in your time of trial.

> *Community:* Show kindness to strangers, advocating for justice and mercy even for those society neglects.

By living this way, the church becomes a visible sign of the kingdom - embodying a countercultural ethic rooted in Christ.

Transitioning to the narrow gate

This section leads naturally to Jesus' next teaching: the narrow and wide gates (Matthew 7:13–14). His command not to judge, His call to prayer, and His summary in the Golden Rule all culminate in a decision point: Will we walk the narrow way of kingdom grace or the broad road of self-righteousness and self-sufficiency?

> *The narrow gate requires humility:* Refusing judgment, embracing mercy, and seeking God's help through prayer all demand humility. These are marks of those who enter through the narrow gate, relying on the Father's grace rather than their own merit.

> *The broad road is marked by pride:* The judgmental spirit, prayerlessness, and disregard for the Golden Rule align with the broad way - self-reliant, loveless, and spiritually blind.

By calling His disciples to prayerful dependence and gracious relationships, Jesus is preparing them to choose the narrow gate: a life surrendered to God and marked by His kingdom ethic.

The flow of the Sermon

Matthew 7:1–12 bridges two major movements of the Sermon on the Mount:

> *Chapters 5–6:* Inner transformation and trust in the Father (purity, love, hidden devotion, freedom from worry).

➤ *Chapters 7:* Final warnings and urgent calls to decision (the narrow gate, true and false prophets, wise and foolish builders).

This passage integrates both: it applies inner transformation (mercy over judgment) and deep trust (persistent prayer) to our outward relationships. It reminds us that kingdom living is both relational and God-dependent.

Grace, prayer, and kingdom life

In Matthew 7:1-12, Jesus weaves together mercy, discernment, prayer, and love into a single tapestry of kingdom living. He calls His disciples to:

➤ Reject harsh judgment in favour of humble self-examination.
➤ Exercise wisdom and discernment guided by prayer.
➤ Persist in prayerful dependence on their Father's generosity.
➤ Live out the Golden Rule, treating others with active grace.

This is life in the kingdom: grounded in the Father's goodness, marked by trust and prayer, and overflowing with mercy toward others. Such a life not only fulfils *"the Law and the Prophets"* but also prepares us for the decisive choice Jesus is about to present - the narrow gate that leads to life.

22

THE NARROW GATE

Matthew 7:13–23

"Enter through the narrow gate. For wide is the gate and broad is the road that leads to destruction, and many enter through it. But small is the gate and narrow the road that leads to life, and only a few find it. Watch out for false prophets. They come to you in sheep's clothing, but inwardly they are ferocious wolves. By their fruit you will recognize them. Do people pick grapes from thornbushes, or figs from thistles? Likewise, every good tree bears good fruit, but a bad tree bears bad fruit. A good tree cannot bear bad fruit, and a bad tree cannot bear good fruit. Every tree that does not bear good fruit is cut down and thrown into the fire.

Thus, by their fruit you will recognize them. Not everyone who says to me, 'Lord, Lord,' will enter the kingdom of heaven, but only the one who does the will of my Father who is in heaven. Many will say to me on that day, 'Lord, Lord, did we not prophesy in your name and in your name drive out demons and in your name perform many miracles?' Then I will tell them plainly, 'I never knew you. Away from me, you evildoers!'"

The urgency of the narrow gate

As Jesus nears the conclusion of the Sermon on the Mount, His tone becomes increasingly urgent. The call to *"enter through the narrow gate"* confronts listeners with a choice: Will we follow Him into life, or remain on the broad road to destruction? This is not theoretical; it is deeply personal and eternally consequential.

The imagery of gates and roads would have been familiar to His audience. Ancient cities were often accessed through gates, some wide and accommodating, others narrow and restrictive.

Jesus uses this image to contrast two ways of living: one easy and popular but fatal, and the other difficult and unpopular but leading to life.

The broad road: ease without life

"Wide is the gate and broad is the road that leads to destruction." (v. 13). The broad road is quite spacious and accommodating. It requires little effort, no repentance, and no surrender. It is crowded because it aligns naturally with human inclination.

This road is marked by self-reliance, moral compromise, and conformity to worldly values. It is appealing precisely because it demands nothing - no discipline, no humility, no cross. But its end is always destruction: spiritual ruin and eternal separation from God.

Proverbs 14:12 warns: *"There is a way that appears to be right, but in the end it leads to death."* The broad road offers comfort now but catastrophe later.

The narrow road: Life through surrender

In contrast, *"small is the gate and narrow the road that leads to life, and only a few find it."* (v. 14). The narrow gate represents Jesus Himself and the life of discipleship He demands. In John 10:9, He declares: *"I am the gate; whoever enters through me will be saved."*

The narrow road is difficult because it requires repentance, self-denial, and submission to Christ's lordship. It is the path of carrying our cross (Luke 9:23). Yet it alone leads to life - true, eternal life in fellowship with God.

Few find it because it runs counter to our natural desires and cultural pressures. It is not crowded, flashy, or easy. But it is worth everything: *"Whoever loses their life for me will find it."* (Matthew 16:25).

The Nature of the Narrow Way

Choosing the narrow gate is not a one-time decision but an ongoing journey. It involves:

> ➤ *Turning from sin:* Genuine repentance and transformation of heart (Acts 3:19).
> ➤ *Following Jesus daily:* Aligning our lives with His teaching and example (John 8:31).

> *Prioritizing His kingdom:* Seeking first His righteousness over worldly pursuits (Matthew 6:33).

> *Enduring difficulty:* Accepting rejection, sacrifice, and hardship as integral to discipleship (2 Timothy 3:12).

This road is narrow not because God is stingy but because it is singular: it passes only through Christ. Salvation is exclusive in its entry point (John 14:6) but inclusive in its offer - open to all who will come.

False prophets: Dangers along the way

Jesus immediately follows His call to the narrow gate with a warning: *"Watch out for false prophets."* (v. 15). He knows that one of the greatest threats to His followers is when we face deception masquerading as truth.

1. Sheep's clothing and wolfish hearts

False prophets appear harmless, even godly: *"They come to you in sheep's clothing."* They speak religious language, claim spiritual authority, and often draw large followings. Yet *"inwardly they are ferocious wolves,"* preying on the vulnerable for gain, power, or self-promotion. Their danger lies in their subtlety. They blend truth with error, diluting the gospel with distortions.

Paul warns strongly in 2 Corinthians 11:14–15 that *"Satan himself masquerades as an angel of light,"* and his servants often disguise themselves similarly.

2. Fruit as the test

Jesus provides a simple test: *"By their fruit you will recognize them."* (v. 16). Just as healthy trees produce good fruit, genuine teachers produce lives of integrity, obedience, and love that align with the gospel.

Bad trees - false prophets - may have charisma and apparent results (miracles, crowds, impressive ministries), but their actual fruit will reveal corruption: greed, immorality, divisiveness, or exploitation.

Galatians 5:22–23 lists the fruit of the Spirit as the evidence of authentic discipleship: love, joy, peace, patience, kindness, goodness, faithfulness, gentleness, and self-control. Any teacher lacking these traits should be viewed with caution.

3. Judgment of the unfruitful

Jesus is stark: *"Every tree that does not bear good fruit is cut down and thrown into the fire."* (v. 19). False prophets may prosper temporarily, but their end is judgment. This echoes John the Baptist's earlier warning we read in Matthew 3:10. Discerning fruit requires time. Wolves can disguise themselves for a season, but character eventually surfaces. Thus, Jesus calls His followers to vigilance: *"By their fruit you will recognize them."* (v. 20).

Not everyone who says, *"Lord, Lord"*

Perhaps the most sobering words in the Sermon on the Mount are in verses 21–23: *"Not everyone who says to me, 'Lord, Lord,' will enter the kingdom of heaven."* Jesus envisions people who appear outwardly devout - even performing miracles - yet are rejected.

1. Empty profession without obedience

These individuals call Jesus *"Lord"* but fail to *"do the will of my Father."* Their confession is verbal, not lived. True discipleship is evidenced not by spectacular works but by obedience to God's will (John 14:15: *"If you love me, keep my commands"*). This warning pierces superficial religiosity. It is possible to attend church, serve in ministry, and even claim spiritual experiences while lacking genuine surrender to Christ.

2. *"I never knew you"*

Jesus' verdict is chilling: *"I never knew you. Away from me, you evildoers!"* (v. 23). The issue is relational: they never truly belonged to Him. Discipleship is not merely external behaviour but intimate fellowship with Jesus Christ, rooted in faith and repentance. This echoes John 10:27: *"My sheep listen to my voice; I know them, and they follow me."* Knowing Christ personally is the essence of salvation.

True discipleship: Doing the Father's will

Jesus defines true discipleship as doing *"the will of my Father."* This does not mean sinless perfection but a life oriented around obedience, trust, and transformation. The narrow way is marked by genuine faith expressed through action (James 2:17).

To walk this path, we must continually ask:

➤ Am I following Jesus' teaching or merely admiring it?
➤ Do my actions align with His commands, or do I excuse disobedience?
➤ Is my relationship with Christ real, vibrant, and personal?

The narrow gate confronts us with this truth: genuine faith cannot be separated from obedience. As Jesus will soon illustrate in the parable of the wise and foolish builders, only those who hear His words and put them into practice will stand firm.

Recognizing false prophets today

Jesus' warning about false prophets is timeless. Throughout history, deceptive leaders have arisen within religious contexts, distorting God's Word and exploiting His people. Their presence today is no less real, making discernment vital for every believer.

1. Signs of false teaching

False prophets often share several characteristics:

➤ *Distorted gospel:* They minimize sin, avoid repentance, or redefine salvation in self-centred terms. Paul warns in Galatians 1:6–7 of those who preach *"a different gospel – which is really no gospel at all."*
➤ *Self-exaltation:* Instead of pointing to Christ, they draw attention to themselves. They crave admiration, power, or control.
➤ *Material greed:* Many exploit their followers for financial gain. Peter cautions: *"In their greed these teachers will exploit you with fabricated stories,"* (2 Peter 2:3).

> *Moral compromise*: Their personal lives often contradict their message. A lack of holiness or integrity is a red flag.

While they may use biblical language and outwardly appear successful, their fruit reveals their true nature over time.

2. Testing Fruit and Teaching

Believers are called to test both fruit (character) and teaching (doctrine).

> *Fruit test:* Does their life reflect the character of Christ and the fruit of the Spirit (Galatians 5:22–23)? Are humility, holiness, and love evident?
> *Teaching test:* Does their message align with Scripture? Acts 17:11 commends the Bereans for examining the Scriptures daily *"to see if what Paul said was true."*

True teachers direct attention to Jesus, not themselves, and their lives reinforce their words.

3. Modern examples of wolves in sheep's clothing

False prophets may appear in various forms:

> *Celebrity preachers* promising prosperity in exchange for faith "seed" offerings.
> *Charismatic figures* who build cult-like followings around their personality rather than Christ.
> *Subtle distorters* who downplay sin, avoid the cross, and recast the gospel as mere self-help or moralism.

Jesus' warning compels us to always remain vigilant, grounded in Scripture, and sensitive to the Spirit's guidance. Spiritual naivety leaves us vulnerable; wise discernment guards us from deception.

True discipleship versus empty religion

Jesus' sobering words, *"Not everyone who says to me, 'Lord, Lord,'"* expose the danger of external religion devoid of genuine faith.

Outward displays of spirituality, even dramatic ones, are no substitute for authentic discipleship.

1. The danger of religious activity without relationship

The individuals Jesus describes here actually prophesied, cast out demons, and performed miracles *"in His name"* (v. 22). These are impressive works, yet Jesus rejects them because they lacked genuine fellowship with Him: *"I never knew you."*

This distinction underscores a critical truth: It is possible to be religiously active but spiritually dead. Mere participation in church services, ministries, or rituals cannot save. Salvation flows from knowing Christ personally and living in obedience to His will.

2. Knowing Christ, not knowing about Him

To *"know"* Jesus (Greek: *ginōskō*) signifies intimate, relational knowledge, not mere intellectual awareness. It mirrors the covenant language of Scripture: God says of His people, *"I know them."* (Exodus 33:12).

True discipleship involves daily communion with Jesus through prayer, Scripture, obedience, and dependence. Without this living relationship, even the most spectacular deeds ring hollow. John 15:4–5 illustrates this vividly: *"Remain in me... apart from me you can do nothing."* Works detached from abiding in Christ are fruitless.

3. Obedience as evidence of knowing Him

Jesus ties kingdom entry to *"the one who does the will of my Father."* (v. 21). Obedience is not the means of earning salvation but its fruit. As 1 John 2:3 says: *"We know that we have come to know him if we keep his commands."*

This aligns with James' bold assertion: *"Faith by itself, if it is not accompanied by action, is dead."* (James 2:17). Genuine faith naturally expresses itself in obedience because it flows from a transformed heart.

Characteristics of true disciples

How can we distinguish true discipleship from empty religion? Jesus and the apostles describe several marks:

- ➤ *Submission to Christ's Lordship:* True disciples will acknowledge Jesus as Lord not just in words but in life. They surrender their will to His and align their decisions with His commands (Luke 6:46: "Why do you call me, 'Lord, Lord,' and do not do what I say?").

- ➤ *Obedience to God's Word:* Genuine followers hunger for Scripture and conform their lives to it (John 8:31: *"If you hold to my teaching, you are really my disciples"*).

- ➤ *Fruit of the Spirit:* Their lives display increasing love, joy, peace, patience, kindness, and other evidences of transformation (Galatians 5:22–23).

- ➤ *Perseverance in Faith:* True disciples endure trials and remain faithful even when it is costly (Matthew 10:22: "The one who stands firm to the end will be saved").

- ➤ *Intimacy with Christ:* Their faith is relational, marked by prayer, worship, and delight in God's presence (Psalm 16:11).

The urgency of Jesus' warning

Jesus' stark language - destruction, false prophets, rejection - underscores the eternal stakes. The Sermon on the Mount is not merely moral advice but a call to action . Neutrality is impossible. The narrow gate demands we choose Christ above all else.

1. Few find it

Jesus says *"only a few find it"* (v. 14), not because God is restrictive but because many resist surrender. Pride, love of comfort, and attachment to worldly desires keep multitudes on the broad road. This echoes His words in Luke 13:24: *"Make every effort to enter through the narrow door, because many… will try to enter and will not be able to."* The kingdom requires intentional pursuit and wholehearted commitment.

2. *The finality of judgment*

Verses 22–23 point forward to *"that day"* - a reference to the final judgment. On that day, words and appearances will not suffice. Only those known by Christ and obedient to the Father will enter His kingdom. This reality presses urgency into discipleship.

The time to choose the narrow gate is now. Waiting or wavering is itself a choice for the broad road.

Avoiding deception: self-examination

Given Jesus' warnings, self-examination is vital. Paul exhorts in 2 Corinthians 13:5: *"Examine yourselves to see whether you are in the faith; test yourselves."*

Key questions to ask include:

> ➢ Do I know Jesus personally, or do I merely know about Him?
> ➢ Is my obedience to Him willing and joyful, or reluctant and inconsistent?
> ➢ Does my life bear the fruit of the Spirit?
> ➢ Am I more concerned with outward reputation or inward transformation?

These questions are not meant to breed fear but to lead us toward genuine, authentic faith rooted in Christ.

Encouragement for the true disciple

While Jesus' words are sobering, they are also deeply reassuring for those of us who truly know Him. The narrow gate may be demanding, but it is secure. His sheep are safe in His hands: *"No one will snatch them out of my hand."* (John 10:28).

True disciples, though imperfect, persevere because the Spirit always sustains them. Their lives are not marked by flawless performance but by repentance, faith, and increasing conformity to Christ. They walk the narrow way not alone but in step with the Shepherd who leads them to life.

Cultivating perseverance on the narrow road

Walking the narrow road is not a single step but a lifelong journey requiring endurance. Jesus Himself warned that following Him would be costly: *"Whoever wants to be my disciple must deny themselves and take up their cross daily and follow me."* (Luke 9:23). Perseverance is essential because the narrow way is neither easy nor popular.

1. Fixing our eyes on the goal

Hebrews 12:1-2 exhorts us to *"run with perseverance the race marked out for us, fixing our eyes on Jesus, the pioneer and perfecter of faith."* The key to staying on the narrow road is maintaining focus on the end: eternal life with Christ. When trials come or the broad road beckons with comfort and ease, we endure by remembering the surpassing worth of knowing Jesus and the joy set before us (Philippians 3:13-14).

2. The role of daily discipline

Perseverance thrives through spiritual disciplines:

➢ *Prayer:* Regular communion with God keeps our hearts dependent and aligned with His will.

➢ *Scripture:* Daily intake of God's Word renews our minds and equips us to resist deception.

➢ *Fellowship:* Gathering with other believers strengthens us, offering accountability and encouragement (Hebrews 10:24-25).

➢ *Obedience:* Consistently practicing Jesus' teaching reinforces the habits of discipleship and deepens trust.

3. Strength in weakness

Perseverance does not mean self-reliant grit. Paul reminds us in 2 Corinthians 12:9 that God's power is made perfect in weakness As we feel our limitations, we lean on His grace, learning to say, *"When I am weak, then I am strong."* (v. 10). This dependence guards against pride and deepens faith.

Avoiding modern deceptions

Jesus' warning about false prophets remains critical in an age of instant information, online platforms, and celebrity-driven influence. Many voices claim to speak for God, but not all are trustworthy.

1. The lure of easy religion

A common modern deception mirrors the broad road: a diluted gospel that promises blessing without repentance, comfort without cost, and heaven without holiness. This *"cheap grace"* dismisses Jesus' demand for surrender. Dietrich Bonhoeffer famously contrasted this with *"costly grace,"* writing: *"Cheap grace is grace without discipleship, grace without the cross, grace without Jesus Christ."* We must resist teachings that remove the call to take up our cross.

2. Charisma versus character

In today's culture, charisma often overshadows character. A compelling personality or polished presentation can mask dangerous teaching. Yet Jesus points to fruit, not flair, as the test of authenticity: *"By their fruit you will recognize them."* (v. 20). True shepherds may lack showmanship but will exhibit humility, holiness, and service modelled after Christ.

3. The importance of sound doctrine

Paul warns Timoth in 2 Timothy 4:3, *"The time will come when people will not put up with sound doctrine... They will gather around them a great number of teachers to say what their itching ears want to hear."* Grounding ourselves in Scripture is the antidote. The Word equips us to discern truth from error, enabling us to evaluate every teaching against God's revealed standard.

Encouragement: The security of the narrow path

Though the narrow road is demanding, it is also secure because it is the road Jesus walks with us. He does not merely point the way - He is the way (John 14:6). His Spirit guides, strengthens, and sustains us.

Isaiah 35:8-10 provides a prophetic picture of this path: *"And a highway will be there; it will be called the Way of Holiness... But only the redeemed will walk there... Gladness and joy will overtake them, and sorrow and sighing will flee away."* This imagery reassures us: the narrow road is not barren but filled with God's presence and an inexpressible joy.

Knowing Christ versus mere works

Jesus' words, *"I never knew you,"* underscore that discipleship is fundamentally relational. Activity without intimacy is empty. We cannot serve our way into salvation; we must be known by Christ. John 17:3 defines eternal life: *"that they know you, the only true God, and Jesus Christ, whom you have sent."* True discipleship flows from this knowledge. Our works become fruit of love, not substitutes for relationship. This truth also comforts believers who worry about inadequacy. Salvation is never about doing "enough" but about abiding in Jesus, who promises: *"If you remain in me... you will bear much fruit."* (John 15:5).

Choosing life daily

The narrow gate is entered through faith in Christ, but the narrow road is walked daily through ongoing surrender. Moses framed a similar choice in Deuteronomy 30:19: *"I have set before you life and death... Now choose life."*

Choosing life means daily decisions to obey Jesus' words even when they conflict with cultural norms, personal desires, or worldly logic. It means turning from sin repeatedly and realigning with His will. These small, daily choices compound into a lifelong pattern of faithfulness, culminating in the joy of hearing, *"Well done, good and faithful servant."* (Matthew 25:21).

The coming transition: Building on the rock

Jesus' warnings about the narrow gate and about false disciples naturally lead into His final parable of the wise and foolish builders (Matthew 7:24-27). This parable clearly illustrates the difference between hearing His words and doing them - a theme He has been pressing throughout this section.

> *Wise builders:* Hear Jesus' words and obey, constructing their lives on the solid foundation of His teaching.
> *Foolish builders:* Hear His words but fail to act, erecting houses on sand that collapse in storms.

This closing image ties directly to the narrow road. Entering the narrow gate and walking the narrow path are not abstract ideas; they are lived out through concrete obedience to Jesus' words.

Decision time

Jesus' Sermon now reaches a decisive point. He has described the kingdom's demands (Matthew 5), warned against hypocrisy and divided loyalties (Matthew 6), and called His listeners to trust the Father, love others, and pray persistently (Matthew 7:1–12). Now He presses for a response: Will we enter the narrow gate, reject false prophets, and live as true disciples, or remain on the broad road of ease and self-deception? The choice cannot be postponed indefinitely.

Matthew 7:23's image of judgment day heightens this urgency. Eternity hangs on whether we truly know Christ and do the Father's will.

Conclusion: Walking the narrow way

Jesus' teaching here strips away illusions. It exposes false confidence in mere words *("Lord, Lord")* or impressive works and directs us to the heart of true discipleship: knowing Him and obeying Him.

The narrow way may be demanding, but it leads to life. It is the road of intimacy with Christ, transformation by His Spirit, and eternal joy in His presence. While few may find it, those who do discover its incomparable reward.

As Jesus now moves to His parable of the wise and foolish builders, He drives this point home: hearing His words is not enough - we must put them into practice. Only then will we stand secure when the storms come.

23

BUILDING ON THE ROCK

Matthew 7:24–29

"Therefore, everyone who hears these words of mine and puts them into practice is like a wise man who built his house on the rock. The rain came down, the streams rose, and the winds blew and beat against that house; yet it did not fall, because it had its foundation on the rock.

But everyone who hears these words of mine and does not put them into practice is like a foolish man who built his house on sand. The rain came down, the streams rose, and the winds blew and beat against that house, and it fell with a great crash."

When Jesus had finished saying these things, the crowds were amazed at his teaching, because he taught as one who had authority, and not as their teachers of the law."

The final *"therefore"*: A call to action

Jesus concludes the Sermon on the Mount with *"Therefore"* - a decisive word which now links all that has come before to this final parable. His message is very clear: hearing His teaching is insufficient unless it is obeyed. The entire Sermon culminates in this urgent call to move from admiration to application, from listening to living.

Throughout chapters 5–7, Jesus has described kingdom life in vivid detail: the Beatitudes, radical love, hidden devotion, trust in the Father, prayerful dependence, discernment, and the narrow gate. Now He presses His hearers to a verdict: Will you act on My words or merely acknowledge them?

The two builders: A sharp contrast

Jesus' parable presents two men, each building a house. Superficially, their houses may appear similar. Both hear Jesus' words, both construct dwellings, and both face storms. The difference lies beneath the surface - in the unseen foundation.

➢ *The wise builder:* Hears Jesus' words and puts them into practice, laying his foundation on the rock.
➢ *The foolish builder:* Hears the same words but fails to obey, erecting his house on sand.

This is not a contrast between those who hear and those who don't hear, but between those who hear and act versus those who hear and ignore. Jesus emphasizes that mere exposure to His teaching is inadequate; obedience is the true measure of discipleship.

The storms of life

Both houses encounter storms: *"The rain came down, the streams rose, and the winds blew and beat against that house."* (vv. 25, 27). The storms symbolize trials in this life and ultimately the final judgment. Jesus' point is sobering: testing is inevitable. When it comes, the strength of one's foundation will be revealed.

1. Present trials

Life's storms: illness, loss, relational conflict, financial hardship, persecution - test the reality of our faith. Those rooted in Christ stand firm, not because they avoid hardship but because their lives are anchored in His unshakable truth. Psalm 62:2 declares: *"Truly he is my rock and my salvation; he is my fortress, I will never be shaken."*

2. Future judgment

More ultimately, the storm points to the final judgment which was described earlier in Matthew 7:21-23. On that day, all superficial religiosity will collapse. Only those whose lives are built on obedience to Jesus - the true foundation - will endure.

The rock: Obedience to Jesus' words

The *"rock"* here represents hearing and doing Jesus' words. In Scripture, God is often called a rock (Psalm 18:2; Isaiah 26:4), but here Jesus identifies His own teaching as the foundation.
His authority is unmistakable: He positions obedience to His words as the dividing line between wisdom and folly, life and

ruin. This obedience is not legalistic rule-keeping but heartfelt response to grace. It flows from faith that trusts Jesus' authority and submits to His reign. As James writes, *"Do not merely listen to the word, and so deceive yourselves. Do what it says."* (James 1:22).

The sand: Hearing without doing

The foolish builder represents those who hear Jesus but fail to act. Their foundation is sand - unstable, shifting, unable to withstand pressure. This may include:

➤ *Nominal believers* who admire Jesus' ethics but never surrender to Him as Lord.

➤ *Churchgoers* who know His words intellectually but resist obedience in daily life.

➤ *Religious hypocrites* who perform outward rituals while neglecting inward transformation.

When storms come, such lives collapse *"with a great crash"* (v. 27). The imagery is devastating: a total, irreversible ruin resulting from neglecting the only secure foundation.

The authority of Jesus' teaching

Matthew closes with the crowd's reaction: *"The crowds were amazed at his teaching, because he taught as one who had authority."* (vv. 28–29). Unlike the scribes, who quoted past rabbis, Jesus spoke directly and definitively. His authority was intrinsic, not derivative.

This astonishment signals a crucial truth: Jesus is not just a teacher of wisdom but the authoritative Lord Whose words demand obedience. His teaching is not optional advice but the foundation of life. To ignore it is not merely foolish but fatal.

Implications for true discipleship

Jesus' final parable presses several key implications for those who would follow Him.

1. Hearing is not enough

Exposure to Scripture, Sermons, or study is insufficient without obedience. Knowledge must translate into action. Kingdom living requires putting Jesus' teaching into practice in real, tangible ways—loving enemies, forgiving offenses, giving in secret, trusting God for provision, and walking the narrow path.

2. Obedience reveals true faith

Obedience is the fruit of genuine faith. Jesus Himself said, *"If you love me, keep my commands."* (John 14:15). Those who truly believe in Him will respond with trust that expresses itself in action. Faith divorced from obedience is counterfeit.

3. Foundations are laid before the storm

When the storm hits, it is too late to rebuild the foundation. The time to obey Jesus is now. Daily practices of prayer, repentance, generosity, and reliance on His Word prepare us for future trials and the ultimate day of reckoning.

The danger of passive admiration

Many admire Jesus' teaching as beautiful and inspiring while ignoring its demands. They nod at the Sermon on the Mount as lofty ideals rather than binding commands. But admiration without action is the hallmark of the foolish builder. C.S. Lewis captured this danger well: *"We are not called to be admirers of Christ but imitators."* Jesus does not seek fans who applaud from a distance but disciples who follow closely, building their lives on His words.

The urgency of decision

This parable functions as Jesus' altar call. Having laid out His vision of kingdom life, He compels His listeners to choose: Will you build on the rock or the sand? Will you enter the narrow gate or remain on the broad road? Neutrality is just not an option. Joshua's challenge to Israel resonates here: *"Choose for yourselves this day whom you will serve."* (Joshua 24:15). Jesus' Sermon leaves no room for delay. The time to hear and obey is now.

Building on the rock: Obedience in practice

Jesus' parable makes clear that the wise builder is not merely a hearer but a doer of His words. The foundation is obedience — applying His teaching to daily life. This raises the practical question: How do we build on the rock?

1. Consistent Scripture engagement

To obey Jesus, we must first know His words. Regularly reading, meditating on, and internalizing Scripture anchors us in His truth. Psalm 1:2-3 describes the blessed person who *"delights in the law of the Lord" and "meditates on his law, day and night,"* likening them to a tree planted by streams of water. Immersing ourselves in Scripture equips us to recognize His voice and discern how to live out His commands in a world filled with competing voices.

2. Daily application of His teaching

Jesus' words must move from head knowledge to heart transformation and practical action. For example:

> *Loving enemies (Matthew 5:44):* Choosing forgiveness instead of retaliation.
> *Generosity in secret (Matthew 6:3-4):* Giving quietly, without seeking recognition.
> *Trusting God for provision (Matthew 6:25-34):* Releasing anxiety and prioritizing His kingdom.

Obedience often comes through small, consistent steps. As we practice His commands in everyday situations - family, work, community - our lives are increasingly built upon His solid foundation.

3. Cultivating repentance

Even the wise stumble. Building on the rock involves ongoing repentance: quickly confessing sin and realigning with Jesus' teaching. Repentance is not failure but progress, keeping our foundation firm. Acts 3:19 calls us to *"repent... so that times of refreshing may come from the Lord."*

Repentance guards against the erosion caused by neglect or compromise. Each time we turn back to Christ, we reinforce our foundation.

4. Practicing obedience in community

True discipleship is not a solo endeavour. Walking with other believers provides accountability, encouragement, and support. Hebrews 10:24–25 urges us to *"spur one another on toward love and good deeds… encouraging one another."*

Building on the rock is strengthened when we share life with others who are committed to hearing and doing Jesus' words together.

The storms that test foundations

Jesus' parable vividly illustrates that both builders face storms. Following Him does not exempt us from trials but equips us to withstand them. Storms expose what lies beneath: a foundation on rock or sand.

1. Storms of life

Life's hardships—illness, grief, betrayal, persecution—test the depth of our trust in Jesus. Those whose foundation is in Him remain steadfast, even amid pain. Isaiah 43:2 reassures: *"When you pass through the waters, I will be with you… they will not sweep over you."* These storms reveal whether our faith is built on mere sentiment or solid obedience grounded in God's Word.

2. Storms of temptation

Temptation also beats against our foundation. A life built on sand easily gives way to compromise when cultural pressures or personal desires conflict with Jesus' commands.

A rock-solid foundation, however, resists temptation by relying on Scripture and the Spirit's power. Jesus Himself modelled this in Matthew 4, responding to temptation with *"It is written."* Knowing and applying His Word fortifies us against spiritual assault.

3. The final storm: Judgment day

Ultimately, the greatest storm is the day of judgment. Jesus has already warned that mere words. or outward works are insufficient. Only those who build on His teaching will stand. This final storm gives eternal weight to our present choices. Building on sand may seem adequate when the weather is calm, but when the storm of judgment comes, it will result in *"a great crash"* (v. 27). Obedience is not optional—it is the difference between eternal security and ruin.

The danger of the sand foundation

What does it mean to build on sand? Sand represents hearing without doing—or acknowledging Jesus intellectually while resisting His authority. This can manifest in several ways:

➢ *Selective obedience:* Picking and choosing which teachings to follow.

➢ *Delayed obedience:* Intending to obey later, while postponing surrender.

➢ *Cultural conformity:* Allowing societal norms to override biblical truth.

➢ *Superficial faith:* Admiring Jesus' teaching without submitting to Him as Lord.

Such lives may appear stable in fair weather, but when tested, their lack of true foundation is revealed.

The authority of Jesus' words

Matthew concludes by noting the crowd's reaction: *"They were amazed at his teaching, because he taught as one who had authority."* (vv. 28–29). Unlike the scribes, who cited rabbinic tradition, Jesus spoke with inherent authority—issuing commands, redefining righteousness, and claiming final judgment power (v. 23).

This astonishment underscores His unique identity. Jesus is not merely a moral philosopher; He is the divine King declaring the terms of His kingdom. His authority demands response—not curiosity or admiration but obedience and faith.

Hearing Jesus today

We stand in the same position as those first listeners. We too have *"heard these words"* through Scripture. The question is: will we put them into practice?

Hearing Jesus today involves:

➢ *Receiving His teaching in faith:* Believing His words are truth and life (John 6:68).
➢ *Submitting to His authority:* Acknowledging Him as Lord in every sphere of life.
➢ *Acting decisively:* Reshaping our priorities, relationships, and habits around His commands.

To hear Jesus but not respond is to risk the foolish builder's fate.

Practical steps to build a rock-solid life

To ground our lives in obedience, we can take intentional steps:

➢ *Daily devotion:* Begin each day with Scripture and prayer, asking, "Lord, how can I obey You today?"
➢ *Immediate action:* When confronted by His commands — whether forgiveness, generosity, or trust — respond promptly rather than delaying.
➢ *Accountability:* Share your commitments with trusted believers who will encourage and challenge you.
➢ *Focus on one command at a time:* Apply specific teachings in tangible ways, gradually integrating Jesus' ethic into all areas of life.

This is how we translate hearing into doing, constructing lives resilient against storms.

The amazed crowds: Authority and astonishment

The crowd's reaction — *"amazed"* — reflects both admiration and unease. They recognized Jesus' authority but had not yet fully understood its implications. His teaching demanded more than appreciation; it required allegiance.

Many today respond similarly: they admire Jesus as a profound teacher yet hesitate to submit to Him as Lord. But Jesus does not leave that option open. His authority is absolute, and His final parable confronts us with a choice: will we build on the rock or the sand?

The link to the Sermon as a whole

This closing parable clearly encapsulates the entire Sermon on the Mount:

➢ *Kingdom righteousness (Matthew 5):* The Beatitudes and Jesus' call to surpass superficial religion.

➢ *Kingdom devotion (Matthew 6):* Hidden giving, prayer, fasting, and trust in the Father.

➢ *Kingdom decisions (Matthew 7):* Judging rightly, praying persistently, entering the narrow gate, and discerning false prophets.

Now Jesus sums it up: His words are not to be admired but obeyed. Only then do we experience the security of lives founded on His eternal truth.

Enduring obedience: A life built to last

Jesus' closing words remind us that true discipleship is not merely about initial enthusiasm but enduring obedience. Building on the rock is not a one-time act; it is a daily pattern of aligning our lives with His commands.

In Luke's version of this parable (Luke 6:48), Jesus describes the wise builder as one who *"dug down deep and laid the foundation on rock."* This image captures the effort required: laying a solid foundation is intentional, deliberate, and often hidden work. Enduring obedience means:

➢ Continuing to trust Christ when His way is difficult.

➢ Persisting in holiness when the world pressures compromise.

➢ Walking by faith when circumstances obscure God's hand.

It is not glamorous, but it is steady and strong, producing lives that remain firm through every storm.

The nature of the storms we face

Jesus does not promise storm-free living. On the contrary, His parable assumes that storms will come. They are part of life in a fallen world, and they test the authenticity of our faith.

1. Personal storms

Health crises, job loss, grief, and relational fractures test whether we truly rely on Christ or merely use Him when convenient. In these seasons, we discover if our confidence rests on circumstances or on His unshakable promises.

When Job faced devastating loss, he declared, *"Though he slay me, yet will I hope in him."* (Job 13:15). His foundation held because his faith was anchored in God rather than prosperity or comfort.

2. Cultural and spiritual storms

We also face cultural winds that challenge biblical convictions — pressures to conform, ridicule for faith, and ideologies that contradict God's Word. Standing firm in such storms requires deep roots in Scripture and courage born of obedience.

Ephesians 4:14 warns against being *"tossed back and forth by the waves"* of false teaching. Only those grounded on Christ's words will withstand the shifting currents of culture.

3. The ultimate storm: Final judgment

Finally, Jesus points to the ultimate storm: the day when every life is tested before God's throne. On that day, appearances will count for nothing. Only those who have built on Christ's words—knowing Him, trusting Him, and obeying Him—will stand secure.

Revelation 6:17 describes that day soberly: *"For the great day of their wrath has come, and who can withstand it?"* The answer is clear: only those whose lives are founded on the Rock will endure.

Worship and surrender: The right response to His authority

The crowds' amazement at Jesus' authority is both inspiring and instructive. They recognized that His teaching carried weight unlike anything they had heard before. Yet amazement alone is insufficient. The right response to His authority is both worship and surrender.

1. Worshiping the King

Jesus' authority reveals His identity: He is not just a wise teacher but the divine Son of God, the rightful King of the kingdom He has described. His words demand reverence because they are the words of God Himself.

We worship Him not only in song or ritual but by honouring Him with our lives. True worship means offering our whole selves to Him as *"a living sacrifice"* (Romans 12:1).

2. Surrendering to His Lordship

To hear Jesus' words and obey them is to submit to His lordship. It means relinquishing control, trusting His wisdom over our own, and yielding to His reign in every single area of life — our ambitions, our relationships, our resources, and our decisions. This surrender is not burdensome but liberating. As we yield to His authority, we find freedom from sin's power, security in His promises, and joy in His presence. His yoke is easy and His burden light. (Matthew 11:30).

Building for eternity

Jesus' parable points us beyond this life. Building on the rock is ultimately about preparing for eternity. Houses on sand may glitter temporarily, but they cannot survive the storm of judgment.

Only lives founded on obedience to Christ endure forever. Paul echoes this in 1 Corinthians 3:11: *"For no one can lay any foundation other than the one already laid, which is Jesus Christ."* Our task is not to invent new foundations but to build faithfully upon the only sure one — Christ Himself and His words.

The beauty of lives built on the rock

What does it look like when someone builds on the rock? It looks like:

> *Steadiness in trials:* A peace that surpasses understanding even amid suffering (Philippians 4:7).

> *Integrity in temptation:* Choosing righteousness even when no one is watching.

> *Resilience under pressure:* Standing firm in faith when mocked or marginalized.

> *Fruitfulness for the kingdom:* Producing good works that flow from deep-rooted faith.

Such lives shine in a world of instability. They become living testimonies of the power and trustworthiness of Jesus' words.

The invitation of the Sermon on the Mount

With this parable, Jesus concludes the Sermon on the Mount—a sweeping vision of life in God's kingdom. Across Matthew 5–7, He has called His disciples to a righteousness deeper than mere rule-keeping, a devotion that trusts the Father, a love that mirrors His own, and a faith that endures through storms.

Now He invites His listeners—and us—to decide. Will we merely admire His words, or will we live them? Will we build on sand or rock? Will we follow the crowd on the broad road or walk the narrow path with Him? This is not merely an ethical invitation but an eternal one. To build on the rock is to align our lives with Jesus Himself, to trust Him fully, and to live in His kingdom both now and forever.

A final call: From hearing to doing

James captures the essence of Jesus' conclusion:

"Do not merely listen to the word, and so deceive yourselves. Do what it says." (James 1:22). Hearing without doing creates self-deception—thinking knowledge alone equals discipleship. Jesus demolishes this illusion. The wise builder hears, obeys, and endures. The foolish builder hears, neglects, and falls.

The Sermon on the Mount ends where true discipleship begins: with obedience that springs from faith and love for the King who speaks with authority.

Conclusion: The rock that cannot be moved

The call of Jesus is clear and urgent: Build your life on Me. Hear My words, trust them, and put them into practice. When the storms rage—and they will—you will stand. When judgment comes, you will be secure.

Isaiah 28:16 offers this promise:

"See, I lay a stone in Zion, a tested stone, a precious cornerstone for a sure foundation; the one who relies on it will never be stricken with panic."

Christ is that cornerstone. His words are the blueprint. His kingdom is the goal. To build on Him is to live unshakable, both now and forever.

As the crowds marvelled, we too must marvel—but more than that, we must bow. We must worship, surrender, and build our lives upon the Rock who is Christ Himself. For in Him, and in obedience to His words, we find both stability for today and security for eternity.

EPILOGUE:
HOW THEN SHALL WE LIVE?

As we conclude our journey through Matthew 5-7, we stand where the crowds once stood, listening to Jesus as He finished His most famous Sermon. Like them, we are left both awed and unsettled.

His words are beautiful, yet demanding; comforting, yet confrontational. They expose our hearts while inviting us into a way of life radically different from the world around us.

The Sermon on the Mount is not merely a collection of moral teachings. It is a portrait of kingdom living, a vision of life under the reign of Jesus Christ. It calls us to a deeper righteousness, authentic devotion, fearless trust, sacrificial love, discerning wisdom, and unwavering obedience. It is both an invitation and a warning—a call to enter the narrow gate and build our lives upon the rock.

The heart of the Sermon: Kingdom life

At its core, the Sermon on the Mount answers the question: What does it mean to live as a disciple of Jesus in His kingdom?

➢ *The Beatitudes (Matthew 5:1–12):* We began with Jesus blessing those the world overlooks—the poor in spirit, the meek, the merciful. Here we saw that kingdom citizens are not defined by power or status but by humility, purity of heart, and hunger for righteousness.

➢ *Transforming righteousness (Matthew 5:13–48):* Jesus called us to surpass superficial religion, to be salt and light, to love enemies, and to reflect our Father's perfection. True righteousness flows from within, reshaping desires as much as deeds.

➢ *Hidden devotion (Matthew 6:1–18):* We learned that kingdom living is not performative but intimate. Prayer, fasting, and generosity are not for display but expressions of love for the Father who sees in secret.

- ➤ *Trusting the Father (Matthew 6:19–34):* Jesus challenged our preoccupation with earthly treasure and anxiety about provision. Instead, He urged us to "seek first His kingdom and His righteousness," resting in the care of our heavenly Father.

- ➤ *Relational grace and prayer (Matthew 7:1–12):* We were reminded to trade judgment for mercy, discern wisely, persist in prayer, and live by the Golden Rule, treating others as we would wish to be treated.

- ➤ *The call to decision (Matthew 7:13–29):* Finally, Jesus pressed His listeners toward choice: the narrow gate or broad road, true discipleship or empty words, the rock or the sand. His teaching demands response — not admiration but action, not vague interest but surrendered obedience.

The King Who calls us

The Sermon's authority flows from its speaker. Jesus is not merely a teacher of ethics but the King who inaugurates His kingdom and calls His followers to live in its reality. His words carry divine authority because He is God incarnate.

Throughout this journey, we have seen that the commands of Jesus cannot be separated from His person:

- ➤ To enter the narrow gate is to enter through Him (John 10:9).
- ➤ To build on the rock is to build on Him, our cornerstone (Isaiah 28:16).
- ➤ To seek first the kingdom is to seek Him, its King (Matthew 6:33).

This Sermon is not simply about adopting a moral code; it is about knowing and following the One who embodies it.

Grace and Obedience: Two sides of kingdom life

The Sermon on the Mount does not present obedience as the means of earning God's favour but as the evidence of it.

Grace comes first: Jesus calls His disciples blessed before they have done anything (Matthew 5:3–12). Yet this grace transforms us, producing lives that reflect His kingdom values.

In *The Cost of Discipleship*, Dietrich Bonhoeffer wrote: *"Only he who believes is obedient, and only he who is obedient believes."* Faith and obedience are inseparable. True belief in Jesus leads to transformed living, not because we are striving to earn salvation but because His Spirit is at work within us, reshaping our hearts to delight in His commands.

The challenge for today

What does it look like to live the Sermon on the Mount in our time? It means:

➢ Choosing humility over self-promotion.
➢ Loving those who hurt us and forgiving those who wrong us.
➢ Praying sincerely, giving quietly, and fasting without display.
➢ Trusting God's provision instead of clinging to material security.
➢ Extending mercy rather than rushing to judgment.
➢ Persisting in prayer with confidence in the Father's goodness.
➢ Resisting false teachings and walking the narrow road of obedience.

Such living is countercultural and often costly. It demands that we relinquish self-rule and bow to Jesus' authority. But it also brings deep joy, unshakable peace, and eternal reward.

Tested and secure

The final parable of building on the rock reminds us that storms will come. Following Jesus does not spare us hardship, but it anchors us in One Who cannot be moved. Whether in personal trials or ultimate judgment, those built on Christ and His words stand secure.

This security is not based on our strength but His. He is the solid foundation who holds us fast. As Paul declares: *"If God is for us, who can be against us?"* (Romans 8:31).

Living as kingdom witnesses

When we live the Sermon on the Mount, we display a different way of being human. Our lives become living invitations to others, showing what it looks like to follow Jesus. We become salt and light, pointing the world to the King who reigns in grace and truth. Our obedience is not only for our own sake but for the sake of the world. As Jesus said, *"Let your light shine before others, that they may see your good deeds and glorify your Father in heaven."* (Matthew 5:16).

A final invitation

As Jesus' words echo across the centuries, they confront us with the same choice He set before His original audience. Will we hear and obey? Will we enter the narrow gate, build on the rock, and follow Him as King? The Sermon on the Mount is both a mirror and a map: it reveals where we fall short and directs us to the only One who fulfils its demands—Jesus Himself. Through His death and resurrection, He not only forgives our failures but empowers us by His Spirit to live the life He describes.

Conclusion: Building on the rock of Christ

This book ends where Jesus ended His Sermon: with a call to action. The choice before us is stark but clear: sand or rock, broad or narrow, admiration or obedience, ruin or life. To hear His words and act on them is to build our lives on a foundation that cannot be shaken.

To trust Him, follow Him, and obey Him is to find ourselves secure in His kingdom, now and forever. May we, like the wise builder, dig deep, lay our foundation on Christ, and stand firm in every storm. And may our lives proclaim to the world that Jesus is not merely a great teacher but the living King, worthy of our faith, our obedience, and our all.

"Thunderously, inarguably, the Sermon on the Mount proves
that before God we all stand on level ground: murderers and
temper-throwers, adulterers and lusters, thieves and coveters.
We are all desperate, and that is in fact the only state appropriate
to a human being who wants to know God. Having fallen from
the absolute Ideal, we have nowhere to land but in
the safety net of absolute grace."

(Philip Yancey)

"Humanly speaking, it is possible to understand the Sermon on the
Mount in a thousand different ways. But Jesus knows only one
possibility: simple surrender and obedience - not interpreting or
applying it, but doing and obeying it. That is the only way to
hear his words. He does not mean for us to discuss it as an
ideal. He really means for us to get on with it."

(Dietrich Bonhoeffer)